AWAKENINGS

Southern Literary Studies

Fred Hobson, Series Editor

AWAKENINGS

The Story of the
KATE CHOPIN
REVIVAL

Edited by Bernard Koloski

LOUISIANA STATE UNIVERSITY PRESS)(BATON ROUGE

PUBLISHED BY LOUISIANA STATE UNIVERSITY PRESS
Copyright © 2009 by Louisiana State University Press
Manufactured in the United States of America
First printing

Designer: Michelle A. Neustrom
Typeface: Seria
Printer and binder: Thomson-Shore, Inc.

LIBRARY OF CONGRESS CATALOGING-IN-PUBLICATION DATA

Awakenings : the story of the Kate Chopin revival / edited by Bernard Koloski.
     p. cm. — (Southern literary studies)
   Includes bibliographical references and index.
   ISBN 978-0-8071-3495-5 (cloth : alk. paper) 1. Chopin, Kate, 1850–1904—Appreciation. 2. Chopin, Kate, 1850–1904. Awakening. 3. Chopin, Kate, 1850–1904—Criticism and interpretation. I. Koloski, Bernard, 1937–
   PS1294.C63Z58 2009
   813'.4—dc22
                                                                              2009014533

The paper in this book meets the guidelines for permanence and durability of the Committee on Production Guidelines for Book Longevity of the Council on Library Resources. ∞

For Kate Chopin's readers

CONTENTS

ACKNOWLEDGMENTS

We acknowledge in our essays many people who guided us in our work on Kate Chopin in the 1970s and 1980s.

We add our thanks to Grace Carino, Dick Walker, Larry Uffelman, Monique Oyallon, Michael Salitrynski, Emily Cole, and Jenny Oyallon-Koloski, who helped us with the preparation of the manuscript. We thank Fred Hobson of the University of North Carolina at Chapel Hill, who offered us invaluable support and suggestions. And we extend a special thank-you to John Easterly of LSU Press, who with his gracious encouragement and expert advice sustained us as we wrote.

AWAKENINGS

Introduction

BERNARD KOLOSKI

NO OTHER AMERICAN BOOK was so maligned, neglected for so long, and then embraced so quickly and with such enthusiasm as Kate Chopin's 1899 novel *The Awakening*. And none has been so thoroughly redeemed as *The Awakening*. Thought vulgar, morbid, and disturbing in Chopin's time, it has for the past quarter of a century been seen as sensitive, passionate, and inspiring. Forgotten for two generations, it is today known by countless people in dozens of countries, and Kate Chopin has become among the most widely read of classic American authors.[1] How Chopin's reputation was transformed in the 1970s and 1980s makes for a remarkable story.

People were captivated by *The Awakening* when a friend gave them a copy or when they came across it in a classroom or a book club or in the mass-circulation magazine *Redbook*, which reprinted the entire novel in a 1972 issue. The effect of the book was immediate and lasting. For most of us whose essays make up this collection, reading the novel was a life-changing event. We wrote books and articles about Kate Chopin— about her novel and her short stories—we gave talks about her to whatever groups would listen to us, we did interviews with newspapers and magazines, we taught her in our classes and urged our colleagues to teach her, and we helped build a network of teachers, students, editors, librarians, journalists, and others to promote Chopin's work.

We explain in these essays how as graduate students and young college instructors we carried out some of the basic research, thought through some of the critical approaches, and developed some of the present directions for reading, studying, and teaching Kate Chopin. Our volume of collective recollection builds what historians would call a literary foundation narrative. It focuses on what happened a generation ago and why—and how that literary activity looks today.

We are all scholars, but our essays are not scholarship of the usual kind. *Awakenings* is not a book of literary analyses or literary approaches or classroom practices, although at moments it may feel like one of those. It is rather a description of our work on a once neglected writer. It is about a decisive moment in American literary history.

The recovery of something forgotten is not unique, since revivals of one sort or another—of architectural styles or trade routes or political parties—occur frequently. In English, according to the *Oxford English Dictionary*, the word *revival* first appeared in the seventeenth century. Then, as now, it was used to mean "the act of reviving after decline or discontinuance," "the act of restoring an old play to the stage, or of republishing an old literary work."

In the United States, the OED notes, the word is often employed in a religious sense to mean "an evangelical service; a revival meeting." One of the earliest American revivals was, in fact, called an "Awakening"—actually a "Great Awakening"—but Jonathan Edwards in the 1730s was more a religious than a literary figure, and his movement was aimed at reforming what he saw as the lapsed morality of his congregation and the rigid formality of his fellow New England ministers. It was the power of Protestant Christianity, not a forgotten novel, he sought to revive.

In spite of its religious connotations, however, *revival* in the United States is also used to describe literary recoveries, and sometimes recoveries of nineteenth-century writers by twentieth-century readers. Emily Dickinson, for one, had little recognition in her own time, becoming famous only after her death. And Herman Melville, successful early in his career, lost most of his audience later in life. But he is widely acclaimed today.

Neither Dickinson nor Melville, however, waited seventy years for most readers to discover them. Emily Dickinson died in 1886, eighteen years before Kate Chopin, but editions of some of her poems were in print from 1890 on, and less-than-satisfactory versions of the poems continued to be available until 1955, when Thomas H. Johnson published accurate texts and readers could feel the full force of what Dickinson had accomplished. Herman Melville died in 1891, thirteen years before Kate Chopin, but reprinted editions of his works began appearing shortly after his death, and by 1923 British novelist D. H. Lawrence was proclaiming him, along with Nathaniel Hawthorne, Walt Whitman, Edgar Allan Poe, and others, to be among America's great writers.

Kate Chopin, unlike Emily Dickinson, was published in America's premier magazines and was the author of two successful books. And Chopin, unlike Herman Melville, was easy enough for readers at the time to understand. No critic of The Awakening echoed a reviewer of Melville's novel Pierre by famously proclaiming in a headline, "Kate Chopin Crazy," because the truth of her work was thought obscure, indecipherable. Just the opposite. The Awakening was perfectly clear, and its author was presumed to be absolutely sane. It was not the truth of her book that came under attack in 1899 but the fact that Chopin had put that truth on paper and published it.

Other nineteenth-century writers have also belatedly found their way into the American literary canon—Frederick Douglass, W. E. B. Du Bois, Fanny Fern, Mary Wilkins Freeman, Charlotte Perkins Gilman, Harriet Jacobs, Sarah Orne Jewett, and Sojourner Truth, among them. But Kate Chopin, with her tempestuous trajectory of broad acceptance, fierce rejection, long decades of neglect, and ecstatic embrace by today's readers, remains extraordinary.

During the closing decade of the nineteenth century, starting when she was about forty years old, Chopin wrote a hundred or so short stories, two novels, and some other works. Her first novel, At Fault (1890), was ignored by readers and critics, but her short stories were very successful. She placed them with some of America's most prestigious magazines— the Atlantic Monthly, the Century, Vogue, Youth's Companion, Harper's Young People—and the American Press Association syndicated several of them. Editors and readers across the country responded with enthusiasm to her charming pictures of life among the Creoles and Acadians of Louisiana, and her two collections of stories, Bayou Folk (1894) and A Night in Acadie (1897), were praised by reviewers. Kate Chopin became well known as a writer of regional fiction, local-color fiction.

The Awakening (1899), however, set off a firestorm of complaints from critics scandalized by its frank treatment of a woman's frustration with her marriage, of her emotional and sexual awakening and her eventual suicide. They attacked the novel mercilessly, calling it disagreeable, flawed, unhealthy—"gilded dirt," as one phrased it, "trite and sordid," as Willa Cather wrote.[2]

Although the book was not removed from the shelves of Chopin's hometown library, as has often been claimed, it was pulled from circulation at a library in Evanston, Illinois, in 1902. And the contract for a third book of short stories, A Vocation and a Voice, was, for whatever reason, canceled by her publisher. Chopin wrote just a few more works before her death in 1904.

The Awakening was reissued in 1906, but after that it went unread for decades. Chopin's short stories fared a little better. Bayou Folk was also reprinted in 1906 and again in 1911, and beginning in 1921 some Chopin stories began appearing in collections. Eight stories were anthologized over the next few decades, some of them in books that went through multiple printings. In 1930 Dorothy Anne Dondore extolled The Awakening as being ahead of its time, and for a brief moment it seemed like the novel might be on its way to rediscovery. But in his biography two years later, Daniel Rankin, a conservative Roman Catholic priest, praised the richness of Kate Chopin's fiction and her emphasis on local color but reinforced what critics wrote in the 1890s by describing The Awakening as "exotic in setting, morbid in theme, erotic in motivation." Although Rankin was, as a later critic phrased it, "disqualified by taste and temperament from doing justice to the original qualities of Kate Chopin's mind," his biography set the tone for critical response to Kate Chopin for another generation.[3]

Then Cyrille Arnavon, a French scholar who in 1946 had written an article about Chopin and in 1953 had been the first to translate The Awakening into French (and whose influence among French Chopin scholars today is still very strong), met a Norwegian graduate student, Per Seyersted, at Harvard and interested him in Chopin's work. Seyersted spent years shuffling between Norway and the United States gathering materials—and in 1969 Louisiana State University Press published his Kate Chopin: A Critical Biography and his edition The Complete Works of Kate Chopin, with a foreword by the great American critic Edmund Wilson. Kate Chopin was back.

It is difficult to overstate the importance of Per Seyersted's work. Most of us writing in this volume are deeply indebted to the man. He was not, it is true, the first to recognize that The Awakening was a remarkable work. George Arms, Warner Berthoff, Robert Cantwell, Kenneth Eble, Edmund Wilson, and Larzer Ziff, all established critics, promoted the novel's reputation throughout the 1950s and 1960s. But Seyersted made available for the first time the breadth, richness, and vitality of Kate Chopin's complete work. He reexamined her subjects, her influences, her themes, her private life. And he redefined her place among American authors by shifting critical focus from the regional nature of her writing to its position in the realm of women's fiction. "The great achievement of Kate Chopin," Seyersted wrote,

> was that she broke new ground in American literature. She was the first woman writer in her country to accept passion as a legitimate subject for serious, outspoken fiction. Revolting against tradition and authority; with a daring which we can hardly fathom today; with an uncompromising honesty and no trace of sensationalism, she undertook to give the unsparing truth about woman's submerged life. She was something of a pioneer in the amoral treatment of sexuality, of divorce, and of woman's urge for an existential authenticity. She is in many respects a modern writer, particularly in her awareness of the complexities of truth and the complications of freedom. With no desire to reform, but only to understand; with the clear conscience of the rebel, yet unembittered by society's massive lack of understanding, she arrived at her culminating achievements, The Awakening and "The Storm."[4]

Per Seyersted's biography and his edition of Chopin's work solidified, accelerated, extended, and enriched a Kate Chopin revival already under way. And his books arrived at a watershed moment in American life. The nation was ready for them.

The women's movement was coming into its own in the 1960s, experiencing a rebirth. The National Organization for Women was formed in 1966, the same year, according to records at the Louisiana State University Press, that Per Seyersted received his contract to edit an edition of Kate Chopin's works. Bella Abzug, Gloria Steinem, Betty Friedan, and other feminist leaders were arguing for legal and social changes— abortion rights, government-funded child care centers, equal pay for women, and an end to economic, political, and educational barriers that blocked women from achieving their potential. As several of us point out in these essays, feminism unquestionably provided the primary motive force for the Kate Chopin revival.

But massive changes and startling events playing out around the world in the 1960s helped set the mood for the feminist movement and for the way that Kate Chopin was received in the United States and abroad in the 1970s and 1980s. Several of us protested against the war in Vietnam, and all of us were aware of the impact of the civil rights movement, of political assassinations in the country (John F. Kennedy, Martin Luther King, Malcolm X, Robert Kennedy), of social upheavals in Prague and Paris, along with the worldwide revolutions in popular music, literature, art, and film, the rise of the drug culture, the emergence of new sexual norms, and the astonishing technological achievements epitomized by human beings walking on the moon. That famous "one small step for a man, one giant leap for mankind" took place in the summer of 1969, as Chopin's *Complete Works* was being printed and bound. We were living, we recognized, at a heady time, one in which, despite setbacks and disasters, almost anything seemed possible. Our essays capture some of that excitement and hope.

Each of us included in this collection published an extended work of Chopin scholarship in the twenty-five years after the appearance of Per Seyersted's *Complete Works* in 1969. Each of us edited a volume of Kate Chopin's fiction or a collection of essays about Chopin or wrote a biography or critical study or assembled a bibliography in those years. Certainly we were not alone in our work. Nina Baym, Harold Bloom, Margo Culley, Sara deSaussure Davis, Kenneth Eble, Sandra Gilbert, Lewis Leary, Peggy Skaggs, and Nancy Walker also wrote or edited books in that quarter century promoting Kate Chopin's work. Jean Bardot, Carol P. Christ, Joyce Dyer, Elizabeth Fox-Genovese, Patricia Hopkins Lattin, John May, Richard Potter, John Carlos Rowe, Lawrence Thornton, Jane Tompkins, Cynthia Griffin Wolff, and others wrote influential essays that helped shape people's response to Kate Chopin in the 1970s and 1980s. And others influenced readers through their discussions of regional literature or women's literature or canon construction—Warner Berthoff, Marie Fletcher, Judith Fryer, Susan Gubar, Anne Goodwyn Jones, Paul Lauter, Ellen Moers, Anne Firor Scott, Elaine Showalter, Patricia Meyer Spacks, and Barbara Welter, among them.

Our essays have several characteristics:

—They are arranged in groups, but each encompasses more than its place in a grouping might suggest. Most of the essays, even those not in the feminist group, contain feminist connections, and many, including some in the feminist group, question some of those connections.

—They are at times highly personal. Even scholars in the sciences and mathematics admit that their professional work may be influenced by their private concerns, that their research may affect their lives and their lives their research. That was true for most of us working on Kate Chopin.

—They are full of surprises. Some of them take turns that are not predictable from reading the first page or two, and several include facts or observations that even seasoned Chopin scholars should find intriguing.

—They contain discussions of *The Awakening*, of course, but also of *At Fault*, "The Storm," "Désirée's Baby," "A Pair of Silk Stockings," "Athénaïse," "Aunt Lympy's Interference," "A No-Account Creole," "Lilacs," Chopin's Guy de Maupassant translations, and other Kate Chopin works.

—They vary widely in rhetorical style. We are all academicians, but some of us work at research institutions while others teach at small regional public and private colleges. At least three of us have been academic administrators—one a president and two vice presidents of colleges or universities—and several of us are retired or near retirement. Some of us have published with commercial houses as well as with academic journals, and one of us is a columnist for the *Chronicle of Higher Education*. Our essays bear the marks of our different experiences since the 1970s.

—They are not only celebratory. A few of us have dealt with disappointments and have backed away from our study of Chopin. And several of us have questioned others' arguments about Chopin's fiction. Some degree of disappointment with and disagreement about what happened in the 1970s and 1980s is inevitable, and documenting such matters is, we think, important for the record.

—And they are history, but history colored a bit by memory, hence the word "Story" in our subtitle. We've checked our facts carefully, but we hope you'll forgive us if we've confused the order in which a couple of events played out, if we've ornamented a detail here and there, or especially if we've neglected to credit someone who helped us along the way. We are fully aware that many people besides us are responsible for bringing Kate

Chopin into the canon. A number of those people are mentioned in our essays; others reside in our memories. If the Chopin revival was anything, it was teamwork—in, of course, the academic humanities' sense of that word, meaning that we mostly worked alone, competed for book contracts and space in journals, and often did not meet or talk with one another. But each of us was aware of what the others were doing. In our own way, we supported one another when we could. And we realized that there was something important at stake in our work. We understood, as Robert Frost phrased it in "The Tuft of Flowers," that people "work together . . . whether they work together or apart."

We have, therefore, many stories to tell that together constitute the story of the Kate Chopin revival. We present our essays in three sections.

Emily Toth opens "Feminisms," the first group of essays, with her rebel's wide-ranging discussion of everything Chopin, including her meetings with Per Seyersted, her founding of the Kate Chopin Newsletter, and her long path to her two Kate Chopin biographies. Barbara C. Ewell describes the events that led to her engagement with feminism and the writing of her early critical study of Chopin's short stories and novels, and she mounts a spirited argument for reevaluating nineteenth-century local-color writing. Helen Taylor internationalizes the Kate Chopin revival by tying it to her native Britain. She tells of her years as a student at Louisiana State University and her return to England, where she edited Chopin volumes and pursued other feminist projects. Barbara H. Solomon explains how she came to edit the New American Library's "The Awakening" and Selected Stories of Kate Chopin and the criteria she used for selecting short works for the volume. And Mary E. Papke writes from a "feminist materialist" perspective about the profound sense of sadness that she finds in The Awakening and other Chopin works. She looks at what she calls partial readings or misreadings of Kate Chopin with a view to rethinking Chopin's position in American literature.

Thomas Bonner Jr. begins "Foundations," the second essay set, in 1956, as he is reading "Désirée's Baby" on a segregated streetcar in New Orleans. His essay describes the motivation behind his book The Kate Chopin Companion: With Translations from French Fiction. Robert D. Arner, who wrote the first Kate Chopin dissertation since Daniel Rankin's in the 1930s and published it in a special issue of Louisiana Studies, explains why he abandoned his work on Chopin. He argues for the importance of close reading of Chopin's short fiction, focusing on "A Pair of Silk Stockings." Marlene Springer describes her work on assembling her volume *Edith Wharton and Kate Chopin: A Reference Guide*, and she includes reflections on the death of the card catalog and the implications for Chopin studies of rapid technological change. And Lynda S. Boren's engagement with Chopin leads her back to the Louisiana of her youth, where she finds classical elements of romantic thought in *The Awakening*, including elements of spiritual vampirism.

Susan Lohafer introduces "Expansions," the third group of essays, by looking at what Chopin offers people interested in short fiction studies and the relationship between genre studies and cognitive science. She concentrates on her preclosure analysis of Chopin's "Athénaïse" and "Aunt Lympy's Interference." Anna Shannon Elfenbein discusses her work on race in Chopin's fiction, including her study *Women on the Color Line: Evolving Stereotypes and the Writings of George Washington Cable, Grace King, Kate Chopin*. She shows how mixed-race women in *The Awakening* enrich the social texture of the novel and illuminate Edna Pontellier's "awakening." And Bernard Koloski, surveying Chopin's two novels and several short stories, emphasizes an undercurrent in Chopin's work—her French connections and her American optimism.

Embedded in our essays are implications for people today who are determined to revive another forgotten writer. It is well to keep in mind that as we were promoting Kate Chopin's work in the 1970s and 1980s, many other scholars were working just as hard as we were to revive the fiction or the poetry of many other writers. A few of those writers now occupy a widely accepted place in the literary canon, but most do not. Our sponsorship of a neglected author was not unique, but it was unusual because it succeeded.

Our essays stress several elements that contributed to that success:

—Timing was critical. Would Kate Chopin have been accepted as she was if we had set out to work on her after 1949 rather than after 1969? If we had set out after 1989? Perhaps, but probably not. The Chopin revival was a literary event, but it was also a social, a cultural phenomenon. We rode a wave—an enormous wave—that was not much of our own making, and it is difficult to imagine so spirited a Kate Chopin revival taking place at another time.

—Textural, biographical, and historical scholarship was essential. Copies of The Awakening alone would almost certainly not have been enough to launch Kate Chopin's nineteenth-century novel so quickly into anthologies and college courses, no matter how powerfully it affected people. Most of us were able to work swiftly and efficiently and to publish our scholarship with established journals and presses because we had at our fingertips much of what we needed to do serious scholarly work—Per Seyersted's accurate texts of almost everything Chopin had written, a good biographical basis for understanding the relationship between her life and her fiction, organized critical and historical documents and analyses—principal materials of literary study. We built on what we had to work with knowing we had solid foundations under us.

—Highly respected scholars smoothed the road for us. It was no small matter that publications by Nina Baym, Harold Bloom, Sandra Gilbert, Lewis Leary, Elaine Showalter, Edmund Wilson, Larzer Ziff, and others gave a legitimacy to our arguments for the importance of Chopin's work.

—Popular sources helped. Redbook and the New York Times ran pieces on Chopin, PBS organized a television production, directors completed films based on The Awakening and "The Story of an Hour," and Robert Stone published a novel about the making of a film of Chopin's book.

—Networking also helped. Emily Toth's Kate Chopin Newsletter early on built a Chopin community—and not only a community of scholars. Several of us mention the importance of Mildred McCoy, who created the Bayou Folk Museum in Cloutierville, Louisiana (which, unfortunately, burned to the ground in October 2008), and most of us are indebted to people from other walks of life who moved our work along.

—We managed the ups and downs. Because we were young and inexperienced, we were sometimes startled to receive book contracts and always honored to have our work accepted and published. We were, it is true, fearless—"confident," as one of us phrases it—in proposing ahead-of-their-time projects, and, as a result, some of us had to deal with rejection. Several of us describe our failures to convince department chairs, funding committees, or publishers that our proposals were viable, only to see such proposals by other scholars accepted a few years later. Premature discernment, we learned—as Kate Chopin had learned—can be a burden.

—Diversity of thought enhanced our efforts. Beginning in her own time, Kate Chopin has been understood in different ways. Feminism drove much of our work in the 1970s and 1980s, but a look at these essays or at a listing of articles and books about Chopin will reveal that people take quite varied approaches to her fiction. Part of what sustains the continuing interest in Chopin today is the freshness and richness of critical thought about her.

In the final analysis, however, despite all we describe in this book and all that others have done on her behalf, it is Kate Chopin herself who made her revival possible, who made her work canonical. We scholars guided readers to Chopin and offered them texts and tools for understanding her, but it is she herself they responded to. The fact is that for countless readers, Kate Chopin at her best is irresistible. She draws people, as she drew the twelve of us, into her imaginative world. She grows with them and continues to speak to them in new ways, surprising ways, as they mature and as their world changes.

For nearly three-quarters of a century, Kate Chopin was neglected. In the 1970s, when the time was right, people rediscovered her—and through their awakenings enriched their lives.

NOTES

1. Chopin's works are available in a great number of editions, anthologies, and textbooks; they have been translated into other languages, including French, Polish, Dutch, Czech, Korean, and Portuguese; and in 2008 an average of more than two hundred people a day from at least ninety countries visited the Web site of the Kate Chopin International Society, seeking information about Chopin and her fiction. KateChopin.org, Kate Chopin International Society, 2 Jan. 2009. Web. 2 Jan. 2009.

2. Janet Beer and Elizabeth Nolan, eds., Kate Chopin's "The Awakening": A Sourcebook (London: Routledge, 2004) 58–60.

3. Daniel S. Rankin, Kate Chopin and Her Creole Stories (Philadelphia: U of Pennsylvania P, 1932) 175. Daniel Aaron, "Per Seyersted: Kate Chopin. A Critical Biography," Edda: Scandinavian Journal of Literary Research 71 (1971): 342.

4. Per Seyersted, Kate Chopin: A Critical Biography (Baton Rouge: Louisiana State UP, 1969) 198.

1

FEMINISMS

1

My Part in Reviving Kate Chopin

EMILY TOTH

"YOU SHOULD READ THIS," said my friend Annette Stadd, slipping a small orange-covered paperback into my book bag. I barely got a peek at the cover drawing—a lady with a chignon—before we rejoined the chant "U.S. Out of Vietnam! Make love, not war!"

It was 1970 in Baltimore, and we were trying to end the Vietnam War. Annette soon left for Colorado to find herself, but I still have that tattered copy of *The Awakening*. It gave me a lifetime of questions that I'm still pondering.

As a snobbish grad student, I was proud that I understood the parrot's French. Edna's honest confusions were true of every woman I knew, and I recognized her pompous husband as one in a long line of patriarchal know-it-alls, including Torvald in Ibsen's *A Doll's House*. The kind of Victorian man who believes that he knows all about women was a cliché—but he was also alive and well and teaching in my graduate program at Johns Hopkins University.

My Dante professor said that the last interesting woman had been Francesca in the *Inferno* (Dante died in 1321). My eighteenth-century-literature professor assigned no women writers, while conceding that a lot of women had been published during that period "but I've never read them. They were all trash." My European-novel professor offered to discuss women in literature if I'd be his "mistress," while a French professor most wanted me to know that he was different from other Frenchmen, who "mostly masturbated."

Then my Chaucer professor, a not-yet-out gay man, got tired of my arguing that he didn't represent women characters' points of view—and threw me out of class. So did the European-novel professor, for that matter, and the Dante professor—my sometime department chair—wouldn't allow me to teach a women writers course for credit: "There's nothing of substance," he said.

So I taught a noncredit course in women writers in the spring of 1971. A dozen brave undergraduates signed up, including some of the first women undergrads ever at Hopkins. In other classes, their male classmates either ignored them or leered crudely, and they were hungry—as I was—for writers who made women important and serious characters. We were hungry for women who didn't take what the patriarchs dished out. (When coeducation was first being considered, one furious alumnus had written to the Johns Hopkins newsletter: "Why waste a first-class Hopkins education on future cooks and bottle washers?")

My students and I were determined not to waste our time. We were creating women's studies at "the Hop"—and we started by reading Kate Chopin. I had read and reread *The Awakening* through 1970 and 1971, and I'd also found "The Story of an Hour" because it was reprinted in *Aphra*, a pioneering feminist literary magazine named after Aphra Behn, the first Englishwoman to make a living from her writing. (As a college English major, I'd never heard of her, either. We'd read Virginia Woolf, but not *A Room of One's Own*, the book that celebrates Aphra Behn as our foremother.)

Of the students who first read *The Awakening* with me, one became Miss Missouri (Kate Chopin's home state), while the others went on to become labor lawyers, judges, and muckraking journalists. Kate Chopin taught us all to take wing, to learn and to soar.

I'd always known I wanted to be a writer, but my education as a woman writer was mostly nonexistent. I'd picked up the message that writing popular fiction about women's thoughts was a little low class (that's still the attitude in many creative writing programs). The only assigned books that moved me were George Eliot's *Middlemarch* and *Mill on the Floss*. Our methods for literary criticism didn't allow us to talk about emotions, especially the war between being a person and being a "mother-woman."

Though I was (and am) married, I didn't want the rest of the traditional package, and Kate Chopin taught me how to resist. In fact, at every stage in my life, she's had wise advice for me. Now, older than she was when she died, I'm most moved by Dr. Mandelet's musings in chapter 38: "Youth is given up to illusions . . . a decoy to secure mothers for the race."

The women's movement, the second wave in the 1970s, was supposed to deconstruct women's illusions. By finding and teaching women writers, we helped destroy the myth that women had never written anything of literary or cultural merit—but for a long time I didn't question those standards of "merit." When I first taught *The Awakening*, I wanted to show that it was respectable by the male standards I'd been taught. It paralleled *Madame Bovary*, *A Doll's House*, and *Anna Karenina*, and yet. . . . As one of the early reviewers of *The Awakening* noted, "There is throughout the story an undercurrent of sympathy for Edna, and nowhere a single note of censure of her totally unjustifiable conduct."[1]

Yes! And it was that sympathy that I wanted to share.

I had started grad school thinking I was a medievalist. But once I was kicked out of Chaucer class, that pilgrimage was shut down. The greatest —and at that time, perhaps the only—mensch in the all-white, all-male Johns Hopkins English Department was Laurence Holland, the newly hired professor in American literature. And so I suddenly became an Americanist, despite never having taken an American lit course in my life. But I knew I'd chosen the best possible dissertation topic: a superb woman writer about whom very little had been written. And to my great relief—and now, more gratitude than I could ever express—Larry Holland agreed to direct my dissertation on Kate Chopin.

The next step was making up my (very short) bibliography. The only scholar who'd published recently on Kate Chopin was someone named Per Seyersted, a Norwegian businessman (manager of the Viul pulp mill, I learned later). He had gone to Harvard graduate school, where a visiting French professor, Cyrille Arnavon, turned him on to Kate Chopin. Seyersted, whose mother, Dakky Kiær, had been a women's rights leader in Norway, was primed to appreciate Kate Chopin. Determined to resurrect her, he spent half a decade crisscrossing the Atlantic to visit libraries, transcribe unreadable manuscripts in pencil, and hunt up anyone who might have known anything about her. His energy and dedication were astounding and resulted in the two-volume *Complete Works of Kate Chopin* and *Kate Chopin: A Critical Biography*. Both were published in 1969, a year before the fateful copy of *The Awakening* fell into my hands.[2]

Three things, though, made *The Awakening* and Kate Chopin different from other women's writings that were being resurrected at the time. *The Awakening* was known to be about sex—a subject of intense public interest. We were, after all, at the height of the sexual revolution in 1970, ten years after the Pill and three years before *Roe v. Wade*. A second difference is that *The Awakening* was being championed by powerful men: the great literary critic Edmund Wilson and the University of Oslo professor Per Seyersted. Other contenders for resurrection, such as Elizabeth Stuart Phelps, were championed mostly by women who were graduate students (Carol Farley Kessler and Susan Coultrap McQuin). Seyersted and Wilson in effect gave *The Awakening* an imprimatur, making it acceptable for other men to read the book and call it "universal."

And there was also the story that *The Awakening* had been banned for its sexual content. In 1969–70, everyone wanted to read banned books, and a lot of us had grown up hotly reading the great dirty book of our generation, Grace Metalious's *Peyton Place* (1956). We were primed for a banned book about women and sex, and *The Awakening* was it on the literary side.

We were brash then—and so, at my first MLA convention ever, I found out that Per Seyersted was staying in my hotel, and I called him up. We had tea in the hotel coffee shop. I wore purple (in honor of Kate Chopin's love of lavender and lilac). He probably didn't notice.

He was very tall and thin, gangly and a little awkward. A Louisiana scholar later said that he resembled Ichabod Crane. He was fiftyish (born in 1921) and had a sharply pointed, sallow, lined face. He looked intensely interested, and I liked him immediately because he treated me as an equal, not as a silly girl who'd somehow come to believe that literature is pretty. (A Hopkins professor had said that to my roommate, who dropped out.)

Seyersted told me how to pronounce his name—"Pair Say-er-sted"— and added that he and his second wife, Brita Lindberg-Seyersted, also a literary scholar, had not stayed in the United States because women academics were treated so badly here. He treated me with great generosity and approved of my not having children. We also gossiped a bit about one Hopkins professor whom he knew as an important scholar. I knew the man as a sexual harasser who destroyed blonde women students' careers.

Before we said good-bye, he'd given me permission to see the sealed Kate Chopin 1894 diary at the Missouri Historical Society (now the Missouri History Museum) in St. Louis. Seyersted had gotten it from her grandson, after cold-calling him from a New York airport and confessing, "I'm in love with your grandmother." Robert Hattersley had never known his grandmother Kate, who'd died before he was born, but he did not hang up on this foreign-sounding loon who claimed to be in love with Kate Chopin. Instead, Hattersley gave Per Seyersted the run of his attic, and when the 1894 diary was recovered from a pile of stuff, it had a large rat hole gnawed in the cover. It contained stunning things, especially the priceless erotic vignette "The Storm." (Seyersted could not get the Missouri Historical Society to publish it in its bulletin.)

Seyersted told me that he'd been hoping that American feminists would take up Kate Chopin. I was the first to contact him; he was very happy; and sometime soon thereafter he signed me up to do editing and clerical chores for what became A Kate Chopin Miscellany.

Two years later, in 1972, Seyersted flew in from Oslo for the first MLA session on Kate Chopin, which I arranged and chaired. It was standing-room only, seventy-five people, to Seyersted's amazement and delight. We discussed about a dozen papers, distributed beforehand, including one by Bernard Koloski, who became a close friend and fellow Chopinist. Another was by Peggy Skaggs, whose Twayne book on Chopin was one of the first full-length studies. That session also inspired me to create the Kate Chopin Newsletter.

That kind of outsider publishing was part of my family heritage. My mother had written and mimeographed protest leaflets for the Communist Party in the 1930s, and I ran a fan club and newsletter for a Cleveland Indians baseball player, Rocky Colavito, in the late 1950s. By the mid-1960s, my Jewish mother was putting out the Unitarians' fair housing newsletter, staking out her claim to the truth as she saw it—just as I did with the Kate Chopin Newsletter.

There were other photocopied newsletters at the time, and I especially remember studying The Mary Wollstonecraft Newsletter for its mix of news and criticism. Like bloggers and authors' societies today, we were making up our own rules.

Meanwhile there were no rules, or any agreed-upon language, for discussing "the literary canon." The term wasn't yet in use because we were supposed to trust that our school books were the best that had been thought and written. Without a term like "male approval" (never mind "phallocrat"), we had no language for contesting what we'd been told—though we did notice that sometimes men got mad. When I asked, "What criteria are used to determine that Chaucer is a great writer?" my professor snarled his contempt: "That's a simple-minded question that only a freshman would ask." But he did deign to answer it later: Chaucer, he said, covered and depicted all the central human experiences.

"What about childbirth?" I asked.

Obviously I was on my way out the door—but Kate Chopin was on her way into the literary canon. The *Kate Chopin Newsletter*, which ran for two years under that title and then for another two as *Regionalism and the Female Imagination*, no doubt helped. I sent it to the few women who were important in MLA and to friends who later became powerful reshapers of the canon: Cathy Davidson, Carolyn Heilbrun, Florence Howe, Annette Kolodny, Susan Koppelman, Mary Jane Lupton, Lillian Robinson, Elaine Showalter, Catharine Stimpson.

The *Kate Chopin Newsletter* was the first to break the story of Kate Chopin's true birth date. Although her tombstone says 1851, French professor Jean Bardot found a St. Louis baptismal record showing her birth in 1850, a date confirmed by the U.S. Census for that year. That discovery, made some thirty years ago, still hasn't penetrated the Library of Congress system, and half the sites on the Net still have the wrong date. (I've given up complaining.)

I began my dissertation at a time when Kate Chopin was just starting to become "hot." The first two biographies had been completed (Daniel Rankin's in 1932, Per Seyersted's in 1969), along with Robert Arner's Penn State dissertation. By the time I finished in 1975, there were nearly a dozen other dissertations, including those by Bernard Koloski and Peggy Skaggs.

We were on a wave, but we didn't know where it was taking us, and we all floundered a bit as we tried to figure out what to say about Kate Chopin's writings. Some of us wrote about images and themes, using the tools of New Criticism, while others gathered Chopin reviews or studied Chopin's rendering of regional accents. I may be the only one who attempted to link Chopin's work with the literary theory that was then emerging at my graduate school.

Paul de Man was my first department head, before he dumped Hopkins and decamped for Yale. One afternoon Jacques Derrida visited our class and ruminated on the theory that "the title is father to the text," a subject of no use at all to me. Much of literary theory (it seemed to me) was ponderous peacocking, vague generalities that could come to destroy our appreciation for good writing and lucid thinking. (I didn't yet know the term "post comprehensible jargon.") Still, I thought I needed to know all about it.

The original plan was that my dissertation would examine Kate Chopin's works in the light of various literary critical approaches, including New Criticism, structuralism, Marxism, and the newly emerging feminist criticism. This proved unworkable, mostly because it didn't grab me—and in the meantime I'd gone on a research trip to the Missouri Historical Society in St. Louis. I got to touch Kate Chopin's papers.

I had never held someone else's diaries or read the handwritten thoughts of a teenager who already knew what it had taken me years to notice. According to her Commonplace Book from the 1860s, Kate O'Flaherty hated the social whirl ("I dance with people I despise; amuse myself with men whose only talent lies in their feet"), and she'd figured out what it takes to be popular: let the other person speak, appear to be totally enthralled, and "twenty to one—he will report you as one of the most entertaining and intelligent persons."[3] Kate O'Flaherty's youthful realism made me laugh out loud. I, too, was falling deeply in love with Robert Hattersley's grandmother.

Kate Chopin's papers made me want to know more about how her mind worked—not the minds of literary critics. I wanted to see her as a writer drawing on other writers (her "influences," we said then; now we might say "intertextuality"). I wanted to see how she adapted other writers' "literary conventions" ("tropes") for her own ends.

Without knowing it, because we didn't have the vocabulary, I was trying to link her into the standard literary canon. A writer who is too different from her predecessors, who truly is a "solitary genius" and "ahead of her time" (terms frequently applied to Kate Chopin), will always be a commercial failure—if she even manages to be published at all. Chopin had to draw on those who wrote before her, and often they were women writers: as Virginia Woolf wrote, we think back through our mothers. Chopin's foremothers were usually women writers unknown to me, so I found myself among those scholars who were reconstructing the women's literary canon. I read such writers as Mary E. Wilkins Freeman, E. D. E. N. Southworth, and Susan Warner in long-out-of-print, locked-away copies at the Library of Congress.

Eventually my dissertation compared Kate Chopin's writings with theirs, as well as with those of white writers in the plantation tradition, works by black and white writers about African American characters, and writings of European and American critics about women's roles. I looked at male writers in the canon (Twain, Flaubert), and showed how Chopin's perceptions diverged from theirs. I was doing cultural studies before it had a name.

But I mainly wanted to learn more about Kate Chopin, teach her everywhere I could, write about her, meet like-minded people—and get an academic job. I was teaching at Morgan State, a historically black university in Baltimore, when *Redbook* reprinted *The Awakening* in 1972 as "a classic underground novel" that many readers thought was a contemporary book. I taught *The Awakening* as a part-time instructor, day and evening, at Hopkins, and I included Chopin in Women's Liberation talks for Essex Community College, the University of Maryland–Baltimore County, Towson State, Goucher, and elsewhere. It all runs together because we feminist activists were so busy.

My first Chopin publication was in a Baltimore activist newsletter called *Cold Day in August*. In "Women and Their Friends: Some Thoughts about Literature," I described Edna as someone torn between the conflicting models of the artist and the mother-woman. The men are far less important to Edna than her sense of herself, I wrote. That was a fairly radical thought, then, or so said one of my dissertation readers.

I was close to finishing when I went on the job market, which was tight even in 1973. I was a lifelong Yankee, imbued with all the usual prejudices. I'd worked in the civil rights movement, and I'd never been south of Maryland. Nevertheless, inspired by my Kate Chopin reading, I applied to be an instructor at the University of New Orleans. It proved to be the only job offer I got—and so, in 1974, my husband and I moved to New Orleans. It was 104 years after Kate Chopin moved there with her new husband, and we did exactly what she'd done. We fell in love with New Orleans.

I was still writing the dissertation, sometimes by hand on the St. Charles Avenue streetcar. The route went all the way up to Carrollton (where Edna Pontellier winds up after her long walks), and it went down to Canal Street, the boundary between the "American" side and the French Quarter (where the Ratignolles and Pontelliers live). On Rampart Street there was still Congo Square, the site of the slaves' dancing in "La Belle Zoraïde" (the site is now Louis Armstrong Park). The levees and the French Market were still there, as were the St. Louis Cathedral and Bayou St. John. We lived not far from Magazine Street, where Kate Chopin gave birth to her first son, Jean, in 1871. The Chopins' last New Orleans home, on Louisiana Avenue, was a stop on our Sunday night walks.

It was easy to see why Kate Chopin loved the color, music, and food of New Orleans. Many people struggle to finish their dissertations, but I wrote mine in a kind of sensory harmony. The only discordant note was Grand Isle, no longer the tropical paradise of Chopin's day. It was mostly a lot of shacks on sandy land, and a huge dead dolphin lay on the beach.

When I did finish, there was so much that I still didn't know. I was, after all, not much older than Edna in *The Awakening*. I was dimly aware that the world outside Louisiana had noticed Kate Chopin, but I still thought of her as mostly a private discovery, the property of a coterie.

That perception began to change, and I wasn't done with her. Per Seyersted's assignments for me included pursuing some leads at the Kate Chopin/Bayou Folk Museum in Cloutierville, Louisiana, where the Chopins had moved in 1879 after Oscar's cotton factor business went bankrupt. Oscar died there in 1882, and Kate stayed on until 1884.

The museum had been founded by Mildred LaCaze McCoy in 1964, just a few years before Seyersted's books made Kate Chopin available to the world. The house where Kate and Oscar Chopin and their six children had lived was small by modern standards but grand by those of Cloutierville: two stories, several bedrooms, outbuildings for servants. A century later, Cloutierville (pronounced "Cloochy-ville") was still a tiny village, a few hundred souls settled around one winding road. As a city person myself, I wondered how Kate Chopin, with her urban ways and her flamboyant fashions, could have functioned in such a small rural world. She must have felt diminished, and I wondered what she thought and how she coped.

And then, thanks to the academic job market, I found myself in rural North Dakota. Like Kate Chopin in Cloutierville, I could look out the back door for miles and see what—to my citified eyes—looked like nothing, emptiness. Country people see a natural beauty that to me was thoroughly lacking.

I wanted to wear purple.

Still, at the University of North Dakota, Kate Chopin had become a more respected and more-taught author. She fit into the local interest in regionalism and place, and that was why I changed the Kate Chopin Newsletter to Regionalism and the Female Imagination. A generous dean funded one printed edition (the only one). Of the two graduate students who helped me with editing and production, one left academia and the other—having read and absorbed The Awakening—left her husband.

Kate Chopin was reaching out.

But the importance of women writers hadn't yet penetrated the English Department at Penn State, where I moved in 1977. I had been hired to "do" women's studies and popular culture, both of which were distinctly unpopular among my colleagues. I was also abrasive, I realize now, as well as politically obtuse: I preferred holing up at home and writing, rather than schmoozing in the halls. (When I did come to campus, I found myself perennially put on panels and committees as a token woman. No wonder academic women of my generation didn't have time to have children.)

I also didn't know how to convince my Penn State colleagues that Kate Chopin was more than "an interesting minor writer." Nor could I persuade them that a course on the history of the literary canon was more than "just a parlor game." It was ten years before I was allowed to teach a graduate course, and despite three books, numerous publications, and a stellar teaching record, I barely got tenure. (I think one of my outside tenure referees was Marlene Springer. I was not supposed to be told their names, but my department chair took pity on me, a bit, when I started to cry.)

All that was material for a later revenge book, Ms. Mentor's Impeccable Advice for Women in Academia, but even at the time, mostly unbeknownst to me, I was winning. In 1979 I gave up producing *Regionalism and the Female Imagination* because there was little or no department support. It was tiring, in those days before computers. I had to type each article myself, on my manual typewriter at home, so I'd have the same typeface, and I corrected errors with Wite-Out. I learned to type with extreme accuracy because correcting errors was so laborious. Once when the backspace key jammed, I learned not to make errors at all. I couldn't afford the time.

But elsewhere, as *Dissertation Abstracts* showed me, people were writing dissertations on Kate Chopin. They were fitting her into literary history and showing that she was not an anomaly. She was becoming a little domesticated. The University of Oslo Press (Universitetsforlaget) and the newly created Northwestern State University Press of Louisiana agreed to co-publish the *Kate Chopin Miscellany* that Per Seyersted had long envisioned.

My part was mostly editorial drudgery, including proofreading the letters and diaries that Seyersted had painstakingly gathered. I worked on translating Cyrille Arnavon's Chopin appreciation and compiled a bibliography of Chopin criticism, expanding on Marlene Springer's work. Seyersted contributed the photos for that book, including the beautiful ones of Kate Chopin in her riding habit and the one of her in an opera gown, photographed from the back.

He and I met for the last time in 1979 at Kate Chopin's house, the Bayou Folk Museum in Cloutierville, for the launching of *A Kate Chopin Miscellany*. No one had exactly told me when I should be at the museum, and so I arrived late, just as Seyersted was signing the last copy of our book. At least the party had been well attended by some legislators and by the local "historical ladies," and the museum's proprietor, Mildred McCoy, was gratified. (She was also hilariously spiteful, and she would write me letters spilling the secrets of the area's "best families": inbreeding, interracial sex, endless scandals. Although she was a widow who'd lived in the area for fifty years, McCoy was still considered an outsider and "not from here"—and she retaliated, she told me with relish, by having an affair with someone else's husband.)

We dined at a local restaurant that evening, on the Cane River, and from the dock Seyersted saw the first turtles he'd ever seen. He was in great spirits, as were we all. We thought A Kate Chopin Miscellany would finally show the world what a fascinating woman the private Kate Chopin was—wise, witty, and worldly.

It didn't quite work out that way. Northwestern University Press of Louisiana was barely viable financially and not well run, and the book was never publicized or shown at conferences. I suspect most Chopin scholars today don't know it exists, especially since I folded most of the material into Kate Chopin's Private Papers—much of which Penn State funded, through research money.

It was an odd liminal time when I was at Penn State (1977–88). We hadn't gotten women securely into the literary canon, except for the great Victorian novelists. It eventually took an accreditation/evaluation team to point out that something was missing: the comprehensive reading list for Penn State doctoral candidates in English was all white, all male, as were almost all the courses. But my older colleagues, especially Daniel Walden, Stanley Weintraub, and Philip Young, liked my doing original research on a less-known author. Sometimes we had lunch and talked about biographical writing, since they'd worked on W. E. B. Du Bois, Queen Victoria, Ernest Hemingway, and many others. Maybe it was their age and stage in life: like Per Seyersted, who was forty-eight when his Chopin volumes appeared, they were professionally secure, not competitive about status and prestige. They welcomed me and helped me with grant and publishing tips—but my contemporary colleagues were wary to hostile. (When I published a popular historical novel, it was one of my contemporaries who called it "a piece of trash.")

I published things that embarrassed my department: not only that novel, Daughters of New Orleans, but also my first book, The Curse: A Cultural History of Menstruation (coauthored with Janice Delaney and Mary Jane Lupton). I also published Inside Peyton Place, a biography of the notorious author Grace Metalious. Kate Chopin was my most respectable subject, and that may be why I had no trouble getting a year-long sabbatical (at two-thirds pay) in 1984 to do biographical research on Chopin.

By then it had been fourteen years since Annette had slipped that slim volume of The Awakening into my eager hand. I was turning forty, Kate Chopin's age when she published At Fault and turned her writing life in a new direction, and it was time to do that myself. I was abetted by my mentors (Walden, Weintraub, and Young) and by my literary agents (Elaine Markson and Geri Thoma) and by the Chopinists I met at conferences (Bernie Koloski, Marlene Springer, and new friends Barbara Ewell and Thomas Bonner).

Finally I would do what I'd wanted to do all along: a biography of Kate Chopin. Before that I'd been too young, or too insecure in my career, but now I could pursue those questions that had been roiling about in my mind for so long: "How did Kate Chopin know all that in 1899?" and "Did she have a happy marriage?" and "After Oscar died, did she really—as Rankin claimed—never look at another man?"

The time was ripe, for biographers no longer had to be keepers of their subjects' secrets. R. W. B. Lewis had published the tale of Edith Wharton's juicy affair with Morton Fullerton, and soon Linda Wagner-Martin would write truthfully about Sylvia Plath's struggles with her powerful, sexy, and violent husband, Ted Hughes. Anne Sexton's and Henry James's private stories were revealed, and even academics' secret lives came out. After his 1983 death, Paul de Man was unmasked not only as an anti-Semite but also as a bigamist. (I finally understood why he'd advised me that "All academics marry twice: once when they're young and stupid, and later when they know more.")

Kate Chopin's biography would be the fruits of my wise early middle age. I got a book contract and a smart editor (Susan Leon) and set out to discover everything I could about Kate Chopin. By then I had allies and hosts in the growing Chopin network. In St. Louis, I stayed with Susan Koppelman; in New Orleans, with Barbara Ewell. In Cloutierville, Mildred McCoy had had a disabling stroke, and the Chopin Museum was being run by Lucille Carnahan, a retired librarian who was the best historian in town, a marvelous storyteller. Cloutierville was still a tiny village, occupied by twenty-seven widows over seventy, all of whom knew everything that had ever happened there. Lucille Carnahan let me, a Yankee outsider, into their world while I sought the answer to my boorish question: Did Kate Chopin have another man in her life?

I knew that Seyersted's formal manner and Rankin's being a Marist priest would have kept people from telling them any racy secrets. I also knew that women in the kitchen are the ones who have all the wisdom and the gossip.

A hint from one of Mildred McCoy's gossipy letters ("Mr. Sampite") sent me to New Orleans, where I visited with Ivy DeLouche, a former Cloutiervillian whose uncle was named Albert Sampite ("Sam-pi-tay"). Back in Cloutierville I visited his granddaughter Leona in her kitchen late one afternoon. After a while she handed me a Coke and a plate of tacos and said, "This was Kate Chopin's table."

I lifted the cover and found a green fuzzy surface. It had been Kate Chopin's pool and game table when she lived in Cloutierville, and when she left to go home to St. Louis in 1884—exactly a century before our conversation—she'd sold or given the table to Albert Sampite.

He had been someone else's husband, and he had been Kate Chopin's lover.

When Lucille Carnahan convened a group of descendants to share what they knew, they began with the conventional statement that "Kate Chopin was beautiful and charitable to the poor"—and then they dished. I learned that Albert Sampite had been a charming man when sober and a brutal batterer when he drank.

His character obviously inspired Chopin's characters named Alcée in "At the 'Cadian Ball," "The Storm," and *The Awakening*. Calixta in the two short stories closely resembles Ivy DeLouche's grandmother Maria Normand, who was Albert Sampite's long-term mistress—and everyone also remembered what Sampite's wife used to say: "Kate Chopin broke up my marriage."

There were those in Cloutierville who didn't want me to publish all that, but Leona Sampite thought the world should know. Her brother Joseph (the mayor of the town of Natchitoches) later bragged that his grandfather had gotten it on with Kate Chopin.

Kate Chopin's St. Louis descendants were intrigued. I'd stumbled upon them one day when my friend Susan Koppelman accidentally left her headlights on, and a helpful neighbor turned out to be named Kate Chopin—the writer's great-granddaughter. The Chopins were cheerful, funny, cooperative, and apologetic: "We don't know a whole lot—too bad we didn't listen to the grownups." One daughter-in-law hadn't wanted any mentions of Kate Chopin, who'd "read herself out of the Catholic Church." But that woman's son gleefully invented, just for me, a story about a wild tryst that Kate Chopin must have had with her doctor on the steps of a church.

I wrote it down, and this is the first time I've published that tale.

But my most startling St. Louis discovery was, well, a deflation. Beverly Bishop, the archivist at the Missouri Historical Society, told me that a dissertation writer, Joan Mayerson Clatworthy, had questioned whether The Awakening had really been banned in St. Louis.

I checked the library records and found out that it hadn't.

When Seyersted had reported that it had been withdrawn, in the chapter in his biography called "A Daring Novel Banned," he relied on an interview with a retired head librarian, as well as Chopin's own breezy statement in an essay, "The libraries! Oh, no, they don't keep it."[4] But it turned out that the libraries had indeed carried it. The copies were thrown out only after they were worn out.

We'd been suckered into reading a banned book that hadn't been banned after all, at least in St. Louis. (Bernard Koloski's recent research has turned up a banning in Evanston, Illinois, in 1902, and as late as 2005, a school board member in Chicago tried to ban it.) But any adult who'd wanted to read The Awakening in 1899 could easily have done so, just as we did from 1970 onward.

Meanwhile, my one-year biographical project morphed into five years. I was learning to write on a computer, struggling with filing, worrying about ailing parents, and looking for another job. By the time Kate Chopin: A Life of the Author of "The Awakening" came out in 1990, I had happily moved to Louisiana State University. It was the realization of a dream, to be in a place where Kate Chopin had always been in the canon. I no longer had to justify or explain anything.

Penguin agreed to publish Chopin's last short story collection, A Vocation and a Voice, ninety years after the original publication date. Seyersted agreed to an updated version of A Kate Chopin Miscellany, including new Chopin manuscripts discovered in Massachusetts in 1992. My graduate research assistants, Cheyenne Bonnell (Penn State) and Janet Wondra (Louisiana State University), transcribed manuscripts and account books. We proved that Chopin had been a careful reviser, not a spontaneous writer. Like so many women, she'd had to present herself as unserious in order to fit a proper public image as a wife and mother.

While doing my part of the research for Kate Chopin's Private Papers, I delved once more into the treasures at the Missouri Historical Society—

and found, in a private folder, a letter to "Mo Hist" from Per Seyersted. He was angry that I'd said The Awakening was not banned, and he thought I was wrong. But he never told me so, and we had no contact after Private Papers was published in 1998. He died in 2005, just after finishing a book on Robert Cantwell, an American critic who had been one of the few appreciators of Kate Chopin during her long eclipse.

In my second Chopin biography, Unveiling Kate Chopin, for the centennial of The Awakening in 1999, I'd come to view Chopin differently—not as a writer inspired by a failed romance but as an ambitious and singular woman whose closeness to her mother inspired much of her work. My mother had passed away in 1990, just before my first biographical Kate Chopin appeared, and the stutterings and wordiness in that book are due to my worries about her health, as well as the self-doubts I'd felt at Penn State. Kate Chopin is full of doubled-over sentences with qualifiers; Unveiling Kate Chopin is a much more confident book, reflecting my coming into my own as "a woman of a certain age." When it appeared, I was the same age as Kate Chopin when she died.

By now, The Awakening is The Novel in American literature courses. When Cathy Davidson was editor of American Literature, she reported that Kate Chopin was the fifth most written-about author in the literary canon (after Hemingway, Faulkner, Hawthorne, and Twain). The Awakening has replaced Moby Dick as the required novel ("So there is a God," says one of my grad students). My Google Alert sends me quotes every day from bloggers about Kate Chopin, and my Unveiling Kate Chopin is one of the top plagiarized books, according to Questia. The world is full of wonders that did not exist in 1970, when that orange paperback found its way into my hand.

I'm still involved in antiwar protests, although it's a different war. Kate Chopin, who wrote "The Locket" and "Ma'ame Pélagie" and whose son Fred enlisted for the Spanish-American War, would have understood that, too. And although I showed in 1990 that it wasn't banned, The Awakening is still displayed during Banned Books Week, and maybe its presence still seduces some randy young readers.

Kate Chopin would have liked that, and so do I.

After all these years, we're still great friends. I still carry her book around, and it still opens to the good parts.

NOTES

1. Emily Toth, *Unveiling Kate Chopin* (Jackson: UP of Mississippi, 1999) 222.

2. Information about Per Seyersted comes from interviews and correspondence with his wife's former student, Elisabeth Sandberg, May–July 2008, and from an entry in the Norwegian Wikipedia: "Per Seyersted," *Wikipedia Den frie encyklopedi*. Wikipedia, 14 Jan. 2008. Web. 2 Jan. 2009. See also Per Winther, "Minnetale over professor dr. philos. Per Eynert Seyersted." *Det Norske Videnskaps-Akademi*. Norwegian Academy of Science and Letters, 8 Sept. 2005. Web. 2 Jan. 2009.

3. Emily Toth, Per Seyersted, and Cheyenne Bonnell, eds., *Kate Chopin's Private Papers* (Bloomington: Indiana UP, 1998) 82, 84.

4. Kate Chopin, *The Complete Works of Kate Chopin*, ed. Per Seyersted (Baton Rouge: Louisiana State UP, 1969) 722. Per Seyersted, *Kate Chopin: A Critical Biography* (Baton Rouge: Louisiana State UP, 1969) 164–85.

2

Linked Fortunes
Kate Chopin, the Short Story (and Me)

BARBARA C. EWELL

As FOR SO MANY OTHERS, my first encounter with Kate Chopin was a tip from a colleague—"You gotta read this!" Or, more specifically, "Put this one in your syllabus!" It was the mid-seventies. I had just finished my PhD at a venerable midwestern Catholic institution, and tenure-track jobs were sparse. After a year in a part-time position at Loyola University New Orleans, I had been offered my first full-time job: teaching three composition courses as an instructor at Newcomb College of Tulane University, just across the fence from Loyola.

When I was interviewed by the Newcomb department chair, he asked if I would be interested in teaching the Women in Literature course, created by the instructor whose departure for California was providing my employment. I was delighted to have a chance to teach a real literature course, but I must have voiced some of my uncertainty about the subject matter. I knew that there was nothing in my freshly typed résumé that indicated any such expertise. Renaissance poetry or Shakespeare I could do, but how could I teach a subject in which I had had no training? The graying chair, a kindly and otherwise enlightened sort of guy, leaned back from his cluttered desk, gave me an appraising glance, and said with a chortle, "You certainly look qualified!"

The notion that simply being a woman qualified me to teach a whole literary field might seem a bit startling (it was to me), but in those days, it shouldn't have been. For one thing, no one was "qualified" to teach women's studies. The first women's studies program had been established only in 1969 (at San Diego State, in California, the epitome of sixties radicalism), and even Newcomb's own women's center (the oldest university-based center in the Gulf South) did not yet exist; it was founded later that fall in 1975. Women's studies was a brand-new discipline, with close links to the politically based women's movement, which was largely focused on passing the ERA, having finally succeeded in securing legal abortion. Given such political and activist associations, "women's lib" was seen by many academics as merely trendy, a bit of a joke, as the flippancy of the department chair indicated. But women-in-literature courses did attract students, and since the lone female tenured professor in the English Department could hardly be expected to teach such a lightweight course, my gender must have seemed like a bonus for the department's bottom line.

I set about preparing the syllabus with all the gusto of a brand new teacher. The departing instructor had helpfully left her syllabus, and I began making it my own, consulting friends and former colleagues for more ideas. I think it was Dawson Gaillard, the department chair who had hired me at Loyola, who recommended *The Awakening*; I know she told me about Hurston's *Their Eyes Were Watching God*—a dreadful title, I thought, as I located a little-used bound paperback copy in the vast Tulane library. I hesitated with Hurston (though it later became another classroom staple), but *The Awakening* was a no-brainer.

In fine New Critical fashion, I was intent that my course should not be too political or biased ("only the best literature"), so I included a few male writers, notably D. H. Lawrence, whom I had always thought of as a liberated sort, making my first course, in effect, an "images of women in literature." But after only one semester of reading these often new (to me) writers, like Chopin and Hurston and Lessing and Plath, in that blindingly intense context of their own female spaces, I promptly stripped the men away. Lawrence's pallid women and phallic figures wilted before the searing images of Adrienne Rich, Margaret Atwood, Charlotte Perkins Gilman, the Brontës, Virginia Woolf, Maya Angelou. At the same time, my stance toward the women's movement completely changed. The timid objectivity, which I had thought appropriately professional and professorial, fell away like scales from my traditionally educated eyes: in one short semester, I had become a full-fledged, card-carrying feminist.

With my Women in Literature course soon expanding to two sections every semester, I became increasingly involved in organized efforts to make women more visible—in the profession as well as in the cur-

riculum. The late 1970s were heady days: founding women's centers, organizing the first women's studies courses (team-taught by volunteers like
me, energized by a cause and eager to teach what we ourselves were just
learning), inventing and sharing syllabi, creating new professional cau-
cuses and women's studies associations, even helping to organize boy-
cotts. At the insistence of some of its more outspoken female members
(including Carol Gelderman and Seraphia Leyda of the University of New
Orleans, Dawson Gaillard—and me—at Loyola), the South Central Modern Language Association was avoiding conventions in New Orleans because Louisiana had failed to ratify the ERA. I made a brief debut on local
television that year, trying to explain, somewhat inconsistently, that we
professors didn't want to hurt New Orleans but the only way to make the
establishment pay attention was to attack a sensitive place: their wallets.
Louisiana never ratified the ERA, but we did found the Women's Caucus
of the South Central Modern Language Association, which still functions
to highlight women's concerns in the profession. Among the many ini-
tiatives generated by women's demands for change was a project called
"Teaching Women's Literature from a Regional Perspective," sponsored
by the MLA Commission on the Status of Women and FIPSE (the Fund
for the Improvement of Post-Secondary Education). In 1979, I participated
in the seminar organized by Elizabeth Meese for the south central region;
other participants included Peggy Prenshaw, Joanne Hawkes, and Viralene
Coleman—women who later all played major roles in the development of
women's studies in the South. It was another one of those transformative
encounters.

  Kate Chopin was central to the readings of that provocative seminar,
which also gave me an essential grounding in the contexts of her work:
southern local color, issues of race and class at the turn of the century, the
history of women's rights and women's writing in America. By the time I
landed my first tenure-track job as an assistant professor at the University
of Mississippi the next year, I was deeply committed to women's studies and hooked on Kate Chopin. Her novel had become a centerpiece of
my Women in Literature course, which came along with me to Ole Miss,
where I had been hired to teach the poetry and prose of the Renaissance,
as the Early Modern Period was known in those distant days.

  In Oxford, I was soon joining the efforts to found a women's center,

developing women's studies courses and programs, helping recruit more
women to the faculty, trying to raise their salaries, and generally trying to
give Ole Miss women more status than as coeds and sorority girls. But if
I was going to continue all these exciting labors, my chief focus had to be
tenure, which required writing a book. Startlingly naive about departmen-
tal positions and specializations, I figured a book was a book, regardless
of its subject. In truth, I probably suffered from a lack of imagination. I
no longer wanted to write about men's "images of women," and the few
women poets I could discover in Renaissance England seemed quite pedestrian beside Kate Chopin; moreover, I was not a little intimidated by
the erudition of my chosen field. Besides, my husband had just written
a book for Frederick Ungar's well-respected small press, and the editors
were looking for writers for their Modern Literature series. In the spring
of 1981, I pitched a proposal for a volume on a writer they hadn't even considered, Kate Chopin. I pointed out how important The Awakening was becoming in the American literary canon and how there was not yet any comprehensive critical study of Chopin's work. They bought it—and I got the
contract, and I thought I had secured the book that would get me tenure.

I was only partly right. The next year, when the English Department refused to give its Renaissance specialist a course release to work on a book
on a "minor" American writer, I was irked. So I started looking for external grants. I was going to write that book. As it turned out, the women's
network came to my rescue. When the director of the Newberry Library
visited Ole Miss that February, Ann Abadie, a comrade in our campus
struggles for women, introduced me, and Dick Brown encouraged me to
submit an application for the Monticello College Foundation Fellowship
for Women. I did so, and by the end of that summer, I was ensconced in a
tiny carrel behind the dark-brick facade of that eminent institution, only
blocks from Lake Michigan, beginning a glorious six months of research
among stimulating new colleagues—writing my book on Kate Chopin.

When the monograph was finished, a year or so later, it did get me
tenure—but at another institution. While I loved the many friends I had
made in Oxford, the siren call of south Louisiana (80 percent of whose
inhabitants are native—like me) remained strong. In 1984, I was offered a
position at Loyola University, back in New Orleans, teaching in City College, which catered to part-time adult students and where specialization

was not necessarily a virtue. By then, I was well on my scholarly way into southern and women's studies, with a new project on Louisiana women writers and a fantastic gig teaching an NEH Summer Seminar on short stories by southern women. As for so many of us in this volume, Kate Chopin turned my head and changed my life.

As I had argued in my proposals to Ungar and to the Newberry, one of my chief objectives in *Kate Chopin* (1986) was to understand Chopin's work in its entirety, "so that her famous novel appears as an inescapable climax, but not the sum of her achievement as a writer." Although Peggy Skaggs's volume in the better-known Twayne series had appeared in 1985, just months before mine, to that point there had been no critical study covering Chopin's complete oeuvre that was not primarily biographical. Daniel Rankin and Per Seyersted had, of course, included critical analyses, but Robert Arner's comprehensive dissertation remained unpublished. I thought I might be the first to appraise Chopin's total achievement in print—and "firsts" are just about irresistible to academics.

What I intended was a careful study of all of Chopin's work—novels, short fiction, poetry, and essays—identifying their merits and shortcomings but ultimately giving her short stories the status and centrality that they deserve. It seemed to me then, as now, that the brilliance of *The Awakening* has tended to obscure Chopin's mastery of the short story, even as it reduces her accomplishment to a single novel, an anomaly that only confirms her (minor) status as a one-trick writer—a common means by which women's work has been marginalized. The short story itself is notoriously lacking in literary status; novels still confirm and confer majority. Certainly, *The Awakening* (not unlike *The Red Badge of Courage* or *The Scarlet Letter*) is a remarkable piece of fiction, but Chopin—like Crane or even Hawthorne—would still be a figure of importance even if that novel had been lost or never written. Happily, neither is the case. Moreover, as with other tours de force, contexts provide helpful, even crucial, insight—clarifying elements of style and content by their reiteration elsewhere. We learn much about *The Awakening* from the short stories through which Chopin honed her craft—the backstories of recurring characters like Gouvernail or Tonie, the connotations of settings like New Orleans's neighborhoods or Grand Isle, the repetition of resistant females and their fates, the links between nature and sexuality, the uses of metaphor and allusion.

Chopin's principal métier was, in fact, the short story. In her lifetime and in the first half century after her death, it was also the basis for her reputation. Even more significant, the short story served as a source of her self-confidence as a writer. Chopin's earliest efforts in 1888 were apparently a couple of short stories and what might have been her first novel, the 30,000-word "Unfinished Story—Grand Isle"; these were either later revised or destroyed. She began At Fault in July 1889, the same year she first appeared in print, with a poem in January and two short stories in October and December. Though she eventually had At Fault printed at her own expense, highlighting its commercial failure, she began "Young Dr. Gosse and Theo" barely two weeks after she finished At Fault, demonstrating her early confidence in the genre.

But while that second effort languished in manuscript through five years and ten submissions, Chopin's short stories continued to be accepted by increasingly prestigious magazines. In an 1895 letter to J. M. Stoddart of Lippincott's, in one of her last attempts to find a publisher for "Young Dr. Gosse and Theo," she noted her dissatisfaction with the book and commented that it had been written "before I had found my way to the short story."[1] She evidently destroyed the manuscript a short time later. Writing a year earlier to Waitman Barbe, the editor of Representative Southern Writers, in which she was being featured, Chopin had already explained that "the novel does not seem to me now to be my natural form of expression."[2] Apparently it wasn't until another prominent editor, Horace Scudder, commenting on a story that was "long enough to run through two or three numbers in the magazine," asked if she wasn't "moved to write a downright novel" that Chopin again ventured beyond the genre that had established her success.[3] But while that final novel, which she began to write just a few months after Scudder's flattering letter, eventually ensured her literary immortality, it also seriously damaged her career. Tracing her way to The Awakening through the successes of the short story thus became my mission.

It was a mission, I should add, in which I was abetted not only by timely fellowships but also by critical friendships—such as my first meeting with Emily Toth at the 1984 Southeast Women's Studies Association Conference at the University of South Carolina. Since she was already a Famous Chopin Scholar, I was not a little intimidated to make her acquaintance. What I discovered was a supportive (and irrepressibly mischievous) fellow traveler, who that very weekend generously shared juicy tidbits of her research on Chopin's love life—and even agreed to read my manuscript. She was, it turns out, only the first of several Famous Chopin Scholars, like Helen Taylor and Bernie Koloski, whose work on Chopin not only smoothed my own scholarly way but also paved paths to friendship.

The Newberry Library was, of course, a more conventional but equally helpful resource for writing about Kate Chopin. Not only did it maintain a strong focus on nineteenth-century American literature with wonderful issues of rare journals, but it also included the papers of Herbert Stone, the Chicago publisher who eventually published *The Awakening*. Stone's earlier partnership with fellow Harvard grad Hannibal Ingalls Kimball (Stone and Kimball's) had a deserved reputation for publishing innovative contemporary writers. The *Chap-Book*, of which the Newberry had lovely copies, was noted for avant-garde fiction and poetry, an American version of London's famous *Yellow Book*, which defined fin de siècle fiction and style. Lamenting she "didn't know how to reach" the latter (in the days before Google), Chopin aspired to "have something—anything over my name in the Chap-Book" and submitted a number of poems and several short stories.[4] But while Chopin never succeeded in publishing anything in the *Chap-Book*, *The Awakening* was eventually produced by Herbert Stone's press. The novel had been accepted by Way and Williams, another Chicago company, just before it was acquired by Stone and Kimball, which then merged to become "Herbert S. Stone." The Newberry contained a fine cache of Chopin materials, including several publicity photographs that Chopin sent her publisher to promote the novel. One of these became the sepia-toned cover for my monograph—and remains my very favorite image of Chopin.

The critical clue to Chopin's career as a writer, however, lay not in Chicago but in her home town of St. Louis. Knowing that the largest body of her manuscripts was in the Missouri Historical Society, I was finally able to visit there in the fall of 1983, where I found conclusive support for my basic argument that Chopin's career was guided by her commercial successes—her account books. Seyersted had provided in the *Complete Works* and in his biography extremely helpful reconstructions of the composition and publication dates for Chopin's stories. From that information (whose pages in my copy soon became ragged from use), I could see that Chopin's choices of material were clearly shaped by what sold. When her novels failed to find publishers, she wrote short stories; when stories about St. Louis kept the mailman busy and tales of the Cane River country appeared in print after only one submission—often to magazines like Youth's Companion or Harper's Young People—Chopin wrote more stories about Louisiana that featured children and young people.

Recently, Bonnie James Shaker has corroborated the notion of Chopin's marketing savvy in her book-length study of Chopin's Youth's Companion stories. With similar attention to Chopin's account books, Shaker argues effectively for the writer's shrewd attention to editorial tastes, providing relatively conservative stories for Youth's Companion while sending more experimental work to "adult" vehicles, such as the new Vogue. Chopin continued to rely on the solid relationship she had built with Youth's Companion, sending stories to that magazine until the end of her career. But as prestigious magazines like Boston's Two Tales or Century (and Vogue) began in late 1892 to accept her more sophisticated material, like "At the 'Cadian Ball," "Azélie," and "La Belle Zoraïde," she ventured even riskier stories of domestic abuse and infidelity, like "In Sabine" and "A Respectable Woman." Louisiana settings continued to provide a constant in her work. Between 1891 and 1894, Chopin wrote nothing set elsewhere, and when she did return to nonsouthern locales, her efforts were clearly prompted by the critical success (and attendant sales) of her first short story collection, Bayou Folk. Chopin understood her market.

It is no surprise that writers are driven by "the commercial instinct"—as Chopin rather ruefully acknowledges in her diary of 1894[5]—but it's still quite unusual to see that instinct played out so explicitly. Indeed, I am unaware of any comparable record by any other nineteenth-century writer. When I finally got to see and study and turn the pages of her account books myself, I was struck by their calculation and detail—at least after I figured out how to decipher their construction. Chopin evidently began by entering story titles across the tops of pages, but when she reached the end of the notebook, she reversed herself and made entries on the backs and bottom halves of empty pages. It's quite confusing at first—and even Emily Toth's laudable and painstaking transcriptions in Private Papers don't quite replicate the effect of the notebooks themselves. This is one case where there is no real substitute for a facsimile.

But it is clear that from the very first stories Chopin wrote she was reckoning their productivity: when they were written, how many words, where and when they were sent, when they were returned or accepted—and for how much money. Success is marked by the word "published," often scrawled across the entry like a mark of victory. The earlier notebook especially (an ordinary school tablet that she seems to have pilfered from her oldest son, Jean-Baptiste) reflects a certain informality—with its crowded notations and eccentric order—but there is no mistaking the seriousness of Chopin's intent. This is no blithely creative spirit, for whom writing is "completely at the mercy of unconscious selection" or an idle pastime when sewing or trying "a new furniture polish" is not more tempting—as she rather disingenuously claims in an 1899 essay, after the rejections of her final novel.[6] These notebooks reflect a woman who was keeping track of what worked and what didn't, how much she was paid, and—especially in her second account book, which is in fact a ledger designed for bookkeeping—how much her writing had ultimately earned, as she totes up the figures for all the stories she has sold over the previous decade, including the sales figures for The Awakening.

Chopin's ambition is evident in other ways, as well. After publishing At Fault herself, she astutely sent copies to a number of newspapers and magazines, including one to Harper's editor William Dean Howells. Later, her children recalled that Howells had sent her a complimentary letter on her sketch "Boulot and Boulotte," which he accepted for publication. As Emily Toth observes, Chopin clearly admired and respected Howells,[7] and his encouragement at that early point must have further confirmed the potential of her Louisiana sketches. Of course, one of the reasons that Chopin's Cane River stories were selling so well was the contemporary popularity of local color, which had created a lucrative market for writers of regional short fiction.

Championed by Howells and others as an important mode of realism, local color attracted writers of great talent, including Mark Twain, George Washington Cable, Sarah Orne Jewett, and Mary Wilkins Freeman. But its popularity also encouraged hundreds of less skillful writers and repetitive stories and plots, and by the 1890s the innovative potential of the genre was beginning to seem limited. Chopin herself clearly understood the threat of superficiality in a genre that emphasized picturesque surfaces and quaintness; in 1894 she famously criticized both the provincialism of the writers' association of northern Indiana and Hamlin Garland's youthful iconoclasm, pointing out that "social problems, social environments, local color and the rest of it are not of *themselves* motives to insure the survival of a writer who employs them."[8] Nonetheless, writers must work with the material and the markets available to them, and Chopin readily exploited both. Even if local color was in decline as a serious literary vehicle, Chopin was hardly unaware of the directions that modern fiction was taking, as the impressionistic style and thematic daring of many later stories reveal. What she needed was the encouragement to pursue those uncharted paths—and she got that from the success of her first collection of local-color fiction.

One of the ironies of Chopin's literary reputation has been its links to local color, whose central vehicle was the short story. In her own time, she was consistently praised for her "faithful, spirited representations" of the "unfamiliar characters and customs" of the "semi-aliens" of south Louisiana.[9] Her name became linked with a number of other well-regarded writers: George Washington Cable, one of the genre's originators, and the popular Ruth McEnery Stuart (whom Chopin met in St. Louis), as well as Grace King and Lafcadio Hearn. Although *The Awakening* could be regarded as a regional novel, its iconoclasm made it seem anomalous to Chopin's early critics. Rankin, for example, dismissed it as such, while the influential Fred Lewis Pattee feared that in 1923, despite the "genius" of Chopin's short stories, the eclipse of her talent was destined to be total.[10] As Bernard Koloski's research has confirmed, for most of the twentieth century Chopin's reputation rested on a few remarkable short stories, particularly "Désirée's Baby," whose poignant rendering of the consequences of racism provided a sting to the conscience of a nation (and sensitive young readers like Tom Bonner) still struggling with Jim Crow.[11]

But local color itself experienced a serious depreciation in the first half of the twentieth century. With the rise of literary modernism, many southern writers identified in local color the sentimentality and superficiality to be rejected by twentieth-century sensibilities. For ambitious young white male intellectuals, like the Fugitive-Agrarians of Tennessee or William Faulkner of Mississippi, local color, practiced and refined by so many prominent women writers (as well as many successful writers of color, like Charles Chesnutt and Alice Dunbar-Nelson), was also distastefully effeminate, another sign of southern defeat and debility. For much of the twentieth century then, even writers of genius (like Chopin) could not be redeemed from their association with an old-fashioned and feminine genre, whose dismissal was essential to demonstrating the relevance and vitality of southern writers and writing.

The recovery of The Awakening in the 1970s, which rode the second wave of the women's movement and the new women's studies, occasioned a reevaluation of both the literary canon and the nature of its construction. Kate Chopin became a poster child for the kind of neglect that mainstream critics imposed on works of art that failed to match their own, often invisible, biases. Those of us writing in this volume were all part of that reconstruction of the canon, asking new questions about what was valuable and what was art. Chopin's well-crafted fiction was a powerful reminder of how contexts determine value and how much can be lost when those contexts are too narrowly defined. Literary critics began reexamining perspectives and genres that had been dismissed or undervalued, including domestic fiction (whose traditions shape At Fault) and local color. Like scores of other women writers, Chopin had embraced elements of both genres and, in consequence, had been relegated to the margins as "minor."

But the chief vehicle of local-color fiction was always the short story, partly because of the demands of the market but also because its brevity accommodated the oblique reassessments of the familial—and specifically not familiar—spaces of identity that were its focus. The general devaluation of the short story, vis-à-vis the novel, only underlined the marginality of local color, while its prominence among women writers further confirmed its insignificance for critics whose perspectives echoed the social dominance of upper-class white men. For southern women writers like Chopin, that marginality was intensified by the South itself, a region that has long served as the "other" of American culture, representing in its military defeat, racial inequities, poverty, and conservative social mores the repudiated dimensions of a progressive national self-image.

If, however, Chopin's links to southern local color worked against the reputation of her short fiction in the twentieth-century canon, the reevaluation of her singular novel helped to bring the entire genre of local color back into the mainstream of the critical conversation. After all, if local color can produce stories of the power and complexity of "La Belle Zoraïde" or "Athénaïse," the genre implies a sophistication worthy of attention. One could thus argue that the recovery of *The Awakening*, in addition to being a central event in reconstructing the history of the American novel, helped to bring about the repositioning of local color in literary history. Early feminist critics initiated that process by trying to appreciate the constraints shaping women's writing and the reasons for the devaluation of their work. In her pioneering essays, Ann Douglas Wood argued that nineteenth-century women often had to disguise their "unladylike" professional ambition under the pretexts of moral or economic necessity. Women wrote because they had a moral mission (like Harriet Beecher Stowe or Susan Warner) or they had children to support (like Fannie Fern).[12]

Later Wood and scholars like Josephine Donovan and Judith Fetterley refined that view, suggesting that by the latter half of the century many women writers were able to assume a more confident attitude toward their profession.[13] Often working in genres like local color and the short story (viewed as having less scope and significance than the novel), they also found malleable new spaces in which to explore their visions. Unfortunately, as Nancy Walker has remarked, these shifts in literary culture ironically affected the careers of women like Kate Chopin, on the one hand encouraging her authenticity as a realist while on the other ultimately dismissing her boldest work.[14] Chopin had important contemporary models (including Freeman and Jewett, no less than Maupassant) for writing "what she saw," and in her short stories she explored aspects of contemporary women's lives with fresh insight. Stories like "A Vocation and a Voice," "Lilacs," "Athénaïse," "Regret," or "A Respectable Woman" expose connections between sensuality and spiritual awakening as well as the ambivalences of passion and childbearing with unprecedented clarity. Unfortunately, Chopin produced her most perceptive text about women's experience just as the definitions of value in American literature shifted toward a more masculine modernity and denigrated the perspectives of women as inherently limited—thus ensuring the eclipse of Chopin's work for a half century.

But as critics have continued to find new dimensions of meaning in *The Awakening*, scholars like Helen Taylor, Elizabeth Ammons, Kate McCullough, and Amy Kaplan have similarly revealed an increasing complexity in the genre that defined its contexts. Recent investigations (including the work I've done with my colleague and friend Pamela Menke, whom I met at the Kate Chopin Conference in Natchitoches, following Emily Toth around on a tour of Cloutierville in 1993) have focused on the cultural work performed by local-color fiction—from the forging of postwar nationalism to the consolidation of racial and ethnic hierarchies—as well as the critical sensibilities that relegated it to a footnote in American fiction. In fact, when the recuperative social functions of local color were completed around the end of the nineteenth century, the genre that had simultaneously privileged both the experience and careers of women was dismissed as too feminine for the modernist aesthetic of the new century. Local color became synonymous with superficial and irrelevant fiction. The precise relationship of local color to midcentury regionalism, its links with realism and modernism, and its political implications remain under discussion, but the genre itself, like the author of one of its most compelling texts, has been reclaimed as a serious contributor to American literature.

Understanding the contexts of Chopin's novel has proved a rich thread of investigation for many scholars, including myself. Appreciating Chopin's "commercial instinct," for example, has provided new perspectives on how women writers viewed their craft and how they negotiated the complex and often contradictory messages about gender and writing at the turn of the century. That Chopin should have pursued her vision of "what she saw" so confidently in her short stories only to find that vision unacceptable in her novel suggests just what contradictory messages women writers were encountering at the turn of the century. The changing assessments of local color and the short story reflect similar ironies. A genre willingly adopted and shaped by women writers as a way to explore the domestic and "local" places to which they had been confined, local color provided writers like Chopin with both commercial success and a flexible tool for examining those realities—and implicitly the means to move beyond that confinement, both economically and imaginatively. But even as women writers glimpsed these other possibilities—to paraphrase Chopin, those worlds within and about them—the holy ghosts of a persistent patriarchy refused more, and local-color fiction became synonymous with the same narrow superficiality that it had aspired to escape. Even so, through the imaginative spaces that these writers opened for us poured the critical reassessments that eventually revealed the spiraling implications of local color in shaping American notions of race, region, gender, and the construction of the short story.

Edna, like Chopin, never really got to see the consequences of her willingness to explore the boundaries of her experience. Such is the fate of pioneers, including scholars and writers like ourselves, who have been able to ensure by our early investigations that Kate Chopin and other women writers can be seen in new ways, ways that allow us all to hear a bit better that seductive voice that whispers important insights about our position in the universe as human beings. Hopefully, others will be able to swim out even farther—with more confidence, greater buoyancy, and altogether better results.

NOTES

1. Emily Toth, Per Seyersted, and Cheyenne Bonnell, eds., *Kate Chopin's Private Papers* (Bloomington: Indiana UP, 1998) 207.

2. Toth, Seyersted, and Bonnell, 205.

3. Per Seyersted and Emily Toth, eds., *A Kate Chopin Miscellany* (Natchitoches: Northwestern State UP, 1979) 127–28.

4. Seyersted and Toth 125.

5. Toth, Seyersted, and Bonnell 179.

6. Kate Chopin, *The Complete Works of Kate Chopin*, ed. Per Seyersted (Baton Rouge: Louisiana State UP, 1969) 721–22.

7. Emily Toth, *Kate Chopin: A Life of the Author of "The Awakening"* (New York: Morrow, 1990) 191.

8. Chopin, *Complete Works* 693.

9. Bayou Folk. Advertisement. *Publishers' Weekly* 17 Mar. 1894: 450.

10. Fred Lewis Pattee, *The Development of the American Short Story: An Historical Survey* (New York: Harper, 1923) 327.

11. Bernard Koloski, "The Anthologized Chopin: Kate Chopin's Short Stories in Yesterday's and Today's Anthologies," *Louisiana Literature* 11 (1994): 18–30.

12. Ann Douglas Wood, "The Literature of Impoverishment: The Women Local Colorists in America, 1865–1914," *Women's Studies* 1 (1972): 3–46.

13. Josephine Donovan, *Sarah Orne Jewett* (New York: Ungar, 1980) and *New England Local Color Literature: A Women's Tradition* (New York: Ungar, 1983). Judith Fetterley, ed., *Provisions: A Reader from 19th-Century American Women* (Bloomington: Indiana UP, 1985).

14. Nancy A. Walker, *Kate Chopin: A Literary Life* (New York: Palgrave, 2001) 17–19.

3

Bringing Kate Chopin to Britain
A Transatlantic Perspective

HELEN TAYLOR

IT IS A TRUTH universally acknowledged that, in Britain as well as the United States, Kate Chopin's The Awakening is now one of the most widely read and critically discussed works of fiction and also one of those most studied in literature courses. If you were a young graduate student contemplating the collections of essays, various biographies, critical guides, and annotated editions, you might be forgiven for imagining that Chopin had always been a fixture in English courses throughout the Western world. Alas, this was not the case.

Once upon a time, happily some decades ago, almost no English literature university course embraced the writing of women, blacks, Third World writers of many races, and popular culture. In Britain, the Cambridge scholar F. R. Leavis is often invoked to remind scholars of the nature of English studies until the early 1970s; in the United States the New Critics and others kept a similarly authoritative stranglehold on the curriculum. In my early years of teaching, I too followed the English canon as it had been taught to me—Chaucer and Shakespeare (of course), a few Romantic poets (Wordsworth and Coleridge, with the odd poem by mavericks Byron and Keats), a large dollop of nineteenth-century novelists, and the odd twentieth-century poet. My London University BA degree course finished its curriculum with Thomas Hardy, and all subsequent literature was regarded as fit for "optional" (i.e., dangerous) courses only. A handful of those writers were women (some with male names)—Charlotte Brönte, George Eliot, and Virginia Woolf, among others—but they were taught within the context of Victorian realism, the modernist novel, and so on. Writers who had "disappeared" from the canon and were no longer in print were judged to have been worthless. No wonder I had never heard of Kate Chopin!

And English meant English (with some honorary Irishmen). During sixteen years of school and college, I had never been required to read an American writer—oh, except for those naturalized Englishmen Henry James and T. S. Eliot. It was a revelation to me when I went to do my master's in 1969 at Louisiana State University, Baton Rouge, and was introduced to a huge body of American literature, including African American. Throughout that MA, however, there was also a dearth of women's writing studied within the context of women's history and feminist politics, even though my professors were aware of a new buzz around feminist criticism and a few encouraged the reading of neglected figures from Margaret Fuller to Tillie Olsen.

My time as a master's student in Louisiana coincided with some of the most exciting years in recent American history, and ever since the sixties became the signifier of a cultural revolution that has transformed the Western world, I have been aware that it was indeed bliss to be alive in such a dawn and that my generation helped transform society, however imperfectly and temporarily. We had emerged from a conformist and grateful post–World War II consensus that kept our parents' heads down and stifled legitimate revolt and critique: McCarthyism in the States and weariness of conflict and desire for stability in Europe. We were expected to rejoice at peace in our time, settled government, and—in Britain at least—the welfare state that was bringing us free health care and education. The cultural explosions of late 1960s and early 1970s America and Europe opened up possibilities of questioning every aspect of our lives: the curriculum we were taught, our familial and sexual relationships, and the extent of our duty to support the national and international policies of our governments.

I had been selected for a graduate scheme by the grand trustees of the English-Speaking Union (hands-across-the-sea stuff, sending "appropriate" young English ambassadors to study in American universities) and was asked to apply to six American schools. Knowing little about the country's history, literature, or institutions, I selected at random, with Louisiana the most exotic-sounding of the lot; LSU, in its wisdom, offered me a graduate assistantship that I duly accepted. I am ashamed to admit my ignorance of the nature of the South, which became my temporary home—despite years of experiencing television coverage of civil rights marches and assassinations of key figures, not to mention listening to B. B. King, Elvis, and black girl groups. But I was not alone. My fellow students and teachers in London were horrified that I intended to accept an assistantship in Louisiana, convinced as they were that I would be murdered, raped, or forced to engage in lynchings. The South lived in British popular imagination (including that of intellectuals) as a febrile and demonic gothic site where Rod Steiger and Sidney Poitier slugged it out, terrible racial crimes were committed beneath the magnolias by moonlight, and round each corner Stanley Kowalski was showing Blanche DuBois who was in charge. Although culture shock lasted a long time, I will always be grateful to LSU for offering me a post, where I learned that the South was as complex, and mundane, as anywhere else and also where I enjoyed two of the most exciting years of my life.

Studying in a conservative southern state at a time when anti-Vietnam feeling was at its height and the black, gay, and women's movements were erupting all around me guaranteed an intoxicating atmosphere in which to both study and teach Freshman Composition. The university's regular "Free Speech Alley" boasted heated debates between radical members of Students for a Democratic Society (SDS) and the future Ku Klux Klan grand wizard David Duke, who was later to run for governor of Louisiana. At the Alley, a few of us raised the prospect of women's liberation; we hit the front page of the student newspaper and began to make waves in our classes, while more mature and sober women friends were joining the National Organization for Women and addressing state and local politicians through pamphlets and public meetings. For young women stirred by the fearless rhetoric of Kate Millett, Betty Friedan, and Germaine Greer, it was thrilling to challenge rather nervous middle-aged male professors with names of women writers we wanted to study and also with analyses (crude and unformed, admittedly) of the way male writers treated women in their work. We were ready to take on the sexism of D. H. Lawrence and Eldridge Cleaver alike; we wanted to study Sojourner Truth, Simone de Beauvoir, the feminist essays of Virginia Woolf, and Zora Neale Hurston.

Those heady late 1960s days required students to demand that their political and educational lives come together and that what they read in

the classroom would have relevance to the enormous sociopolitical upheavals happening all around. The idea of the academy as an ivory tower,
or even a quiet space for intellectual reflection unaffected by the rest of the
world, seemed to many of us an abrogation of civic, national, and international responsibilities. This concept was something exhilaratingly new in
my own life, and one that has sadly faded away in recent years; students in
the past couple of decades have seen their university education as a preparation for professionalization, themselves as "customers" or "clients" of a
service. During the late 1960s in Louisiana, education—the very books I
read daily—was about transformation, reeducation, and new political understanding. It still feels like a privilege to have sat side by side with black
and white scholars reading Richard Wright, Ralph Ellison, James Baldwin,
Eudora Welty, and Adrienne Rich. The problem was that there was far
more writing by men than women and very little by Native American or
other minority groups. When we read black writing, there was no Nella
Larsen or Toni Morrison; these writers would emerge later when feminist
presses began to publish for teachers eager to enlarge their syllabi. In my
final days in Louisiana, a couple who had inspired me and led feminist political groups in the earliest years of Baton Rouge's feminist engagement,
Robbie and David Madden, gave me two of the earliest feminist studies of
literature published by the same mainstream publisher, Harcourt Brace
Jovanovich: Mary Ellman's brilliant, witty study of conceptions of femininity, from Jane Austen to Norman Mailer, *Thinking about Women* (1968),
and Elaine Showalter's *Women's Liberation and Literature* (1971), a collection
of "Major Texts of Feminism" (Mary Wollstonecraft and John Stuart Mill),
"Literature by and about Women" (from Henrik Ibsen to Mary McCarthy),[1]
and other materials from literary critics, psychologists, and contemporary feminist writers. Both these critics focused on male as well as female
writers, but very quickly feminist presses began to provide much-needed
teaching editions of novels, poetry, and drama by women writers hitherto
neglected or marginalized. Thus women's studies, and specifically female
literary criticism, was in business.

As the second wave of feminism grew stronger, the works pouring out
of the first feminist presses and the feminist publications by orthodox
publishing houses confirmed the fact that women's writing had come of
age and was in demand in its own right. Introductions by feminist scholars

to works by women such as Louisa M. Alcott and Sylvia Townsend Warner
were offering fresh perspectives on a tradition of writing by women—
and this practice opened the floodgates to an outpouring of historical
and critical studies about a female tradition of literary production that
hitherto had been celebrated only by Virginia Woolf's important A Room
of One's Own (1929). The 1970s saw publication of texts that helped define
the whole project, namely, Ellen Moers's Literary Women (1976), Showalter's
A Literature of Their Own (1977), and Sandra Gilbert and Susan Gubar's The
Madwoman in the Attic (1979). None of these writers celebrated or recognized a separate tradition of southern writing, though all (especially Ellen
Moers) mentioned Kate Chopin.

I returned to Britain in 1971 and spent six months in London working
for the publisher William Collins. Part of my job entailed meeting staff in
other publishing houses, and very early on I came across a small group of
women who were considering establishing feminist presses. Virago and
the Women's Press were set up around the same time, and—like many
other women—I was thrilled with their reprints of earlier texts (often unknown to me). Virago's Modern Classics series reprinted southern writers
such as Ellen Glasgow and Zora Neale Hurston, and Virago was the first
British press to publish Maya Angelou's I Know Why the Caged Bird Sings
(1969; Virago 1984). The Women's Press launched its list in 1978 with four
titles, two of which came from North America—Alice Munro's Lives of
Girls and Women and Kate Chopin's The Awakening, for which I was invited
to write a new introduction.

The director of the Women's Press, Stephanie Dowrick, had discovered
this novel around the time I had, though she had yet to see The Complete
Works of Kate Chopin, which had been sent to me by Robbie Madden, then
an editor at Louisiana State University Press.[2] I was already so excited
about Chopin that I had registered as a part-time PhD student at Sussex
University, under the supervision of Cora Kaplan, an American and British literary and historical scholar and feminist theorist. Cora, who was
to write an introduction to another of those first Women's Press titles
(Elizabeth Barrett Browning's Aurora Leigh), invited me to join a literature
collective, which was preparing a paper on the Brontë sisters that nine
of us delivered polyphonically at an Essex University conference. It was
in that intellectually challenging but informal and friendly group that I

read Marxist cultural criticism, psychoanalysis, and feminist theory, all
of which fed into my PhD dissertation and later writings. The Awakening
seemed the perfect text with which to begin my feminist writing career,
bringing together as it did so many of my literary interests, personal concerns, and aspirations.

Despite my two years in the South, when I first read Kate Chopin,
there were gaps in my knowledge of the political and cultural history of
Louisiana. I had read few "regional" American writers, since my degree
courses had both focused on literature as national or international and
even my Louisiana State master's course sidelined southern writing to
the occasional optional course taught by Southernists—most notably the
English Department's omniscient raconteur and guru Lewis P. Simpson.
Simpson's South was one of eminent white men of letters who engaged
with one another about the fraught issues of slavery and the Civil War,
power, and identity in a backward-looking and guilty region; although he
barely mentioned gender himself, to his credit, he was happy for students
to discover new voices and encouraged me to undertake research into the
Grimké sisters and—later—Grace King. There was little historical writing
available to guide feminist reading of women's texts; when Anne Firor
Scott's book The Southern Lady: From Pedestal to Politics, 1830–1930 appeared
in 1970, my fellow students and I fell upon it with huge excitement, realizing how little we understood of the region's gendered cultural fabric
and how important Scott's work was in fleshing out literary history. At a
conference I attended many years later, the author admitted to astonish-
ment that The Southern Lady had the impact it did—even she had not been
aware of how thirsty feminists were for such material.

The edition of The Awakening was hugely successful, outselling other
Women's Press titles and capturing media and popular attention.[3] There
were newspaper articles about Chopin; I was interviewed repeatedly about
her work; university and high school teachers contacted me, thirsty for
more information. By this time, I was teaching women's writing courses,
both at my own university and at adult classes in the city of Bristol. I recall
a heavily pregnant woman slipping and sliding her way through the snow
to come to discuss The Awakening because it had so struck a chord with
her. Critics and readers alike shared the pleasures of a text that appeared
so effortlessly and elegantly written and that captured so vividly the reso-

nance of desire, frustration, and yearning for profound transformation in one's society and personal life. Chopin was unknown to British readers (Seyersted's edition was available only through scholarly outlets), and there was a clamor for more. The following year, 1978, I selected some of her stories for a further Women's Press edition, Portraits[4]—though I remain sorry I was unable to persuade the editors to include Chopin's first published novel, At Fault. This novel recently appeared in a popular edition, but during those first decades of fascination with her writings, it was unobtainable outside the Complete Works. Reading the two novels together helps illuminate struggles Chopin had with her own Catholic upbringing and with the complexities of Louisiana's French heritage—be it Creole or Acadian. At Fault is a flawed and sometimes ponderous novel, but its unorthodox characters (especially the magnificent Thérèse Lafirme) and its treatment of the issues of divorce, alcoholism, racial and ethnic conflict, and violence offer insights into Chopin's developing independence of thought and expression, as well as anticipating the more accomplished and nuanced achievement of the final novel.

When preparing my introduction to the Women's Press edition, I made copious use of my fellow European Per Seyersted's edition and biography[5]—finding myself wondering how a Norwegian had discovered Chopin's work and feeling jealous that Chopin had been so scrupulously presented to the world by a male scholar. I was also grateful for American feminist literary critical texts and even more to Emily Toth, who had discovered both Chopin and Seyersted (with whom she coedited the Kate Chopin Miscellany[6]) and was distributing a Xeroxed pamphlet of the kind one can no longer find except in archives, the Kate Chopin Newsletter. This informal newsletter, so reminiscent of political leaflets and early kitchen-table feminist free sheets I had found exciting in other contexts, proved an invaluable collection of scholarship, news, gossip, and general Chopiniana. I loved its well-researched but unashamedly personal accounts of the writer, containing as it did new insights into the work and authoritative information such as the crucial birth date of Chopin—something Toth had established via a French scholar, Jean Bardot, correcting Per Seyersted's claim of 1851 to 1850. Happily, I discovered this just before the Women's Press edition went for printing and so was able to correct an error many a writer has since repeated. I have no idea how I knew about the *Newsletter*, since there was no Internet, Chopin Web site, or e-mail correspondence available. I was still writing snail-mail letters to my American friends (phoning was so costly it was out of the question), and at that time I had been unable to return to the States to undertake research. I can only surmise that my friends and former colleagues in Baton Rouge heard about it and sent me early copies of the KCN, which ran for two years under that title and then for a further two under the broader name *Regionalism and the Female Imagination*. Emily Toth and I learned more about each other from our mutual contact, Mildred McCoy.

Mrs. McCoy (as she was always addressed) was one of those maverick enthusiasts who are so vital in disseminating literary culture and who often bring together disparate groups and individuals. A glorious lapsed southern belle with emphysema and a wicked twinkle in her eye, Mrs. McCoy wrote me a letter shortly after the publication of *Portraits*, telling me she owned Kate Chopin's Cloutierville home in northern Louisiana and wanted to visit me in Britain. On a whistle-stop tour of Europe of the kind Americans used to make ("if it's Tuesday, it must be England"), McCoy arrived one evening in 1980 at her Bath hotel. I drove over to meet her, and we fell enthusiastically upon each other (I had never met anyone else immersed in Chopin); she gave me various clippings, copies of the *Chopin Newsletter*, and tidbits of information about the writer and her home. Inviting me to visit her in Cloutierville, she was off to the next stop of her tour. The following spring, fired with enthusiasm, my partner and I traveled to Louisiana, catching up with my old friends in Baton Rouge, then took a deliciously long drive up to the Cane River area, where we dropped in on the painter Clementine Hunter and visited Melrose Plantation to learn about the region's unique "forgotten people," the Creoles of color. To my delight, this bewitching region of Louisiana came to life for me in all its racial, historical, and cultural richness—so that when we reached Cloutierville, I felt an enriched empathy with Chopin and the people she had brought to life in her fiction and poetry. The Bayou Folk Museum, established at great personal expense and after many tussles with national heritage organizations by Mrs. McCoy in the former Chopin home, and at that time very simply furnished, was a moving tribute to the writer. I never returned during Mrs. McCoy's lifetime but was brought back in 1995 during the Fourth International Kate Chopin Conference at Northwestern State University. By this time, the museum had expanded into the blacksmith's shop next door and contained period furniture, newspaper cuttings, and books and articles from many countries about Kate Chopin. I was startled to see in a file a typed letter from myself, written to Mildred McCoy in 1980, thanking her for hospitality and kindness. She had clearly preserved everything!

It is sad that there is no such memorial to Chopin in New Orleans or Grand Isle, the sites of her best-known fiction. Chopin's contribution to New Orleans letters is documented in studies and articles, and at the annual Tennessee Williams New Orleans Literary Festival she features in the renowned literary tours of Kenneth Holditch and others, as well as in panel discussions. However, to my knowledge there is no "Chopin literary trail," and, except in her native St. Louis, her name is nowhere inscribed in museums or streets (unlike lesser writers such as Frances Parkinson Keyes). In 2007, when I visited Grand Isle for only the second time, expecting this sportsman's paradise to acknowledge the novel that so hauntingly represents its pre-1893-hurricane social exclusiveness (something that— before the devastation of Hurricanes Katrina and Rita—it had reestablished with luxurious camps), I was disappointed to find that the tourist office bore no reference to The Awakening or the writer herself.

As may be seen from my description of travels to Louisiana at different periods, I have become somewhat obsessed with the place, its writers and culture. Soon after my visit to Cloutierville in 1980 and funded by the American Council of Learned Societies, I spent some months researching in Baton Rouge and New Orleans archives for my doctoral dissertation on Chopin and two of her contemporary postbellum writers, Grace King and Ruth McEnery Stuart. Supported by friends in the English Department and librarians such as LSU's Evangeline Lynch (how could I resist such a perfect southern name?), I was astonished at the wealth of material in the form of diaries, journals, fiction (published and unpublished), and photographs relating to postbellum Louisiana. The Civil War had liberated some people and devastated others, saving and ruining lives in many different ways; the wealth of writings it had produced proved how significant a catalyst to creative production such a momentous event had been—for white and black alike. I imagined myself in virgin territory (the papers of Grace King had been little examined, though in years to come they would establish her as a significant southern woman of letters[7]), but others were already digging. I shared an office with one of the researchers for the major project on Mary Boykin Chesnut's diaries, led by C. Vann Woodward and Elisabeth Muhlenfeld, and left Louisiana just as Anne Goodwyn Jones published her groundbreaking *Tomorrow Is Another Day*.[8]

My project—which had at first seemed so straightforward—was to become increasingly challenging as I tried to explain the sheer weight and political thrust of women's writing in the decades following the war. This anaylsis involved reading Chopin within a wider context of southern writing, especially by women such as King, McEnery Stuart, Sherwood Bonner, Augusta Evans, and Ellen Glasgow. Chopin herself was usually seen as exceptional, avoiding the political alliances and defensiveness of middle-class white women of her class and eschewing overt descriptions or analyses of fraught race and class relations during Reconstruction and Redemption. Through archival research, I was able to make thematic links between her work and that of her contemporaries and to discover material concerning the racially conservative and violent White League (of which Oscar Chopin was an active member) as well as Grand Isle's devastation and New Orleans's social life during the time Chopin lived there. In later years, Christopher Benfey's and Emily Toth's revelations of Edgar Degas's presence in the city offered new insights into the contexts of *The Awakening*,[9] but at that time I had to rely on my own imperfect research findings. In the years that followed, there was a welcome explosion of excellent publication focusing on the important role of southern women in the region's history, especially in the critical examination of the meanings of slavery, the Civil War, and its long legacy into the twenty-first century.[10]

The narrative that emerged, paradoxically, from my immersion in Louisiana archives was one of European influences, and the narrative I have continued to develop has been one of international influence and exchange. The strongly French culture and tradition of Francophone writing within New Orleans have led me into understanding New Orleans writers within a transatlantic context—especially through writers' Parisian visits and allusions, references to French reading, literary quotations, and so on. Kate O'Flaherty's indebtedness to her mother's French culture, underscored during marriage to French Creole Oscar Chopin, helped her feel immediately at home in the Crescent City, where she lived in early married life, and enabled her to capture in writing the exoticism of a city that retained a strong European flavor—despite its increasing "American" governance. The hauntingly suggestive sketches and paintings of New Orleans by Edgar Degas (in temporary exile from Paris and possibly a close acquaintance of the Chopins) point to a loss of French hegemonic power in the city, as well as a lingering nostalgia about the socioeconomic decline of the Creole community to which his own late mother had belonged.

An attentive reader of Kate Chopin's work will note its repeated stress on linguistic and social differences between French-speaking regions of Louisiana and the rest of the United States. Quotation marks are frequently appended to phrases, sayings, and aspects of Louisiana life and artifacts, and Chopin has an acute ear for specific dialects—mainly black, French Acadian, and French Creole. Writing at a distance in St. Louis, Missouri, following the deaths of her husband and mother, she captured the peculiar culture of a New Orleans that was being forcibly homogenized into postcolonial "America." I have argued elsewhere that New Orleans already lived in popular imagination as a city of unique racial mixtures, sexual pleasure, and immorality and that it was often compared to Paris, the capital city of its former colonizer—specifically in relation to a metaphoric femininity, with both seen as sites of romance, glamour, and sexualized street life, particularly prostitution.[11] By the end of the nineteenth century, both were defined as the sex capitals of their nations, sexualized female spaces within "masculine" nations and continents.

In my readings of The Awakening, developed through a focus on the transatlantic cultural relationship between Paris and New Orleans, I have been interested in the way the writer complicates that easily simplified notion of "local color" through her play on languages, dialects, and colloquialisms, deliberately creating in her New Orleans a multicultural, multilingual urban space that defies the parochial expectations of "regionalist" writing. For her—as for nineteenth-century Parisian flâneur writers—the streets of New Orleans offered liberating possibilities of erotic spectacle and freedom of movement, though for Chopin these streets suggested new ways of being and thinking for women. French Creole isolationism (identified with the interior domestic world away from the street) is satirized in her stories about monolingualism and excessive restriction on women's metaphoric as well as geographic mobility (as in, for instance,

"A Sentimental Soul" [1895], "Athénaïse" [1896], "Charlie" [written in 1900, published in 1969], and the novel At Fault [1890]). The tension between the French and English languages spoken by her characters is a reminder of social and sexual conflicts within a city of racial and ethnic hierarchies.

Unlike earlier stories, The Awakening uses much French dialogue and expression, providing no translation or footnote. The novel opens with a linguistic challenge (via a French-speaking parrot) and continues in that vein—frequently reminding the reader that its female protagonist cannot understand all the language around her and is thus uneasy about her ability to read and understand others. Moving away from a tendency to translate French culture for a national reading public, Kate Chopin in this novel exposes most mercilessly the insularity of the Creole community and its inability to communicate with a wider Anglophone world, to which—by the end of the century—it had become increasingly irrelevant (something Edna Pontellier's own physical and emotional movement away from the community underlines). The Creoles, who read French novels and tell risqué stories about the tenor at the French Opera, draw Edna into a web of sexual innuendo and playfulness without realizing how powerful such discourse might be to this Protestant "solitary soul." Edna, who cannot fully understand the Creoles' language and nuanced behavior, falls for their eroticized culture and then comes up against its tragic limitations for a married mother. Chopin's play with French fictional themes of sexual awakening, adultery, and suicide is well documented; of relevance also is the way she alludes to New Orleans's fin de siècle moral panics about prostitution, notably the presence of "fallen women" sharing the streets with "respectable women," with whom they were in danger of being confused. Her many streetwalking female characters occupy an urban space that the writer knew had become fraught with legal and moral threats to women. Chopin was writing about New Orleans in the city of St. Louis, which had passed an ordinance in 1870 to mandate licensing, medical inspection, and police control of prostitutes; after four years of controversy, this "experiment with legally regulated prostitution" was brought to an end.[12] The whole question of the control of women's bodies was a national obsession, and it culminated in the establishment of New Orleans's notorious prostitutes-only "Storyville" District in 1897—just as The Awakening was taking shape. Chopin's antennae for sociopolitical developments have sometimes been underestimated; I find myself returning to her work for oblique insights into how daily life must have felt for late nineteenth-century southern women during a period of obsessive focus on, and rapidly changing definitions of, their sexuality and very identity.

While preparing this chapter and reflecting on my own humble contribution to Chopin scholarship, I realized how rarely academic writers celebrate the ways their research has enriched and transformed their own lives. I began to have pleasurable flashes of memory: my first visit in 1969 to see the site of Edna Pontellier's sexual awakening, Grand Isle, where a friend's family lived in a house with a monkey that—to my amazement but the residents' sangfroid—delivered droppings onto a birthday cake; the extraordinary sight of elderly, semidisabled Mildred McCoy driving her Lincoln Continental like the legendary bat out of Hell up the tiny main street of Cloutierville; a few magical nights in a quaint Natchitoches bed and breakfast while speaking at a Kate Chopin conference; shared enthusiasm and wicked laughter about Chopin with Emily Toth and Barbara Ewell on a panel at the Tennessee Williams Literary Festival; impassioned arguments with students about the "unsatisfactory" ending of The Awakening; a visit in 2007 to Grand Isle two years after the devastation of Hurricane Katrina and—mindful of Edna Pontellier's magical boat trip with Robert Lebrun—a sight of the desolate "Cheniere" Centennial monument "in memory of the hurricane of 1st October 1893."

My Chopin research and publication have forged transatlantic links and friendship trails that have stretched from Glasgow and Warwick to Lafayette and San Francisco. The novel has opened doors to new British readers of southern literature in ways other southern works (notably those by William Faulkner) have failed to do, and—although, when I started research, there were hardly any—Britain now boasts a respectable number of southern scholars who have made a significant contribution to scholarship and helped ensure that southern writing courses are some of the most popular. I have lost count of the number of European women who claim The Awakening changed their lives. It did for me, too—not because it was my first encounter with profound female dissatisfaction or feminist revolt but because it led me into a feminized South that had rarely emerged from southern textbooks and courses. It has been three decades since I first read *The Awakening*, and I am still turning to Chopin's and other southern women's writing for new understandings of the South, southern culture, and a cornucopia of female experiences, warts and all.

NOTES

1. Elaine Showalter, *Women's Liberation and Literature* (New York: Harcourt Brace Jovanovich, 1971) vii (titles of Part 1 and Part 2).

2. Kate Chopin, *The Complete Works of Kate Chopin*, ed. Per Seyersted (Baton Rouge: Louisiana State UP, 1969).

3. Kate Chopin, *The Awakening* (London: Women's Press, 1978).

4. Kate Chopin, *Portraits: Short Stories Selected and Introduced by Helen Taylor* (London: Women's Press, 1979).

5. Per Seyersted, *Kate Chopin: A Critical Biography* (Baton Rouge: Louisiana State UP, 1969).

6. Per Seyersted and Emily Toth, eds., *A Kate Chopin Miscellany* (Natchitoches: Northwestern State UP, 1979).

7. Helen Taylor, *Gender, Race, and Region in the Writings of Grace King, Ruth McEnery Stuart, and Kate Chopin* (Baton Rouge: Louisiana State UP, 1989), and Melissa Walker Heidari, ed., *To Find My Own Peace: Grace King in Her Journals, 1886–1910* (Athens: U of Georgia P, 2004).

8. Anne Goodwyn Jones, *Tomorrow Is Another Day: The Woman Writer in the South, 1859–1936* (Baton Rouge: Louisiana State UP, 1981).

9. Christopher Benfey, *Degas in New Orleans: Encounters in the Creole World of Kate Chopin and George Washington Cable* (Berkeley: U of California P, 1997); Emily Toth, *Unveiling Kate Chopin* (Jackson: UP of Mississippi, 1999).

10. For example, see Sarah E. Gardner, *Blood and Irony: Southern White Women's Narratives of the Civil War, 1861–1937* (Chapel Hill: U of North Carolina P, 2004); Tara McPherson, *Reconstructing Dixie: Race, Gender, and Nostalgia in the Imagined South* (Durham: Duke UP, 2003); and Diane Roberts, *The Myth of Aunt Jemima: Representations of Race and Region* (London: Routledge, 1994).

11. Helen Taylor, "'The Perfume of the Past': Kate Chopin and Post-Colonial New Orleans," *The Cambridge Companion to Kate Chopin*, ed. Janet Beer (Cambridge: Cambridge UP, 2008); Taylor, "Walking through New Orleans: Kate Chopin and the Female Flâneur," *Southern Quarterly*, 37.3–4 (1999): 21–29.

12. Alecia P. Long, *The Great Southern Babylon: Sex, Race, and Respectability in New Orleans, 1865–1920* (Baton Rouge: Louisiana State UP, 2004) 106.

4

Creating the New American Library's Awakening

BARBARA H. SOLOMON

SINCE THE AWAKENING IS now regularly referred to as a classic of American literature as well as a classic of women's studies, it might be helpful to describe some of the qualities associated with a literary "classic." The one of greatest importance, it seems to me, is that while reading a classic we are engaged—we care about the characters and their problems, or the actions, or the ideas that emerge through these or from the narrator's observations.

Occasionally, some male readers have dismissed The Awakening as a women's novel about a woman's problems, and of course it is, in a narrow sense, about a woman of a certain time who is trapped in a marriage through a misjudgment in her choice of a husband and by motherhood, as well as by a restrictive vision of what her role typically would be in any marriage at the turn of the twentieth century. Obviously, it is also a novel about Edna's love for Robert, a conventional man who is embedded in the Creole community.

Of course, the broader topic is the human condition, human freedom, and the restrictions we accept or reject in our relationships (whether female or male): loneliness, living fully, being trapped in the present by any kind of mistaken choices we have made in the past, discovering our essential identity, and articulating who we are as well as how we have changed over time as the result of new experiences.

The second major characteristic of a "classic" novel is that while we care about what happens, about the events, when we have finished a reading of the work, we don't have the sense that it would be pointless to return to the novel, since we now know how it all turns out. On the surface there is an amazing simplicity about a first reading of The Awakening. There are only a few important characters and no subplot, for Chopin is not interested in exploring the differences that other perspectives might contribute, such as Robert's or Mademoiselle Reisz's view of the events. Only briefly does she depict Léonce's irritation and bewilderment as he consults Dr. Mandelet, and this scene serves to dramatize his reaction to the changes in Edna.

Another—and very broadly defined—category of elements of a classic might well be described as its texture, such matters as its setting, enriching symbols and images, of ironies, connections, and subtleties with relationships, and cultural attitudes. It might well include the economic and powerful prose style of the narrative. This category has, naturally, inspired an immense number of analytical articles about the novel.

Finally, a rather subjective test of a literary work that concerns only academics is that in compiling a course syllabus we find that we cannot omit teaching a particular item even though we might like to put it aside for a while. By this I mean that if we choose not to teach a certain novel or play or poem, no other work adequately replaces it. For example, two novels in volumes that I edited—Herland by Charlotte Perkins Gilman and Miss Lulu Bett by Zona Gale (coedited with Eileen Panetta)—represent rediscovered and excellent fiction and certainly add an element of richness to a course in women's literature. But omission of either of these would not leave the kind of void in a reading list that occurs by omission of The Awakening.

During the period when I was teaching this novel for the first few times, I never thought of it as a classic; to me it was simply one of a group of works that I was going to have a chance to teach in a new context—a course devoted to fiction by women. Generally, this fiction was often given short shrift in standard surveys of American literature as well as in elective courses. It was fitted around or in between a group of works by authors such as Anderson, Fitzgerald, Faulkner, Hemingway, Dos Passos, Lewis, and Bellow. Working with crowded syllabi, professors were often at a loss over which (if any) women to choose to fill the limited available places on their reading lists. In addition, the study of one or two women's novels or collections of stories in these courses often proved to be surprisingly disappointing or unsatisfactory, since there was little time to devote to important cultural and gender issues that might make the analysis of the works so much more meaningful.

During the winter of 1975, Constance Ayers Denne of Baruch College and I decided that we would solicit original essays from women to be published in an anthology that we would coedit. We were hoping that such an anthology might encourage teachers of literature to include more fiction by female writers in courses that were sadly lacking in such choices or that the volume would prove useful in the new courses with a new perspective that were now appearing on American campuses. We drew up the following list of twelve books that would be the subjects of the essays:

The Awakening—Kate Chopin
The House of Mirth—Edith Wharton
Three Lives—Gertrude Stein
To the Lighthouse—Virginia Woolf
The Short Stories of Katherine Mansfield
Flowering Judas and Other Stories—Katherine Anne Porter
Selected Stories of Eudora Welty
A Good Man Is Hard to Find—Flannery O'Connor
The Golden Notebook—Doris Lessing
The Group—Mary McCarthy
Wheel of Love—Joyce Carol Oates
The Bell Jar—Sylvia Plath

At that time, Connie Denne and I were two assistant professors of English with no experience with the process of compiling essays for publication and no special credentials in the study of women writers; she had written her dissertation on James Fenimore Cooper, and mine had been on Joseph Conrad. What we did have was considerable enthusiasm for the project. Martha Kinney of New American Library had indicated an interest in the collection we proposed when I met her for the first time at MLA at the book display. She suggested that we submit a table of contents of contributors, hopefully some of whom were well published and whose name recognition would enable her to "sell" our volume to her colleagues.

A few of the women we contacted agreed to write an essay for the collection, but I particularly cherish a letter from Diana Trilling, who explained why she would not consider contributing to the book. More important, she took the time to explain to us why our letter to potential contributors was not appropriate. In part she wrote:

> You solicit an essay of 4000 to 5000 words. A critical piece of this length constitutes what is called a "major" piece; I think that for most serious critics and certainly for me it would involve at least a month's hard work. Yet you propose such a commitment in the wholly casual tone in which you might ask for a jacket comment which would take no more than a few minutes to formulate. You specify no deadline and, most important, no fee beyond the assurance that some kind of stipend will be paid upon publication. I cannot know what kind of response you are getting from other women to whom you are writing but I cannot suppose that my own negative response will not be duplicated wherever you are dealing with an experienced writer of some critical repute.
>
> I take the liberty of saying this to you because I think the idea of a volume of feminist literary criticism is an attractive one and I would very much hope that it would be of high quality. I am afraid that you will be frustrated in reaching such a goal unless you approach potential contributors in a more professional way.[1]

Trilling continued by suggesting that if we did not "have a substantial budget to pay for new major critical essays," we should consider combining "new essays with reprints of already published pieces" and referred to her previously published essays on a Eudora Welty story collection and on *The House of Mirth*.

As it turned out, Martha Kinney was unable to convince others at NAL that our collection was viable, but she did say that she thought a good case might be made for publishing an edition of *The Awakening* combined with a selection of Chopin's stories. So you might say that I got to edit the novel by default.

The idea that I would produce such a volume was rather startling. In my experience, those who edited works of fiction and wrote book introductions were generally well-known scholars who had published extensively. When Martha asked about my publications, I fear my answer was not very encouraging: my bibliography consisted of two articles. The first, "Conrad's Narrative Material in 'The Inn of the Two Witches,'" had appeared that year in *Conradiana*. The second, "Father and Son in DeSica's

The Bicycle Thief," had been included in The Classic Cinema: Essays in Criticism, edited by my husband, Stanley J. Solomon, and published by Harcourt Brace Jovanovich in 1973. I sent her copies of both.

I certainly never asked Martha why she did not search for a more experienced writer or better-known critic. This was an exciting period of opening doors and welcoming new influences, new perspectives, new topics, new literary works, and NAL, which has been my publisher for more than three decades, did, in fact, open the door wide to let me inside.

It is interesting to explore the milieu in which I and other professors selected texts during the early 1970s. I had arrived at the Department of English at Iona College in the fall of 1969, the first semester during which this formerly all-male private college had accepted women for its entering class for the first time as Iona transformed itself into a coed institution. The paint had barely dried on the hastily renovated men's bathrooms that had become women's rooms. At Hagan Hall, the large women's restroom had a long, oddly shaped Formica bench that ran the entire length of one wall. Only after several weeks did I realize that this commodious bench neatly covered the line of urinals behind it.

The text that I assigned students in my required sophomore courses was a multivolume anthology titled American Literature Survey, edited by Milton R. Stern and Seymour L. Gross. First published in 1962, it was revised and expanded in 1968 and 1975. The attitude of many academics toward female writers—even those of considerable note—is clearly reflected in the editors' introduction to the poetry of Emily Dickinson. They wrote, "Perhaps the most amazing aspect of Emily Dickinson's personality is the fact that such rebellious, strong-souled, hard-minded, iconoclastic, and excellent poetry came, not from a robust man, but from precisely the kind of old maid with whom one would associate the production of scatter-brained verses of turgidity, and convention."[2]

By 1975, Stern and Gross (who reprint "The Story of an Hour" and "Regret" as the Chopin selections) do refer to The Awakening as "her best work" and devote a long paragraph to an analysis of their view of the quest for freedom of her women characters "within a context which suggests that male dominance and female submission are so deeply imbedded in history, psychology, society, and circumstance that women's liberation can never completely transcend a sexually determined identity."[3]

If, however, I had consulted any standard literature reference works during my first years of teaching, I would have found little to encourage me to read The Awakening. In fact, the third edition (1963) of the Literary History of the United States, edited by Spiller and others, makes no mention that Chopin wrote any novels. Instead, the one-page entry compares her very favorably with two writers of regional fiction, George Washington Cable and Grace King. It begins: "The writing career of Kate Chopin, one of the shortest in the annals of the ordinarily long-lived regional writers, began in 1899 [sic] with some indifferent poetry and followed a meteoric course which ended a year or two before her death in 1904." The entry does present a number of positive observations about her prose style in the stories, asserting that

> at their best the bayou tales displayed a clean economy of line, and were rounded off with a kind of Gallic finesse which suggested that Mrs. Chopin's study of Maupassant had not gone unrewarded. She knew, better than many of her contemporaries among the regionalists, how to begin, develop, and conclude a story without waste motion or observable self-consciousness. Her feeling for character was supported by an almost instinctive grasp of form and pace.[4]

In spite of the complimentary description of her style, the entry includes an unusual criticism of Chopin's writing practices, complaining that "many of her stories fell short of excellence because she wrote too swiftly and impulsively, leaned too heavily upon the suggestions of the moment, and impatiently shrugged off the burden of correction and revision."[5]

In another standard reference, The Oxford Companion to American Literature, by James D. Hart, the entry reflects that with so little interest in Kate Chopin and her work, literary authorities were content to pass along inaccurate, second-hand descriptions. It asserts that "Mrs. Chopin's last novel, The Awakening 1899, caused a storm of criticism that ended her literary career because readers of the time were shocked by the realistic treatment of morbid psychology in this objective account of mixed marriage and adultery."[6] Similarly, Max J. Herzberg in The Reader's Encyclopedia of American Literature declared that Chopin "turned to novel writing, not with great success. *The Awakening* (1899), which treated the themes of extramarital love and miscegenation, aroused a storm of criticism that practically silenced her for the rest of her life."[7]

Since I always teach *The Awakening* in both my undergraduate and graduate courses on images of women in modern American fiction, I am usually rereading the novel along with my students. With each reading and discussion comes a somewhat different emphasis in the class's analysis and reactions, as the attitudes and experiences of the students have changed over the decades. Today's young people have very different views of gender roles, family, relationships, sexuality, political issues, career expectations, and values than did the groups who studied the novel in the 1970s. These changes in views mean that I never teach the novel in exactly the same way twice. Rightly or mistakenly, today's students, generally, believe that women's lives have changed dramatically for the better and that many of the problems of women have been solved since the days of the rediscovery of *The Awakening*.

It is, however, Chopin herself who is responsible for the freshness that the novel retains year after year. For example, only recently did I begin to connect a few of the entertaining comic observations of characters with the pattern of serious critical remarks of Léonce that are so hurtful to Edna. With Chopin's perceptive grasp of people's motives and behavior, she describes characters for whom the urge to criticize others is central. Occasionally, the expression of criticism seems harmless, and even amusing. On the occasion of Victor's overseeing the preparation of an ice cream dessert for his mother's pension guests, Chopin depicts the ways in which many comment on the treat: "It was pronounced a great success—excellent if it had only contained a little less vanilla or a little more sugar, if it had been frozen a degree harder, and if the salt might have been kept out of portions of it."[8]

A less pleasant example of the tendency to criticize appears in the relationship between the elderly Monsieur Farival, one of the summer guests, and Beaudelet, the owner of the boat that he sails in taking Edna, Robert, and others to church on the Chênière Caminada. From the outset, Beaudelet is displeased to have the old man "who considered himself the better sailor of the two" as one of his passengers.[9] Just as Beaudelet seems to have anticipated, "Old Monsieur Farival talked incessantly of what he knew about handling a boat, and of what Beaudelet did not know on the same subject."[10]

Mademoiselle Reisz is particularly characterized by her habitual criticisms. At one point, she offers Edna some of the chocolates that she claims have saved her from starving that summer, since she considers that "Madame Lebrun's table was utterly impossible; and no one save so impertinent a woman as Madame Lebrun would think of offering such food to people and requiring them to pay for it."[11] Later, at Edna's dinner party, when Mademoiselle Reisz is asked her opinion of the season's symphony concerts, she has only negative remarks to make about them "and insulting remarks to make of all the musicians of New Orleans, singly and collectively."[12]

It is only with Léonce, however, that we find the habit of criticizing to be unfair, unpleasant, and destructive. It is this characteristic, in fact, that makes us exceedingly sympathetic to Edna, who is the target of his dissatisfaction.

The novel opens with his peevish criticism of Edna's choice of a time for a swim, since he, having swum hours earlier, has been left alone and is thoroughly bored. Later, that same evening, he criticizes Edna as being uncaring about her children. This accusation proves particularly offensive, since Raoul is not suffering from any fever, as Léonce asserts, and Edna is unable to defend herself.

In this scene, Chopin summarizes Léonce's complaints after Edna fails to respond to his attempt to awaken her in order to tell her about his day of gambling at Klein's Hotel: "He thought it very discouraging that his wife, who was the sole object of his existence, evinced so little interest in things which concerned him, and valued so little his conversation."[13] Occasionally, students accept this description of Léonce's ideas in a straightforward way, but, of course, Chopin is clearly depicting his remarks as the perception of an insensitive egotist. He is the father who has forgotten to bring back the candy and nuts he had earlier promised his sons, the husband who believes that when he disturbs his wife's deep slumber, her appropriate response ought to be an intense interest in the details of his entertaining jaunt and the gossip he has heard. Having left "the sole object of his existence" because he found he was having a dull Sunday, he is convinced that he deserves an appreciative audience for his anecdotes.

In a scene a little later, after Léonce returns to their cottage ready to retire, his criticism of Edna for wishing to remain outside grows increasingly harsh. She wishes to remain in the hammock just outside the cottage although it is after one o'clock on this Saturday night when she has experienced unusual emotions upon hearing the music played by Mademoiselle Reisz and discovering how to swim on her own. Almost immediately Léonce refers to her preference in an irritable manner as "folly." Shortly afterward, he orders Edna to come inside immediately. Intent on having the last word, Léonce stations himself in a rocking chair on the house's gallery, drinking wine and smoking cigars until Edna is ready to enter the cottage. With Léonce intruding on her solitude, "Edna began to feel like one who awakens gradually out of a dream, a delicious, grotesque, impossible dream, to feel again the realities pressing into her soul."[14]

Back in New Orleans and displeased by the change that has come over Edna, Léonce criticizes her behavior with no thought of being tactful or of understanding her. On the evening of the first Tuesday when she has abandoned her at-home afternoons, he vents his anger by criticizing all the food presented at dinner. He blames the poor quality of the meal on Edna for she has failed to properly supervise the cook, and he angrily leaves to get dinner at his club. He compares her "failure" with his own successful supervision of the clerks who work for him. This criticism is familiar to Edna and has caused her considerable unhappiness in the past.

When her painting becomes increasingly important to Edna, Léonce tells her that her time would be much better spent "contriving for the comfort of her family."[15] His criticism is of the most disagreeable kind: he compares his wife's behavior with that of another person, one whom he considers superior to his wife, a person who should become her model. He tells Edna: "There's Madame Ratignolle; because she keeps up her music, she doesn't let everything else go to chaos. And she's more of a musician than you are a painter."[16] Edna, who has put up with a number of his criticisms, responds to this one angrily, telling Léonce, "Let me alone; you bother me."[17]

With a few economical segments of dialogue, Chopin has sketched the void that exists in the relationship of this couple. But she has also suggested the ideals of American society concerning the institution of marriage at the turn of the century. Underlying both Léonce's and Edna's discontent is their awareness of the roles that the culture prescribes for wives and husbands. In the ideal marriage, the spouses would be entirely compatible and would perform very specific roles in different spheres. The husband, the head of the household and breadwinner, would make the major decisions for the family and function in the larger world. The wife, his helpmeet, would be responsible for child care and for maintaining domestic comfort. With each assigned to specific tasks based on rigid ideas of gender, marital conflict would be kept to a minimum. If some issue were to arise upon which the couple disagreed, the solution would be simple and recognized by all. The husband would prevail, and his wife would submit to his authoritative judgment, a hierarchy with biblical as well as secular support. Without lecturing the reader about these cultural expectations, Chopin depicts two characters who are well aware of them. Léonce believes his demands to be normal and reasonable. Edna believes her response to his behavior to make her obey his wishes is a personal problem and never analyzes the subordinate role assigned to wives. The novel could not be a better example to dramatize questions about the unrealistic, inappropriate, and unexamined ideals about marital relationships.

One significant issue with which I had to deal as I began editing the New American Library edition of *"The Awakening" and Selected Stories of Kate Chopin* was choosing a small selection from the considerable number of fine stories available to me. As it turned out, there was room for seventeen of them. There was never any question of including the "best" of the stories because many were interesting tales about vivid characters and demonstrated Chopin's consistent narrative skills, but I quickly discovered that I had a few standards that helped make my task easier. The central audience that I had in mind was one of readers interested in feminist literature. Naturally, I wanted to include stories to dramatize Chopin's range of subjects, but I particularly wanted to reprint some stories with women as central characters, specifically women who thought about female-male relationships, about wifehood and motherhood, and who were self conscious enough to raise questions about their growth and fulfillment beyond the day of wedding vows.

Thus, I quickly chose two stories—"Wiser Than a God" and "A Point at Issue!"—because the young women depicted in them had serious artistic and intellectual goals and did not believe that a conventional marriage, even one based on sincere romantic love and respect, would resolve the issue of the kind of lives they would lead as wives. In "Wiser Than a God," Paula Von Stolz, a gifted and serious pianist, has spent her life preparing for a career. In Chopin's era, generally any conflict in fiction between a woman's pursuing a career and accepting a marriage proposal would be short lived and end with the choice of the proposal. This would be especially true if the suitor, as in this story, was well educated, affluent, handsome, caring, and deeply in love.

Chopin's view of the incompatibility of the goals of Paula and George Brainard, the man who wishes to marry her, must have been startling to her audience, and it sounded an early unconventional note in her fiction. A union between a loving man and woman would end with very different outcomes for each of them as spouses. Each marriage, the author seemed to realize, would really be two different marriages because the roles assigned to husbands and wives by society were so dramatically different.

The second early choice was "A Point at Issue!" Contrary to the typical belief that marriage completes and fulfills a woman, in this story Chopin proclaims that marriage often restricts a woman's intellectual growth. The newlywed Eleanor and Charles Faraday plan to spend most of their first year of marriage apart, she in Paris studying French and he back in America teaching at his university. Their plan was based on their determination to ignore the marriage laws that usually restrict wives to a routine of domestic responsibilities and to create a marriage that would preserve their individuality. This experiment, which demands that the couple ignore the prejudices of a scandalized society, again suggests Chopin's continuing concern with the American institution of marriage in her era that was so often unquestioningly accepted as divine law by young people.

Probably among the easiest and earliest choices I made was the inclusion of two stories for which there was no possible alternate, "The Story of an Hour" and "The Storm." "The Story of an Hour" is a meditation about marriage and patriarchal privilege; it makes for a valuable prologue to a reading of *The Awakening*. In a groundbreaking way, the author's central character, Louise Mallard, dismisses the matter of whether a husband and wife love one another and goes on to insist that the institution of marriage warps human nature and imposes controlling and destructive roles.

"The Storm," though written in 1898, was never published during the author's lifetime, and I cannot imagine that the editor of any of the magazines of that era would have accepted it. In it, Chopin ignores two powerful literary taboos of her era. She supplies a detailed description of the intense physical attraction and pleasure of a man and woman as they commit adultery—and the adulteress is not punished for her transgression. Alcée Laballiere takes temporary shelter in the home where Calixta lives with Bobinôt, her husband of five years, and her young son. Alcée looks at the woman who had aroused his unbearable passion five years earlier: "Her lips were as red and moist as pomegranate seed. Her white neck and a glimpse of her full, firm bosom disturbed him powerfully."[18] Their sexual relations result in an extraordinary sensual awakening beyond that either had known with a spouse. Chopin seems to celebrate their erotic union as a transcending joyful experience: "When he touched her breasts they gave themselves up in quivering ecstasy, inviting his lips. Her mouth was a fountain of delight. When he possessed her, they seemed to swoon together at the very borderland of life's mystery."[19]

If we compare Chopin's explicit sexual scene with the scene in Theodore Dreiser's *Sister Carrie* (1900) in which Carrie is about to have sexual relations with Charles Drouet for the first time, we can begin to gauge the degree to which Chopin's readers would have been shocked by her details and positive tone.

In fact, contemporary students who read Dreiser's description about the way in which the couple's eyes meet, his holding her hand, and the dreams that night of Carrie's sister, in which Carrie disappears down an old mine shaft, often have no idea that the author is depicting the night on which the couple embark on a sexual relationship.

The second unusual element in this story that signals how different Chopin was from her contemporaries is her description of the level of happiness of all involved at the story's conclusion. Both Calixta's husband and Alcée's wife have not been harmed in the least by the extramarital passion of their spouses. Calixta suffers from no awkward or guilty feeling as she and Bobinôt look forward to a pleasant meal and a comfortable family evening. Even a cursory glance at the depiction of women who engage in illicit sexual relationships in literature written before 1960 reveals a startling lesson. While male characters engage in sexual liaisons before marriage and commit adultery, typically the price for illicit sexuality of women is death. Thus, the experience of Emma Bovary, Anna Karenina, and even Lily Bart in *The House of Mirth*, who only appears to have had an improper relationship, reveals a subtext that is a message to all readers about the grim consequences of forbidden behavior.

Two stories that were paired in my mind and quickly chosen were "Regret" and "A Pair of Silk Stockings." Although Chopin could brilliantly depict Edna's complicated attitude toward her children and understood that a healthy adult woman could not live through and for her children as society often preached (though this ideal was not extended to men), in "Regret" Chopin dramatized the extraordinary pleasure of caring for young children. The discovery of this kind of fulfillment by a woman who had never imagined it, at a time when it is clearly too late for her to hold on to these pleasures, reveals the way in which Chopin understood the variety and depth of female experience and the cost to a woman who had been ignorant of the simple joys of motherhood.

In contrast, "A Pair of Silk Stockings" emphasizes the extent to which a woman must empty herself of personal preferences and desires in order to care for her children. When Mrs. Sommers—the mother of at least four children—unexpectedly makes the first purchase of the stockings, the intense longings she must have put aside in her straitened circumstances will no longer be denied. Interestingly, Chopin describes the process by which this mother responds to her desires as not involving any thought. Instead, Mrs. Sommers abandons "herself to some mechanical impulse that directed her actions and freed her of responsibility."[20] The intellect has provided restraint, but another, more powerful, force is at work here.

In at least two stories that I chose, Chopin surprisingly depicts two young women for whom she has considerable scorn. In "A Shameful Affair," Miss McEnders is an intolerant and self-righteous snob who discovers that a seamstress who is working on her elaborate and expensive trousseau is raising an illegitimate young daughter. From her pinnacle of moral indignation, Miss McEnders orders that all her work be withdrawn from this tainted woman. In a very satisfying scene, Chopin dramatizes the way that this foolishly ignorant and harsh young woman is forced to face some very unpleasant truths about her own life. Sometimes women are oppressed not by males but by judgmental and rigid other women.

In "The Kiss," Chopin presents a young woman who has made a calculated decision to marry for wealth. While Edna, too, married knowing
that she felt no passion for Léonce, her motivation stemmed partly from
her disillusionment with romantic love, which in three instances led to
nothing. Nathalie, however, expects to continue to enjoy the passion she
has for an attractive young man, a long-time friend of the family.

Chopin seems pleased that Nathalie's design to have both men in her
life will be thwarted. The author's arch comment as the story ends reminds us that she is not always sympathetic to female characters.

In reading the stories recently, I found that they had retained their
interest for different reasons. Some, on marriage and motherhood, dramatized problems that remain somewhat as they were in Chopin's time.
Others remind the reader of the roles and expectations of women at the
turn of the century that have vastly changed. Still others are wonderful
examples of human nature that seems universal and unchanged. While
at least five or six of the stories I originally chose could easily be replaced
by five or six different ones, that idea simply reflects the fact that there are
so many fine stories that any selection will inevitably omit some that have
become favorites of the author's readers.

Over a period of time, those of us who were at first attracted to The
Awakening because of its subject were perhaps taken aback by the extent to
which the style and structure of the novel began to reveal the consummate
artistry of its author and the extent to which it lends itself to analysis at
different levels. Thus, the novel has become both a high school text as well
as a graduate course text, one that is often chosen by graduate students for
extensive study.

One entirely unanticipated situation is the way in which the novel
lends itself to a variety of modern teaching techniques, including the use
of technology. For example, this year a graduate student of mine worked
on a curriculum project of using the novel to teach the elements of fiction to high school seniors. This project fulfilled a three-credit course
requirement for a master of science in teaching degree. It consisted of an
extensive review of the literature about teaching The Awakening, a class-
by-class detailed description of instructional activities for students, and
an appendix containing a variety of handouts. The completed project
presented forty-two lessons to be utilized over a nine-week period. Many

of the assignments required the students to use computer skills for research as well as to make a PowerPoint presentation to the other members of the class.

Among the handouts was a list of Web sites on topics such as realism in American literature, Cajun culture, and women's studies as well as photographs of women's clothing of that era and selections from etiquette and advice books of the period. These would prove particularly helpful to students of *The Awakening*, since they described ideals of wifehood including the duty of presiding over reception days and the supremely important duties of motherhood.

The importance that *The Awakening* assumed in the canon of American literature came, no doubt, as a surprise to many of the early scholars who taught the novel. The factors that influence the popularity of particular authors over time are unpredictable. For example, novels by Nobel Prize–winner Sinclair Lewis and experimentalist John Dos Passos that once seemed so significantly American or so modern in narrative structure seem to have lost their privileged status. Their criticism of American institutions and values, of the sterile middle class and ruthless corporate moguls, now seems off target and dated. At present, it appears as though *The Awakening*, thirty-five years after the critical reassessment that introduced it to a new generation, remains a vibrant and compelling text. It continues to reward the reader with descriptions and insights that are timeless.

NOTES

1. Diana Trilling, letter to Barbara H. Solomon, 23 Feb. 1975.

2. Milton R. Stern and Seymour L. Gross, eds., *American Literature Survey: Nation and Region, 1860–1900*, 3rd ed. (New York: Viking, 1975) 34.

3. Stern and Gross 198.

4. Robert E. Spiller, Willard Thorp, Thomas H. Johnson, Henry Seidel Canby, and Richard M. Ludwig, eds., *Literary History of the United States*, 3rd ed. (New York: Macmillan, 1963) 859.

5. Spiller et al. 859.

6. James D. Hart, *The Oxford Companion to American Literature*, 4th ed. (New York: Oxford UP, 1965) 155.

7. Max J. Herzberg and the Staff of the Thomas Y. Crowell Company, The Reader's Encyclopedia of American Literature (New York: Thomas Y. Crowell Co., 1962) 176.

8. Kate Chopin, The Complete Works of Kate Chopin, ed. Per Seyersted (Baton Rouge: Louisiana State UP, 1969) 905.

9. Chopin, Complete Works 914.

10. Chopin, Complete Works 914.

11. Chopin, Complete Works 930.

12. Chopin, Complete Works 971.

13. Chopin, Complete Works 885.

14. Chopin, Complete Works 912.

15. Chopin, Complete Works 939.

16. Chopin, Complete Works 939.

17. Chopin, Complete Works 939.

18. Chopin, Complete Works 594.

19. Chopin, Complete Works 595

20. Chopin, Complete Works 502.

5

So Long As We Read Chopin

MARY E. PAPKE

I WAS A POOR GRADUATE STUDENT living in a cold-water basement flat in a city in which I did not speak the majority language. I had just that day found a paperback copy of Kate Chopin's *The Awakening*, a book I had seen passing reference to in one of the early overviews of women's literary production. I certainly had not heard of it during my undergraduate study of American literature at a premiere American research university. Neither was anyone promoting Chopin's work at McGill University, where I was pursuing study in American Marxist literary criticism and radical drama. I had found the copy in what was then, I think, the only English-language feminist bookstore in Montreal. I stayed up all night, one arm hanging outside the bedcovers holding up the book, exposing as little of myself to the cold air as was possible. And when I got to the end, I was profoundly shocked, so much so that I shifted the focus of my work to the American women writers Kate Chopin and Edith Wharton, who wrote so powerfully about, within, and against the literary forms and themes I had been taught were the best. I had never before read a novel that so assaulted my senses and left me so distraught at its end that I had to return to it again and again to determine why.

Many of my students over the past twenty-five years have also been distressed, if not by the book's focus on a woman's right to self-definition (and there are some who still find this mightily disturbing in the case of a woman who is also a mother), then by Edna's final defeat in the face of a repressive system in which she has long been complicit. I have sometimes asked students to invent another fitting ending—fitting, that is, in terms of plot, time, and characters—but only one person in all this time has come even close to a possible alternative end. As my students concede, Chopin's ending seems the only one possible for Edna's story. One might go on to argue, perhaps, that the novel should then be read as a thanatography, to use the terminology of forensic experts, a "written account of a person's death" that "selectively relates aspects of a life that set a deadly sequence into motion,"[1] and students familiar with the many crime investigation and medical emergency television series would probably relish the quest for the answer. But approaching the novel as a thanatography suggests that there is a definite reading that would satisfy by providing all the necessary answers to what has appeared heretofore mysterious or unthinkable, a simple solution to the case of Edna Pontellier. This approach would necessarily be a refusal of the purposeful lack of closure in this novel. That is, we cannot persuasively argue that Edna finds meaning in her death from the evidence given, though the jouissance inscribed in the final lyrical images is unmistakable, albeit potentially deceptive. We do see that Chopin writes Edna through her life experience, through memories, and then into what Mircea Eliade calls profane space, "the homogeneous and infinite expanse, in which no point of reference is possible and hence no orientation can be established."[2]

It is this extreme ambiguity, relativity, and existentialist profanation of the life force, the abrupt leaving of Edna in an untenable state of liminality occasioned by traumatic loss, self-abjection, and grief, that is so disturbing for most readers as to remain unspeakable. While I agree with my colleagues that Chopin was a rebel, a protofeminist, and a trailblazer, I also believe that her work is imbued with a sadness and a sorrow so deep that when one catches a glimpse of it—as one does at the end of her last novel—one turns away in self-defense against a sight so vulnerable and yet so brave. Indeed, one almost willfully misreads the novel in order not to have to deal with its sensibility of grieving for that which is already always lost and the impossibility of any meaningful recuperation. The fearlessness of Chopin's writing, her insistence on staring the truth in the face, both frightens and enraptures us, much as the interior voice murmuring about freedom does to Chopin's protagonist in her "The Story of an Hour." But as much as we find Chopin's work seductive, we seem not to want to acknowledge the totality of its philosophical message, and I am as guilty in this as are many other devoted readers and scholars. Maybe we can grasp only a measure of the aesthetic/philosophical import in any one reading. Let me now offer not a definitive reading, of course, but perhaps a helpful supplement to already received wisdom. I will approach what remains to be said by describing the misreadings, or, more precisely, the partial readings, however profitable ones they are for the most part, that I and other readers have done and the directions in which they might lead us to reconsider Chopin's stature and future position in the American literature canon.

In my *Verging on the Abyss* and several complementary pieces, my subject was Chopin's focus on woman's right to subject position and agency, and I attempted a materialist reading of true womanhood ideology and its dramatization in the social fiction of Kate Chopin and Edith Wharton. In many ways, my work simply reflected the usual process of feminist recuperation of lost works—first, finding the text(s), then positioning the work in terms of the female or the feminine, in particular the gender ideology of the time, the consequences of which we still experience today. I was especially interested in a structural and epistemological pattern I saw emerging in her fiction as she approached the writing of *The Awakening*, that which appears in her descriptions of the process of a woman's coming to self-consciousness through sensual apperception followed by philosophical reflection on what might constitute her subjectivity rather than her subjugation, only for her to be defeated by the quotidian demands of her community of husband, children, lover, friends, by their needs that the now awakened woman knows she can never satisfy without sacrificing her newfound self. Chopin thoroughly imagined each phase of what Raymond Williams calls a new "structure of feeling,"[3] a nascent consciousness that reimagines the world as a more equitable, compassionate space, even as it leads to disillusionment with the present. She illustrated as well the consequences of self-desire and betrayal of self-faith. Much to the discomfort of many readers, in her work women's quest for self-determination set against women's capacity for self-betrayal trumps issues of race and class as the central matter in Chopin's fiction even as the fiction effectively manipulates gender politics to expose the perversity of racial hatred and class antagonisms. Chopin's fiction is multivalent, then, but any full social critique it offers is subtly made, sometimes ironized, rarely written out in bold. Instead, Chopin asks of her readers

that they, too, experience a coming to new consciousness as they engage
with her work.

This emergent consciousness that Chopin's women cannot yet fully articulate is most boldly presented in such works as "The Story of an Hour,"
"A Pair of Silk Stockings," "Désirée's Baby," "Her Letters," "An Egyptian
Cigarette," At Fault, and The Awakening, but it also appears in modified
forms in many of the stories once categorized simply as local-color or
regionalist fiction. The fiction to which I am most drawn and that I have
long contemplated is often strangely erotic in its appeal to the senses
but at the same time haunted by the specter of imminent loss and self-
annihilation. This description is particularly well realized, for instance,
in "Désirée's Baby," in which a woman of unknown background is cast
out by her once adoring husband for giving birth to a multiracial child
and then disappears into the abyss of the bayou rather than return to her
adoptive family, which accepts her as she is, or in "An Egyptian Cigarette"
in which a betrayed lover seeks rescue from grief in suicide by drowning
and, pathetically, imagines in her final death throes a perfect reunion with
her lover, only to be doubly cast out as her death vision is rejected by the
woman who has dreamed her story. As these stories illustrate, romantic
blandishments too often prove to be empty, delusory, or overdetermined,
as if they are taken from an old script that the characters woodenly perform even though the dialogue no longer makes any sense. Just think
of Robert's last letter to Edna, the meaning of which is always a point of
contention between my male and female students. As Kevin Brockmeier
writes in his very provocative apocalyptic novel entitled The Brief History
of the Dead, "love doesn't always generate hope. Anyone who has ever experienced love knows that you can have too much love or too little. You can
have love that parches, love that defeats. You can have love measured out in
the wrong proportions. It's like your sunlight and water—the wrong kind
of love is just as likely to stifle hope as it is to nourish it."[4] And so it proves
in the works cited above in which even a mother's unconditional love cannot save a daughter from suicide if she be rejected by both husband and
self or in which children's selfless love for their mother cannot satisfy or
compensate for her need for sensual satisfaction and room of her own.
Once awakened, Chopin's women cannot again delude themselves into
believing that they can achieve self-determination in a world created nei-

ther by nor for them and, in some cases, in which the deck is too obviously stacked against them. I do not, then, read Chopin as romantic or
provincial or genteel. Rather, her gaze returns again and again to abysmal
sublime exaltation as it is experienced by women and the immense tragedy, in Julia Kristeva's words, of the "inhuman loneliness of a self bereft
of itself,"[5] which they too often find is the consequence of their desire for
selfhood.

I am not surprised, then, that it took a scholar from a country not
noted for the naive optimism of the United States and the son of a wom-
en's rights advocate to reclaim her work as important or that the French
honored her work long before it became so common in American undergraduate courses; the concept and the lived experience of the abysmal
sublime were not so strange to them as they still are to American readers. Neither did I feel it at all strange to position Kate Chopin and Edith
Wharton alongside one another as documentarians of woman's conditions and struggle for self-worth, both of them transatlantic in scope, pessimistic in philosophical temper. While both lived rich lives in terms of
opportunities, emotional bonds, and public recognition, either could have
written the haunting line in Wharton's conclusion to her autobiography:
"Life is the saddest thing there is, next to death."[6]

My use above of the term transatlantic is meant to be provocative. A
more recent development in feminist theory than is reflected in my work
is to read the fiction of women writers through a variety of lenses—for instance, those of psychoanalysis, postcolonial theory, queer politics, critical
race studies. All such lenses zero in on a discrete subject—the economic,
libidinal, nationalist, racial, or sexual—in order to enrich what might
otherwise remain a naive reading by attending to elements of the text that
might better elucidate its overarching raison d'être and thus call into account its critical reception and possible misprisions. An excellent example
of a necessary refocusing of our attention from the pure blandishments of
the text is Bernard Koloski's insistence throughout his advocacy of Chopin
upon the importance of our recognizing Chopin's biculturalism, her ability to move comfortably between the French world of her mother's family
and the American immigrant world of her father. In terms of her cultural
affiliations, we would also need to take into account her self-identification
as a Confederate sympathizer and her experience as the daughter of a slave

owner as well as her multiple transitions between matriarchal and patriarchal milieus. Each cultural affiliation complicates enormously how we
read her writing. Like many of her characters, Chopin had to make sense
of sometimes complementary, sometimes contradictory expectations of
what it meant to be a girl and then a woman in whichever society she
was positioned in and, later, chose. Unlike Edna Pontellier, Kate Chopin
seemed to be a successful fusion of different cultural sensibilities in that,
while both are American women, only Chopin was also, simultaneously,
French. Too often we set one cultural identification against the other, as
was the case in the French city in which I studied, or reduce our purview
to a monocultural gaze, as still occurs in many American literature classrooms. It might profit us more to consider her interculturalism, her lived
experience of multiple identifications and ways of self-knowing, and how
one builds oneself out of the fragments of one's intercultural inheritance
in the process of self-construction and imagining a new structure of feeling that can be expressed in words and actions.

From all we know of her biography, Chopin seems to have experienced
her interculturalism as an advantage rather than as a burden. She read and
wrote equally well in both French and English; she early on acquired what
we now term cultural competencies that are evident in her careful delin-
eation of the cultures and peoples of her southern and urban settings. In
many of her works, she purposefully sets culture against culture, introducing issues of race, class, and gender as cultural manifestations to which
attention must be paid. Her work transcends national or dominant Anglo-
American cultural narratives, however, as if to show us that interculturalism
—multiracial, multinational, and cross-class understanding—rather than
the American dream of personal self-satisfaction is what is necessary to
constitute a good life. It is not simple happenstance that her second novel
was set in both Paris and America, that Edna Pontellier speaks of moving to Paris as a possible means of increasing her self-worth, and that
Désirée's husband's mother, a French woman of color, never leaves her
motherland for America precisely because of that nation's racialist agenda.
And Edna, we know, reads both contemporary French novels and essays
by Emerson—reading the novels embarrasses and excites her, and reading the essays puts her to sleep as if to indicate that such self-reliance as
Emerson trumpets is not for her, his vision of nature and man without a

clear meaning for a woman. Extrapolate from these examples and one sees how very rich in cultural histories are the regions, states and cities, and people central to her work. These reminders of Chopin's bicultural and intercultural investment serve again to underscore the central issues of her work: what constitutes subjectivity, to whom is it granted, how might it be won, and at what cost. Despite the multiple grievous losses that would have crippled a lesser individual's self-development and the many conflictual cultural demands she faced, Chopin was a loving wife, a devoted mother, a most productive artist. How interesting, then, that she focused in much of her work—certainly the work we most often teach and read—on women who are stigmatized by particular cultural identifications, constrained from crossing between cultures, or simply unable to use cultural directives to their own advantage, even in the private sphere of the home, less they be marked as unfit, unclean, unwomanly, the abject.

Why did states of liminality and abjection resonate so with Chopin? Her early writings offer little insight, though surely it is unusual for a seventeen-year-old girl to carefully write out the last words of numerous famous personages, among them Aristotle's "I entered this world in sin. I have lived in anxiety. I depart in perturbation. Cause of Causes pity me" and Goethe's call for "Mehr Licht."[7] As Emily Toth's biographical project makes clear, Chopin's life was marked by a series of too early deaths and forced exiles that robbed her of father, half brother, her female soul mate, her husband, and her mother. Prostrated by grief again and again, and in midlife left in debt to care for six children, she repeatedly recuperated herself from the space of mourning by taking up a new subject position, the most empowered of which was as an artist, reintegrating herself into society after each crisis. Yet at least at some of those crisis points—I would guess the death of her husband and the death of her mother—she also must have experienced the longing for rest and the consoling defiance of saying "no more of this." No doubt certain works of literature spoke to her, just as her works speak to us, offering not so much consolation as reaffirmation of the toll grief takes. We know, for instance, that she was particularly influenced by the work of Mary Wilkins (Freeman), whom she considered a genius. We do not know for certain all of what she read by Wilkins, but even a cursory familiarity with Wilkins's work will reveal striking similarities, if not in regional affiliation, then in the lives of the

characters not taken into or taken in by society. Ironically, both Chopin
and Wilkins share a similar critical history—praise in their own time for
their regionalist or local-color fiction, categorizations that immediately
qualified the extent of their contribution to American letters; a falling off
of critical interest and a long period of relative silence; a renewed interest in the women's issues evident in the works; and then a move toward
sophisticated theoretical readings focusing on issues of class and gender
and, in the case of Chopin, race. I have often wondered whether Chopin
read *Pembroke*, that very strange novel that few today read and even fewer
teach. Wilkins's graphic depiction of the negative legacy of puritanical/
patriarchal moral strictures that literally cripple the central characters by
rendering sexual appetites repulsive and deep engagement with another
impossible is as powerfully dramatized in Chopin's own work, in which
men and women go mad with passion, lovers betray one another for the
sake of their love, and people who do not conform are cast out, sometimes
by themselves. Both authors address with extraordinary psychological insight the lived experience of intense self-repression and the consequences
to the individual and her or his world.

Similarly important for Chopin was the work of Guy de Maupassant,
so much so that she translated a series of his stories and tried valiantly
to have these published in one volume only to be told, in so many words,
that such a bicultural investment simply wouldn't pay in America. Indeed,
it still doesn't play in American literature classrooms, where a writer's influences are often cited but primary texts in another language, even in
translation, are rarely included for study. It is, of course, necessary to place
Chopin's work within American regionalism, realism, and naturalism and
in the tradition of American women's writing, but think of how it would
invigorate discussion to place her work also in the bicultural setting of
French and American literary developments. This is not to suggest that
some such work has not been offered by various critics, but it is still most
unusual to find a comparative approach to Chopin's work taken in the
classroom, and I am as guilty as many another in merely paying lip service
to Chopin's influences rather than doing justice to the complete works of
Chopin, including those—specifically her translations of Maupassant—
that are not available in any volume that purports to offer the reader all of
Chopin.

What was it about Maupassant that spoke so directly to Chopin that she devoted considerable time and energy to the translation of eight tales? Even a cursory glance at the titles—short titles of between one and three words that include "divorce," "mad," "solitude," "night," and "suicide"—supports my assertion that themes of grief, loss, and self-abjection are always central to Chopin's artistic project. Out of Maupassant's oeuvre Chopin chose eight short stories that are far from the genteel literature then finding favor in America. As we know from her papers, she began serious study of Maupassant's fiction around 1888 and then labored on the translations from 1892 to 1898, the period of production of her greatest work preceding The Awakening. Chopin chose stories that elaborate intensely disturbed states of mind, what the characters themselves refuse to admit may be sociopathological states of being but in some cases clearly are. In the very short pieces, men repeatedly experience the consequences of "that which we love too violently ends by killing us."[8] In "A Divorce Case," one man's idealization of woman leads to a complete degradation of that sex and a displacement of erotic engagement from that with a particular woman to an obsession with hothouse orchids, obscenely described as "these strange girls from marshy, burning and unwholesome lands" whom he can nurture, fondle, ogle, and imprison "as long as its [the orchid's] existence" for his own perverse delectation: "I stay near it, ardent, feverish and tormented; anticipating its approaching death and watching it fade whilst I possess it, inspire it, drink, gather its short life in an inexpressible caress."[9] Chopin's "Her Letters," written in the same year she translated "A Divorce Case," also attempts to describe in almost clinical detail what she identifies as this "man-instinct of possession."[10] While the woman in this first translation uses the judicial system in order to free herself from an untenable bondage, Maupassant's "Mad?"—which Chopin also translated in the same year—ends with the murder of a woman whose husband's jealousy leads him to conceive of her as "the human beast, less than that: she is but a morsel of soft round flesh which harbors Infamy," finding sexual satisfaction not in him but in a "fiery brute," the horse she rides daily away from him.[11] In light of the innate "perversion" of any "woman's sensuality," the husband argues, can he be held accountable or deemed mad for freeing himself from her filthy grasp? "It?" in turn makes clear that men seek out women not for love or sexual pleasure but as a shield against solitude, or, more precisely in this case, to avoid having to live only with and within themselves. Marriage is a convenient stopgap measure to keep fear of aloneness at bay. Interestingly, this translation was accepted for publication, perhaps because its take on marital relationships did not seem unreasonable to contemporary editors.

Three of the remaining translations, completed by Chopin in 1895, directly reflect themes that Chopin develops in her late stories and in *The Awakening* and perhaps influenced Chopin's original title for her last novel, "A Solitary Soul." "Solitude"—as if in response to "It?"—elaborates on the essential, irremediable estrangement of each human being from another and cites Flaubert's famous statement that "we are all in a desert where no one person understands another."[12] Indeed, as the central character bemoans, "Whatever we may do or attempt, despite the embraces and transports of love, the hunger of the lips, we are always alone," each of us keeping a "sanctuary self where no other soul penetrates."[13] "Night" and "Suicide" offer the only possible respite from such existential angst in the face of a dead world—in the first, surrender to the freezing waters of the Seine; in the second, a loaded revolver. As "Suicide" informs us, it is not great catastrophes that drive one to suicide but "the slow succession of life's little miseries; the fatal disorganization of a solitary existence left without illusions."[14] The central character's admonishment that "we are the everlasting playthings of stupid and engaging illusions forever renewed"[15] is then translated once more, as it were, directly into Edna's confession to Dr. Mandelet that "the years that are gone seem like dreams—if one might go on sleeping and dreaming—but to wake up and find—oh! well! perhaps it is better to wake up after all, even to suffer, rather than to remain a dupe to illusions all one's life."[16] Further, the water and bird imagery in "Night" and "For Sale," the recollection of hope proffered but unrealized in "Suicide" in the form of a love letter written by another young Robert, and the powerful "memory of a sensation, fleeting, exquisite" in "For Sale," particularly of "moments of profound, physical joy; the joy of the animal that runs through the grass and that floats through the blue ether in the sun,"[17] bear striking resemblances to complementary elements in Chopin's masterpiece. And, of course, the loss of the ability to maintain illusions of hope resonates throughout Chopin's work and is also the subject matter of Maupassant's *Une Vie*, available in translation now as *A Life: The*

Humble Truth, in which a woman of the haute bourgeoisie suffers a most unhappy marriage and profound disappointment in her experience of motherhood.

But what can we make of Chopin's last translation, done in 1898, entitled "Father Amable," ostensibly a character study of feudal peasantry in Normandy? If we do not immediately dismiss it as local-color fiction, albeit of a region American readers do not know, or as just another manifestation of Maupassant's exceptional short story technique—quick but bold establishment of character types, some sort of economic or familial crisis (or both), an ending with a poignant twist—we might recognize that its bleak tale of miserliness, subhuman living conditions, and the roles of chance and accident, usually fatal, in one's life reads as of a piece with the work of Zola, Crane, Norris, and Sinclair of The Jungle. Chopin's choice of this last piece to translate is quite telling, then, indicating to us, if we have not already surmised as much from her previously published work, her intellectual attraction to determinist philosophies and sciences. To investigate this investment fully, we would now need to include in a master course on Chopin not only Maupassant's stories in translation and the fiction of the naturalists named above but also works by Zola, Spencer, and Darwin, all "scientists" the writing of whom she studied. And since this dream course seems to have no time or space restrictions, some representative works of Flaubert, the Goncourts, and Daudet could be thrown in for good measure. One would in this way open up serious discussion of Chopin's intercultural and intellectual breadth, a necessary prelude to positioning her within American literature of the determinist, transatlantic, aesthetically experimental bent—that is, alongside the work of the aforementioned naturalists as well as of Mary Wilkins (Freeman), whose pessimistic determinism and hope in the face of destitution I continue to admire, and of Sarah Orne Jewett, whose work Bill Brown has opened up for me with his reading of the cultural souvenirs in the Pointed Fir stories and why they matter.

I have not yet had the luxury to teach the course I have been describing here, but I have tried to move in that direction. I believe my greatest success so far in introducing The Awakening in much of its complexity and ambiguity came last spring in a graduate seminar entitled "The Culture of Consumption in Late 19th Century American Fiction," a course I team-taught with an economic historian. Discussion of The Awakening followed study of works by Rebecca Harding Davis, Howells, James, Garland, and Crane; each discussion was informed by a focus on various economies in the text that determine character/plot formation and limitations and that also reflect the author's philosophical standpoint and reformist or radical sympathies. The course concluded with consideration of work by Dreiser, Dunbar, Wharton, Sinclair, and Cather. Chopin's novel is now one of the most frequently read and taught works in the undergraduate curriculum, so much so that I gave up teaching it for a while when I learned that many of my students had already "studied" it four or five times. The overall grouping of texts in my graduate seminar and the juxtaposition of each text to the others in terms of economic foci and a realist/naturalist aesthetic drive served to make "strange" Chopin's novel and, so, opened up at least the possibility of a reinvigorated reading. This sort of critical estrangement is necessary, I believe, since Chopin's work is now so far from lost to us that we are beginning to take it for granted. In particular, the reputation of The Awakening as a manifesto of rebellion and its popularity today as a paradigmatic feminist text work against our striving for a deep appreciation of Chopin's sophisticated aesthetic agenda and achievement. In important ways, if familiarity does not breed contempt, it does enable an oversimplified interpretation that elides the consequences of rebellion against social/gender proscriptions, the very stacked deck from which Edna is dealt a hand to play in a fixed game. Edna's death leaves everything against which she has struggled intact; her final protest can be erased by one carefully worded newspaper or critical note. By placing Chopin's work with that of a more capacious company than one solely determined by gender or class or regional affiliation, we allow the text a chance to play itself out in full.

Unlike reviewers of her time, we do not now dismiss her work as either snapshots of a quaint backward region or casebook studies of various psychic imbalances bordering on the pathological. Yet postmodern critics can also contain a text's volatility through certain modes of reading. For example, even when the female characters act against their own self-interest or, obversely, are selfish in the extreme, even in cases when a character chooses self-abjection rather than self-determination, it seems almost required by some feminist critical prescriptions that we nevertheless celebrate female "essence" and demonstrate how Chopin's women are always already victims of rather than in any way complicit in the injustices they suffer. Like Maupassant's benighted men, we, too, idealize a heroine of a feminist text, even if she be, as are so many of Chopin's heroines, culpable only by virtue of her already compromised degree of agency in an overly determined environment. Yet, let me be clear, this is not to argue that these fictive women are to blame for their own sadness and suffering. As Chopin herself admonished one reader who considered Fanny Hosmer the one at fault in the novel of the same name, that is an egregious misreading. Rather, as Chopin insists, those who force a repressive morality on others are the ones at fault for much futile suffering. She might, then, have found wanting critical views that seem content in merely pointing out futile suffering and, so, in a strange way celebrating victimage.

For most contributors to this volume, discovering Chopin was a life-changing event. For some, her work complemented feminist/political activism; for others, it opened up the southern or regionalist or realist canon and made it a site of emerging consciousness rather than twilight sleep. Her work also figures centrally in many narratives of personal achievement and, for some, made a career in academia a reality. We all have, then, a great deal invested in Chopin and a visceral understanding of why her work matters not only to us but to her future readers. My own career trajectory, for example, was in significant ways determined by one night's reading. I went on to teach the first course in American women writers at my graduate institution. I successfully defended a dissertation the subject of which was as new to my committee as it was to me (my dissertation director, to whom I am indebted for his enormous help in smoothing the way for a feminist study of American women writers, was a specialist in the early modern period). My first book on Chopin and Wharton, a much expanded and revised version of my dissertation, found ready acceptance at a press whose expanding list in women's studies it fit, and its publication was instrumental in my hire and then in my earning tenure because of the positive recognition it received from other Chopin scholars. I am certainly treated locally as the Chopin expert on call, and, I'm sure like other Chopin scholars, I often receive e-mails from high school and college students near and far pursuing study of her work.

My advocacy of Chopin's merit has also led to some of the most unforgettable moments—good, bad, and ugly—in my professional life as a feminist scholar. For instance, at the party welcoming me into the professoriate at the University of Tennessee, a senior specialist in modern fiction, after congratulating me on my hire, said, "Chopin's work is certainly interesting. [Pause] Not that she's really a good writer. [Longer pause] Not that I've ever read any of her stuff." Moments such as this only underscored for me the continued importance of feminist analysis and the ongoing and never ceasing reclamation of women's work. In that light, however, I have sometimes been amused and sometimes disturbed by the repeated attempts in print, in public, and in the media to make Chopin "sexy" to potential consumers by focusing on her love plots, real and imagined, and therefore more marketable, more easily digestible than the hard issues on which I focus. Certainly, one can gain a great deal of public "capital" by presenting Chopin in this way, and it is a source of capital I rely upon in order to entice some of my students into deeper analysis. However, that sort of commodification also has clear limitations, for it undersells the overall importance of her work by making the product fit a packaging that simply cannot accommodate recognition of the intense and long-term investment Chopin made in producing radical new social fiction in which her brilliant and seductive women are both necessarily flawed and too often left inconsolable or, in the most disquieting cases, altogether erased from their own texts. Désirée walks into the void, and the narratorial eye turns back to the man who has so cruelly pronounced her abject; Edna swims away from her antagonists and then through her memories back to an elemental sensual world in which she no longer figures as an individual. But she also swims into our cultural memory.

For some twenty years now, I've contemplated giving a presentation for an annual series that invites professors from across my institution to share their work with their colleagues. My intellectual come-on title would be "Who Was the First Naked Lady in American Literature?" Such a talk would give me the opportunity to celebrate Edna Pontellier's moment of unburdening and her sensuous apprehension of pure physicality, but I've never offered to give this piece because I can imagine how disappointed my audience would be as I went on then to note that this ecstatic experience is but one short-lived moment and achieved only at the cost of the woman's life. Perhaps it is my own temperament, my feminist materialist standpoint, my life as a woman, and my own experiences of loss and the endlessness of mourning that oblige me to balance the celebratory with the cautionary, the lyrical with the elegiac, whenever I speak about or teach Chopin. In her work, life is, indeed, in so many instances, the saddest thing next to death, especially for those who have lost mothers, those who have been denied a childhood by virtue of their having to take up the position of dead mothers, for those who have lost children and then dulled their pain through alcohol, for those whose families have cast them out, those who have lost husbands and been left insolvent, those who have been abandoned, those whose attempts at rebellion have been neatly co-opted, those who sleepwalk through their lives precisely because it would be too appalling to awaken and see the truth of their compromised existence. Life is bitterly cruel for those who cannot find the space or time to mourn the losses they have sustained or anyone who will grieve with them without doing so as a cover for their own infatuations or to feed their narcissism. Chopin's women walk or swim into the void, they weep piteously on doorsteps strewn with lilacs, they are betrayed by accident, by their own bodies, by friends and lovers, and they come to realize the awful truth, as Lily Bart will in Wharton's The House of Mirth, that they have never had any real relation to life. These women's hold on life or the resolve to be doing something meaningful is as fragile as Désirée's delicate slippers or a too expensive pair of lavender silk stockings.

I realize that my reading of Chopin may seen both overly grim and shortsighted in that it fails to take into account the short works that proffer hopeful resolutions to the human longing to know and be known, but I would argue that even these works address the central life struggle of testing one's power of agency and determining for what reason one lives. While we studiously recite the fact that the mass of men lead lives of quiet desperation, we too often do not acknowledge that women share in that sorrow. Chopin observed that "human impulses do not change and can not so long as men and women continue to stand in the relation to one another which they have occupied since our knowledge of their existence began."[18] One might read this fatalistically by emphasizing the "do not change and can not," but I believe Chopin's subtle social critique is embedded in the words "so long as." Kenneth Burke famously called literature equipment for living, and I am certain that Chopin, whose papers

indicate clearly her insistence on the necessity of right reading, affirmed
through her work the philosophical and sociopolitical importance of telling the right stories. She did not have a sentimentalized or particularly
optimistic view of the future, but neither was hers a hard deterministic
outlook. Like other American pragmatist philosophers, she seemed to es-
pouse the belief that, as Henry James put it, while we cannot be certain
free will exists, we must nevertheless act as if that were so. The equipment
for living Chopin gives us insists, even in negative fashion, on our making
a similar choice to live as if free and to choose what nurtures life. Even in
her bleaker tales of longing, loss, and mourning, Chopin intimates a new
structure of feeling in which women's rights to self-determination and
fulfillment are central givens. Further, her work calls for that revolutionary moment of change in human impulses to arrive through the agency of
women and men working together. She does this by chronicling the grief
we will suffer should we let that opportunity for radical social change slip
out of our grasp and by reminding us how very near we always are to the
abyss of despair and nothingness. Out of grief and loss, she creates for us,
still, the radical hope that we might choose to live better lives. So long as
we do not lose faith in that promise, so long we will read and celebrate the
works of Kate Chopin.

NOTES

1. Stefan Timmermans, *Postmortem: How Medical Examiners Explain Suspicious Deaths*
(Chicago: U of Chicago P, 2006) 93.

2. Mircea Eliade, *The Sacred and the Profane: The Nature of Religion*, trans. Willard R.
Trask (New York: Harcourt, Brace, 1959) 21.

3. Raymond Williams, *Marxism and Literature* (Oxford: Oxford UP, 1977) 131–32.

4. Kevin Brockmeier, *The Brief History of the Dead* (New York: Pantheon, 2006) 108.

5. Julia Kristeva, *Possessions: A Novel*, trans. Barbara Bray (New York: Columbia UP,
1998) 18.

6. Edith Wharton, *A Backward Glance* (New York: Appleton-Century, 1934) 379.

7. Kate Chopin, "Commonplace Book," *Kate Chopin's Private Papers*, ed. Emily Toth, Per
Seyersted, and Cheyenne Bonnell (Bloomington: Indiana UP, 1998) 27–28.

8. "Kate Chopin's Translations," *The Kate Chopin Companion: With Chopin's Translations
from French Fiction*, ed. Thomas Bonner Jr. (New York: Greenwood, 1988) 199.

9. "Kate Chopin's Translations" 182–83.

10. Kate Chopin, *The Complete Works of Kate Chopin*, ed. Per Seyersted (Baton Rouge: Louisiana State UP, 1969) 401.

11. "Kate Chopin's Translations" 186–87.

12. "Kate Chopin's Translations" 196.

13. "Kate Chopin's Translations" 195–96.

14. "Kate Chopin's Translations" 203.

15. "Kate Chopin's Translations" 203.

16. Chopin, *Complete Works* 996.

17. "Kate Chopin's Translations" 207.

18. Chopin, *Complete Works* 693.

2

FOUNDATIONS

6

My Life with Kate Chopin

THOMAS BONNER JR.

WRITING ABOUT HOW KATE CHOPIN and her fiction entered my life
and the lives I've touched professionally in the critical and social context
of a generation ago suggests not only that something significant had occurred in the world of letters but that the event provided the beginnings
of a series of changes in the way a writer and her works have affected
that generation and subsequent ones. The task before us is somewhat difficult, especially for those of us who in our early years in the profession
were admonished to avoid the first-person singular in our examinations
of literary texts and who were directed toward considering texts solely on
their own merits.

With this complex condition in mind, I begin by reviewing my first
encounter with Kate Chopin as a high school student and proceed to my
rediscovery of her in graduate school. At this point, it seems fruitful to reflect on the influence of New Criticism in the choices I had begun to make
as well as the schools of social criticism that were emerging in the 1970s.
Simultaneously, I encountered somewhat by accident bibliographical and
textual criticism with work on William Faulkner and Frederick Douglass,
respectively, during which time I had begun and concluded a dissertation
on Chopin. The confluence of critical approaches moved me toward a
contextual approach to Chopin and the importance of developing basic
tools for her study, tools generally available on writers in the mainstream
of most literary traditions. Over the years, three facets of Chopin's writing
have kept my attention: the art of her novels and stories, the development
of specific aspects of her craft, and the intellectual development that affected her writing.

My first encounter with Kate Chopin's writing came in the fall of 1956, and I have lived happily with her in personal, scholarly, and professional ways ever since. As a freshman at Jesuit High School in New Orleans, I had an anthology of literature devoted to introducing students to reading on a level that led young readers beyond their concern for suspense. While students were reading more seriously, they were doing so in the context of studies in theology, history, and classical as well as modern languages. There was a strong moral temper that accompanied discussions of the readings. The emphasis on language and history provided further intensity. The times, however, provided easy applications for the relation of art and life in 1950s New Orleans, especially in matters of race.

Brown v. Board of Education in 1954 had a major impact on the city of New Orleans but even more so in my own neighborhoods. When this decision of the Supreme Court of the United States was enacted, the blue-collar neighborhoods surrounding Jackson Barracks, the military post where I lived, were directly affected as two nearby elementary schools were chosen for integration of Caucasian and African American students. Many of the Caucasian men worked on the docks and in related areas like the sugar refinery and slaughterhouses as well as in small shops. Their ethnicities ranged from Irish to Italian, and there was the feeling of displacement to a lower rung on the social scale, almost a parallel to the Anglo-Saxon "poor whites" response to social change in the wider South. The African American men and women in these neighborhoods often lived across the fence or down the block, although there were a number of concentrations over several blocks in both the Eighth and Ninth wards. Black men often had jobs similar to those of many of the Caucasian men, although many worked in yard care and lesser positions; black women worked most often as domestics. Despite the close proximity of the races, Caucasians felt on a higher social and economic plane than their African American neighbors, whose color ranged from dark to nearly white. The forthcoming changes allowed tensions, largely camouflaged by good manners, to emerge into the open.

In the fall of 1956, I traveled by streetcar through these neighborhoods to Canal Street and out to Carrollton Avenue to Jesuit High School. Despite the changes under way and ugly scenes that were to occur as the two elementary schools were integrated, I sat in front of the "For Colored

Only" sign that moved back and forth on the car depending on the numbers of white and black riders. Public accommodations legislation would
not be enacted until the mid-1960s. I had been using public transportation
for five years without any memory of questioning the peculiar arrange-
ment of riders or finding the environment in the least bit uncomfortable.

The rides to and from school were long, usually more than an hour,
and the streetcar bumped about and vibrated to the point that doing
written homework was nearly impossible, and so I read and memorized
paradigms of declensions and conjugations in Latin. One morning on
the streetcar, I was reading Chopin's "Désirée's Baby." It was the first time
that I was reading anything by her, and I had no notion that this was the
most frequently anthologized story by Chopin at the time; nor would that
knowledge have been relevant for a fourteen-year-old reader. It certainly
was not important for my teacher and his purposes.

As usual, the car was filled with people going to work and school. I
began reading it with increasing interest, as the story had an exotic quality much like fairy tales and medieval romances with their high contrasts,
auras of mystery, faraway times, and unfamiliar places. Then the ambivalence of racial identity struck me as a subject that was forbidden and yet
attractive, like many sins. Reading this in public caused a rising sense of
embarrassment, as adolescents often have the illusion that everyone is
paying attention to them. As the story closed, I looked up at the riders on
the streetcar, who were, of course, not paying me the slightest attention.
Relieved, I quickly closed the anthology. When I looked up again, something else caught my attention: the people in front of the Jim Crow sign
were frequently darker than the people behind it. It was the nearest that
I had ever been to what I later learned was an epiphany, the opening of
an unforeseen question, but as a teenager with the events of life speeding
by, I thought about this scene and the fictional images of black features
only for a day or two. I do not recall whether there was an application of
the story to contemporary life in English class, but I do remember the
term "local color" from the teacher's presentation. Over the next twelve
years, I often remembered "Désirée's Baby" and the scene of my reading
it but never the name of its author. When I thought of the Chopin story, I
placed it in the context of another story, "The Most Dangerous Game," by
Richard Connell, for its exotic rather than for its literary qualities.

In the early 1960s during undergraduate studies at Southeastern Louisiana College (now University), neither the story nor its author was mentioned in American literature classes. For the local-color tradition in the South, George Washington Cable's "Jean-ah Poquelin" seemed the story of choice, but as that tradition had such low standing then, little attention and time were spent on it. Teachers reflected two generations of criticism, the biographical-historical and the New Critical. Among American writers the only female writer to get much attention—and that was largely out of class at the campus Newman Center—was Flannery O'Connor, who spoke and read from her work at the center. She had been invited because of her Catholicism rather than her gender.

John Thibaut Purser, who had been a graduate student at Louisiana State University when Cleanth Brooks and Robert Penn Warren were there and who had worked with them on the series of anthologies based on the New Critical mode, taught at the college, advancing New Critical approaches. His association with Brooks and Warren influenced students as well as some of his colleagues. Reading introductions to writers and their works in those anthologies was a liberation from the often narrow ones based nearly completely on the lives (and social transgressions) of the authors. The logic of focusing on the text, the art itself, rather than on its creator was appealing.

At Tulane University New Criticism formed the basis of literary approaches that varied somewhat according to the individual professors. Joseph Patrick Roppolo emphasized the revolutionary nature of New Criticism in the rejection of the author's biography as a dominant influence on the reading, especially in his teaching of Poe and American drama. An admirer of John Crowe Ransom's *The New Criticism*, Roppolo emphasized the independence of the text, although he introduced me to bibliography as a scholarly model. My reading Faulkner through the lens of the evolved New Critical approaches of Brooks led toward contextualism and through Richard P. Adams's *Faulkner: Myth and Motion*—with his emphasis on mythic patterns—toward formalism.

But it was in Donald Pizer's seminar on the American 1890s that critical approach and Kate Chopin as a subject came together. It was here in January 1969 at the first meeting when he distributed a list of writers on whom we could work that Chopin's name reminded me of "Désirée's

Baby." That winter I began doing an introductory study of Kate Chopin, aided, of course, by Pizer but also by Larzer Ziff's The American 1890s: Life and Times of a Lost Generation, the basic text for the seminar. The major secondary source, however, was Daniel Rankin's 1932 biography of Chopin (dusty and little used in the open stacks of the Howard-Tilton Library). There was something exciting about this personal rediscovery and Per Seyersted's biography and edition of the complete works of Chopin then in the process of being published at Louisiana State University Press.

My unpublished seminar paper asked more questions than it answered and served as more of a document of my inquiries than a coherent statement of findings. The manuscript having been lost with all my work in the flood following Hurricane Katrina, I can now only point to the issue of whether Chopin was a major writer or a minor writer with a major novel. Those modes of distinction that Matthew Arnold would have appreciated often dominated critical discussion then. The understanding that I advanced was that Chopin was a minor writer with a major novel, all of this based on comparing her writings with the volume of high-quality fiction by writers like Hawthorne, Melville, James, Cather, and Faulkner.

An incident at the outset of the seminar served as a precursor to what would happen in subsequent years when, in negotiating for the opportunity to work on Chopin, a woman graduate student, whose name was already next to Chopin's on the list of subjects for the students, said that she had been at Tulane for several years and that this was her first opportunity to work in a substantive way on a woman writer. She kindly made another choice after I explained my long-term interest. Her gesture turned out to be an extraordinary gift.

When I began searching for a dissertation topic, I kept coming back to Chopin. At the time the Department of English at Tulane was reluctant to allow the writing of dissertations on writers who were not considered major. By 1973, with further study, I was still caught between the major-minor divide, but I was convinced of Chopin's importance and that her value went beyond the traditions of national boundaries. It also was becoming apparent that the major-minor distinction was not always helpful in considering writers and their works. Furthermore, the feminist readings of Chopin had begun, and I was concerned that the spirit of the age might overwhelm the need for basic scholarly tools for and studies of Chopin.

After all, standard scholarly tools had been published for all the writers I considered major, and concordances had begun to enter that arena of study as well. Finally, with the support of Roppolo, I submitted a dissertation proposal that incorporated my concern that Chopin be studied in the comprehensive manner that the artistry of her texts demanded: "A Critical Study of the Fiction of Kate Chopin: The Formal Elements." After much discussion on the graduate committee, the topic was approved, and my work began amid that of others on dissertations devoted to Chopin across the country.

At this point Seyersted's fine biography and edition of Chopin's writing had had a signal impact. His work superseded the only sustained effort thus far, that by Rankin, but interestingly he showed a respect for Rankin's efforts that kept his volume an important source. I felt a kinship with Rankin because of the sense of discovery in his treatment of Chopin, and his moral approaches revived some familiar feelings from the exegeses that the Jesuits had used in my youth. Seyersted, however, combined the approaches that I had been developing. In his critical biography, the emphasis was clearly on how the life contributed to the work, rather than the work reflecting the life. It was this contextual effort that offered me encouragement that I was taking a valid direction. As I began the basic research, Roppolo's bibliographical training encouraged me to assemble an annotated bibliography for publication, which appeared in *Bulletin of Bibliography* in 1975. I had participated in two early Kate Chopin sessions at MLA while developing the dissertation, benefiting from the papers and discussions. In retrospect, as I had analyzed Chopin's fiction honoring the integrity of their forms of publication, it might have been more helpful to have drawn her similar and dissimilar works accordingly in appropriate groups. Another re-visioning would have brought about a stronger conclusion tying the various compositional strategies together in greater detail. Despite these over-the-shoulder glances, it was important to attend to compositional techniques and structures, as those had not been addressed when I started work.

Despite my New Critical bias, I was and have been strongly appreciative of John R. May's essay "Local Color in *The Awakening*" on several grounds.[1] It reminded me of the importance of basic elements like setting and custom and their control over a text's development. It also made clear how much this novel was on the margin of what one found then in most anthologies of American literature. Even now while he reminded readers of the novel's origins, he also had us look ahead as the issues of local realism (similar to the principle behind Flaubert's concerns on the local origins of realism) moved toward what now has been termed "island theory." It was this essay that also encouraged me to examine Chopin's stories that were set abroad to see whether there were similar patterns of "local" influence. Finally, May's essay and the work on the dissertation, especially my seeing repeated appearances of characters, varied place-names, and linguistic elements, made me recognize the usefulness of a glossary of names, places, and related items over the body of Chopin's writings.

As I worked on the research, I began keeping a formal set of notes on characters and places in much the same way that I had handled bibliographical items. Shortly after completing the dissertation, I began to write a dictionary of Chopin references from these notes that I had assembled. The strategy, which included compiling names of characters (legal and informal), involved identifying family relationships, repeated appearances in stories and novels, and brief descriptions related to plot and themes. What would have added value to the work was an etymological treatment and inquiries on other sources of names. Emily Toth did some of this kind of work in her first biography of Chopin. Place-names in Chopin's writings also seemed important to describe and locate for readers, as many of the areas of Louisiana, in particular, that Chopin used were far from common knowledge.

More extensive examination of symbolic possibilities embedded in the names would have been helpful in light of Chopin's often moving between strategies associated with romanticism and realism. Working with French expressions, which I should have expanded, provided the third component of the dictionary. An aspect that could have been helpful was to have, as George Reinecke once suggested in a conversation, a look at possible variations in Chopin's French in the context of Creole and Acadian dialects in use at the time of her writing.

It was this work with the French expressions that brought me to examine Chopin's translations from French fiction. The fact that she had systematically over a decade translated Guy de Maupassant and Adrien Vely at the same time that she was making significant changes in her

approach to writing short stories and developing The Awakening in a manner far different from her first novel, At Fault, suggested that those translations were critical to her writing. Their neither having been collected
nor republished separately led me to expand my original concept of the
project by republishing them as part of the dictionary. Having worked
with a small poem in manuscript by Frederick Douglass helped develop
strategies using varied light and magnifiers to work from the soft pencil
lead of the manuscript of "Father Amable," for which no published version existed.

I had wanted to write a full essay introducing these translations, but
while working on them, I met Jean Bardot of the American College in
Paris, who had just completed a dissertation on Chopin at the Sorbonne
and had begun working on the translations, and I decided out of respect to
address them only briefly in my manuscript. Jean Bardot never completed
this aspect of his work, but Richard Fusco addressed Maupassant's influence on Chopin in an excellent essay some years later. Subsequently, other
scholars as well have made connections between Chopin's translations
and her fiction, especially in treatments of The Awakening. Annotating the
translations with references to Chopin's stories and her life would also
have established more immediate and useful connections. Much remains
to be examined in both the linguistic and cultural contexts of French and
European writings and experiences that affected Chopin's approaches to
her writing.

Because Chopin seemed wedded to Flaubert's idea that all realism begins in the local place, it seemed important to provide maps that reflected
as closely as possible the period of her writing stories, especially those set
in Louisiana. It is important to remember that Louisiana then was only
forty years removed from the frontier of what became known as the "Old
Southwest." In fact, all one has to do to realize the proximity of this moving frontier is to consider that the title character in "Désirée's Baby" as a
child had been left on the Texas Road by a family traveling to the West.
The backwoods and bayous of the state remained inaccessible to most
through the mid-twentieth century. When Kenneth Eble visited Louisiana after the publication of his essay on Chopin in Western Humanities
Review and his Capricorn edition (with the essay as the introduction) of
The Awakening,[2] he was astonished at the deeply rural areas of Louisiana

and yet their sometimes close proximity to established urban areas. The photographs of the maps selected for the book were clear and detailed enough, but their reductions for the format of a non-oversized book made them useful for the most part only with magnification.

In completing what came to be *The Kate Chopin Companion: With Translations from French Fiction*, it was evident that a bibliographical element would complement the other parts of the book. It was important to be comprehensive on the primary sources and selective on secondary ones. After all, at this point, in addition to my earlier bibliography in *Bulletin of Bibliography*, there were others of a comprehensive nature, and so my efforts here would form a guide, making some distinctions about where readers and scholars might go initially and suggesting some dimensions in relative helpfulness of published secondary ones. The essay form seemed then, and still does today, the appropriate form for this guide.

The last item added to the book, although it was placed in the beginning, was a chronology. Both the 1932 and 1969 biographies at this point had no chronology, and Toth's biography had not appeared as yet. Most readers and scholars had little grasp of the range of Chopin's life. The correction of Chopin's birth date from 1851 to 1850, which Bardot had discovered in church archives in St. Louis, also seemed important to establish fully, as I had published his essay with the correction in *Xavier Review* earlier.[3] Shortly after, the New Orleans *Times-Picayune* in a column by its then book editor Mabel Simmons had made the date available to the general public. The brief chronological annotations for the dates should have been expanded both in number and in detail, but I was concerned about chronologies that were not easily accessible and that often seemed closer to short essays, like those in some of the Library of America editions. Happily, Toth's biography in 1990 included a chronology that provided an effective balance of detail and brevity.

A curious and brief essay, "Something about Kate Chopin," by Joseph J. Reilly in his 1942 collection of literary reflections *Of Books and Men*, captured my interest early and moved me toward considerations of her craft in fiction. Reilly devoted his attention to Chopin's two collections of stories published in her lifetime; he does not mention *The Awakening*, nor does he suggest an awareness of her work on the novel. Interestingly, he includes the essay on Chopin in a section titled "Some of Our Contem-

poraries," grouping her with Joseph Conrad, Lytton Strachey, John Gals-
worthy, Thomas Hardy, Louise Imogen Guiney, J. M. Barrie, and Mary
Coleridge. Then and now his use of the word "contemporaries" seems to
have extraordinary chronological range, but one must consider the presence of the classical world in education of the first half of the twentieth
century and how that tended to expand the context for such a term. Reilly
places Chopin in the tradition of place-centered realism by including her
among Hamlin Garland, Mary Wilkins Freeman, and Thomas Nelson
Page and then distinguishes her writing from those in Chopin's immediate settings: Grace King and George W. Cable.

Nowhere does Reilly address Chopin as a woman writer in any kind
of feminist sense, for he plunges right in to addressing her narrative techniques in the manner of Maupassant. What impressed me then and now
was his consideration of her as a writer aside from any disparaging attitudes toward women writers commonplace for the times—despite his
courtly style, using "Miss" and "Mrs." to identify them in his texts. In a
way one might find a patriarchal attitude underlying his essay on Chopin,
but in no way is it negative, and his observation on the English poet Mary
Coleridge offers a clue to his broad position: "My concern is . . . with the
danger of overlooking real poetry because its author was a woman who,
being dead, can depend on no clique to press her claims."[4] It is clear that
he felt an obligation that the art be recognized, and it is this sense of purpose that pervades his treatment of Chopin's fiction. His sense of duty
toward literary works that are truly distinguished as art suggests a professional virtue that was immediately attractive.

Reilly avoids the term modernism in discussing these "contemporaries," but it is evident that the elements of Chopin's craft lift her from
those he might have included among fiction writers characteristic of
the earlier century. Three aspects of Reilly's consideration of Chopin—
language, technique, and characterization—engaged me in my own
studies of Chopin. He devotes much attention to her ability with the sentence, especially its economy and impact both early and later in her stories. For example, Chopin writes in "The Locket," "The peace and beauty
of a spring day had descended on the earth like a benediction."[5] Most
readers of Chopin can quote these singular sentences that hit them like
well-launched and sharply aimed arrows. Reilly sees a close and subtle

integration of technique and content with the effect that her conclusions appear "inherent in the situation or in the psychology of the chief character." The characters, according to him, are more than names but often "endowed with three dimensions in a sentence or two," and he emphasizes with many examples from the stories that her focus is on "character rather than situation."[6]

Despite Reilly's being in an era of criticism that flowered before the New Critics, he makes a transition into their world in this series of studies or, more precisely, reflections on British and American texts and writers. It is interesting that this may be the first time that Chopin had been placed in an international or transatlantic context. The book, published during the dark days of World War II, certainly had no significant impact on increasing interest in Kate Chopin at the time, but Seyersted quoted an observation of his in the critical biography,[7] and as a consequence he brought Reilly's work to a wider and newer group of scholars and students in the late 1960s. For me Reilly expressed real insight and honesty in his treatment of writer and writings, as his and Seyersted's work created further avenues of interest for me.

Like Reilly, I was really interested in how Chopin structured her fiction. She seemed supremely aware of how she would assemble a story and how she would choose the various components. Reilly is responding to the stories with exclusive Louisiana settings, works to which he had access through libraries, but if Maupassant had such an influence on these works as he and Fusco rightly indicate, Chopin was working beyond Maupassant in other works that were unpublished and uncollected at the time. For example, the style of story with Louisiana settings often differs from those set in Europe and St. Louis, as well as with those having no named setting.

The effects of these variations suggest that Chopin had different purposes in her fiction. Bayou Folk (1894), Chopin's first collection, has a closer connection in narrative technique as related to setting to her first novel, At Fault (1890), with storytelling qualities amid the Maupassant-like structures. She was working with form, as one can see with the deus ex machina device in working out the conclusion of At Fault, an awkward solution at best, but in the next four years after the novel was published she had begun the intense work of translating Maupassant's short fiction. As a result, one can see the more integrated narrative and the more convincing solutions to problems and conflicts she develops in her stories in Bayou Folk. As her translations continue over the decade of the 1890s, Chopin has a growing consciousness of form, first noticeable in A Night in Acadie (1897), and certainly evident in her planned but then unpublished collection A Vocation and a Voice (1991). While I charted these changes in my dissertation, I only incidentally approached their underlying causes in later work. This kind of inquiry should still yield helpful results, as Chopin, like Walker Percy, often seems poised between the art of the story and the pragmatic impulses in the expression of ideas generally found in nonfiction, especially in stories that have no specific setting.

While Maupassant certainly touched her compositions directly, Chopin was always a wide-ranging reader, and the 1890s brought about a transformation of her narrative techniques of fiction, especially in the novel. All one has to do is look at the vast differences in narrative technique between At Fault and The Awakening (1899), published just nine years later. The orthodox structure of the former with its similarities to popular fiction of the nineteenth century stands apart from the latter with its tight focus, restrained point of view, and organically structured sentences. For all of the early comparisons made to Flaubert's Madame Bovary (1857), The Awakening stands alone as a novel more characteristic of modernism—not American modernism but European modernism—closer to Camus's The Stranger (1942). Chopin had a visual acuity in giving her fiction shape that seemed to have permeable and concrete qualities in readers' imaginations.

The growth of Chopin's imagination and its effect on her techniques and approaches to fiction developed as a subject for me in my later years working with her writing. For example, when I was visiting a class on The Awakening taught by Max Despain at the United States Air Force Academy, the discussion reminded me of a previous day's visit to Richard Lemp's class on criticism and theory during which the conversations centered on the Roman writer Horace. I noticed in the translated Latin the poet's use of wings and shoulders. The connection started me thinking about the development of winged imagery in Chopin's imagination and led to a jointly written article by Despain and me tracing the exposure of Chopin from youth through adulthood to visual images as well as literary ones and their effect on her imagination and her writing.[8] This interesting exercise, much of it conducted via e-mail after Despain was sent to South Korea for a year, convinced me that there were other images and related topics that, if explored and examined in this context, would bear fruit not only for reading Chopin's fiction but for getting closer to her own imaginative and literary development.

In this context I have become interested in the walking motif in Chopin's writing, not only in her fiction but also in the other genres in which she wrote. Nearly everyone who has written about *The Awakening* has examined this aspect in some way, as there is a tour de force of walking in this novel. Throughout the years of reading Chopin, I have been persistently reminded of an auctorial intellect at work, one that had grown in a nearly systematic manner. From her juvenilia through her most mature writing, the motif of walking has endured. Examining this aspect of her writing using her diaries, commonplace book, and letters should provide a basis for seeing how this element develops chronologically through her writing career. Initial inquiries suggest a relation between expanding ideas and her articulated experiences of walking as journey in fiction and nonfiction. Her own appreciation of the classical literary and intellectual tradition, one in which walking is associated with the increase of knowledge, indicates that it has a presence in the formulation of both her ideas and her art. Accordingly, Chopin seems to have established definite links between the physical and the intellectual in her writing. The acts of walking then frequently become acts of the mind at work, often reflections of an acquisitive mind.

From her youthful years Chopin records her broad reading in several languages and the texts in which she has particular and often intense interest, emphasizing a strong intellectual inclination that continued through her adult life. Bernard Koloski's *Kate Chopin: A Study of the Short Fiction* addresses with real insight Chopin's linguistic capacities. She had read a number of Greek and Roman writers, the full range of English writers, a substantial number of European writers, and a significant number of American writers from her own century. Her participation in salons in both St. Louis and New Orleans and the influence of Dr. Kolbenheyer offer definite markers outside of those in her writing to indicate that she led an intellectual life as well as a literary one. The essays Chopin wrote for *St. Louis Life* provide overt indications of the intersections of her intellectual and literary lives. In a way Chopin gathered people who would not only complement but also challenge her interests, somewhat like the role Mabel Dodge Luhan had in Taos, New Mexico, a generation later. Chopin's two-year participation in Charlotte Eliot's salon in St. Louis and her withdrawal from it emphasizes an intellectual independence that all three of her biographers have noted. Despite their good work on this aspect of Chopin, an intellectual biography of Chopin is needed to address the formal sources and influences of the questions that inform her writing but also those that inform her life as articulated in documents and other sources. This is a project that I have pursued thus far only in fragments.

From my earliest scholarly efforts on Chopin in Pizer's seminar, I have had an interest in "organizing the Chopin canon," as Bernard Koloski, the editor of this volume of essays, has suggested to me in correspondence. The phrase and its implications were not immediately clear to me, but they have grown in clarity as I have considered and reconsidered my scholarly work and that of others on Chopin. Indeed, I attempted to get my arms about Chopin's works in such a way as to provide means for others to do so as well, but I have not been alone in this quest. The company of scholars who have been active since the 1960s as well as those from earlier decades have done for her and American, if not world, literary culture a noble service. Barbara Ewell's *Kate Chopin* is exemplary in offering perspective on the Chopin canon.[9] In this spirit, it is important that Heather Kirk Thomas's dissertation, "'A Vocation and a Voice': A Documentary Life of Kate Chopin," with its emphasis on the documents and their applications, be published as a book.[10] It is possible that this work could have an effect on Chopin studies similar to that which Samuel Schoenbaum's documentary biography has had on studies of Shakespeare. Similarly, I have long been interested in working on a new edition of Daniel Rankin's 1932 biography of Chopin, accompanied by annotations and appendixes, making it not only more easily available but more useful to contemporary students and scholars. Despite its being superseded by Seyersted's and Toth's biographies, it has singular value, much in the way that Dumas Malone's biography of Thomas Jefferson still has merit despite the avalanche of biographical studies of Jefferson that have followed.

My life's work on Chopin has been a humbling experience, for after all the efforts, there are even more questions to consider, and that, of course, is both the pleasure and the pain of our kind of work—in fact the very symptoms of the nature of this work. It has been an honor for me to be in this devoted company. Just as I completed my own dissertation in 1975, Robert Arner's revised dissertation on Chopin that was published as a special issue of *Louisiana Studies* made me sit up to take note of issues that I had not as yet considered. And so it has gone over the years, as more studies emerged in what has been an extraordinary cornucopia of scholarship. Lastly, the constant through the reading, thinking, and writing has been Chopin's writings with their gifts of language, form, and theme. My original, sun-faded, well-thumbed, and annotated two volumes of her complete works were destroyed in the flood of 2005, but the texts of the newly acquired, bright red one-volume edition have already begun to pose new questions.

NOTES

1. John R. May, "Local Color in *The Awakening*," *Southern Review* 6 (1970): 1031–40.

2. Kenneth Eble, "A Forgotten Novel: Kate Chopin's *The Awakening*," *Western Humanities Review* 10 (1956): 261–69.

3. Jean Bardot, "Kate Chopin: Her Actual Birth Date," *Xavier Review* 7 (1987): 70–72.

4. Joseph J. Reilly, *Of Books and Men* (New York: Julian Messner, 1942) 166.

5. Kate Chopin, *The Complete Works of Kate Chopin*, ed. Per Seyersted (Baton Rouge: Louisiana State UP, 1969) 562.

6. Reilly 331, 332.

7. Per Seyersted, *Kate Chopin: A Critical Biography* (Baton Rouge: Louisiana State UP, 1969).

8. Max Despain and Thomas Bonner Jr., "Shoulders to Wings: The Provenance of Winged Imagery from Kate Chopin's Juvenilia through *The Awakening*," *Xavier Review* 25 (2005): 49–64.

9. Barbara C. Ewell, *Kate Chopin* (New York: Ungar, 1986).

10. Heather Kirk Thomas, "'A Vocation and a Voice': A Documentary Life of Kate Chopin," diss., U of Missouri–Columbia, 1988.

7

On First Looking (and Looking Once Again) into Chopin's Fiction
Kate and Ernest and "A Pair of Silk Stockings"

ROBERT D. ARNER

> If a writer of prose knows enough about what he is writing about he may omit
> things that he knows and the reader, if the writer is writing truly enough, will
> have a feeling of those things as strongly as though the writer had stated them.
> ERNEST HEMINGWAY, *Death in the Afternoon*

OF COURSE, NEITHER HEMINGWAY'S gender nor his general (I would argue undeserved) reputation for misogyny would seem to hold out much hope that his remarks on writing could tell us anything we need to know about how to read a late nineteenth-century woman author whose subjects and themes are for the most part as far removed from Hemingway's own concerns as anyone might imagine or desire. Even in this famous formulation, Hemingway seems to take for granted that any worthwhile writing will be done by men rather than women (hence the masculine pronouns), although we know that he admired a number of women writers of his own generation or somewhat earlier, including Marie Belloc Lowndes and Isak Dinesen. There is in unconsciously prophetic response to Hemingway's sort of culturally reflexive exclusionary thinking a wonderful moment in *The Awakening* when Chopin notes, through Edna, that Edna's father, who served as a Confederate officer and still proudly sports the title of Colonel, "wore his coats padded, which gave a fictitious breadth and depth to his shoulders and chest,"[1] and that striking image, so economically deflating a posed and postured and unwittingly self-parodic masculinity, is just about all the commentary that anybody needs (although there is plenty more elsewhere in Chopin's fiction) to understand how distant is her imagination from the military mystique and male code of values that

so fascinated and beguiled, not to say beset and bedeviled and eventually
destroyed, Ernest Hemingway. And yet Hemingway, or, rather, a deep appreciation for his writing, is the most important critical equipment that I
could bring to bear when I started reading my way through Kate Chopin's
novels and short stories in the summer of 1969, newly if still unofficially
out of grad school with only ABD in hand, in preparation for writing
what turned out to be (I did not know this at the time) the first modern
American dissertation on her fiction. If Hemingway at times steered me
amiss in my expectations and thus in my interpretations, particularly in
the masculine metaphors of approval that, I can see in retrospect, pep-
pered my commentary on her writing, praising stories that seemed to me
to work as "strong" and "direct" (that is, male) and dismissing those that
did not as "weak" or "unclear" (that is, feminine), he nevertheless stood me
in good stead throughout most of the enterprise, at least to my critical eye
even at this moment so far removed from the original act of writing, so
that what I wrote back then thinking about how a writer may know things
truly and what these things might be and how the writer might best go
about getting them into the reader's understanding of the story still seems
to me mostly on target, although in some important regards long since
superseded by nearly four decades of subsequent criticism and analysis of
Kate Chopin's fiction.

I want to return in due time to at least a brief consideration both of
those subsequent decades of criticism, to which I hasten to add I have
contributed nothing since 1975, and of the idea or strategy of leaving
things out of a story in order to have the reader feel the unstated things
more deeply and disturbingly than if they had been overtly articulated,
as well as to suggest at this juncture that these same passing decades of
critical attention have revealed for Hemingway but, I think, less clearly for
Kate Chopin the kind of absent things that might easily have been missed,
or at least only partially sensed and comprehended, upon a first reading.
For Hemingway, the new information would include such things as the
many drafts and false starts preserved for scholarly and critical analysis in
the Kennedy Library, as well as the wealth of historical detail that has been
turned up by researchers since the 1960s about the events and people ly-
ing behind, for instance, the intertexts of In Our Time, while for Chopin it
would be primarily the wealth of mostly biographical material exhumed

by scholars such as Emily Toth and a handful of others, perhaps still only superficially applied to readings of her fiction. I have in mind here as a superficial application of the biographical information more or less newly available about Kate Chopin, for example, commentary on a story such as "A Pair of Silk Stockings" that merely notes that Chopin herself was a single mother living on the economic margins of American society as if that were an adequate explanation of the genesis or implications of that story.

Before turning back to the topics outlined above, however, and in keeping with the theme of this volume of essays on Kate Chopin's discovery by the first generation of (mostly American) scholars to work on her writing and how that discovery came into being, I think it only fair to disavow any credit for being among the first American graduate students to discover Kate Chopin and to award it instead to the late Professor Joseph Jay Rubin of Penn State, to whose memory and merry sense of humor I here wish to pay an affectionate homage (both of us had, of course, been antedated by Kenneth Eble and George Arms, among others). In the spring of 1966, Professor Rubin, who was especially interested in John W. DeForest and who, through his Bald Eagle Press, was in the process of issuing a number of DeForest's long out of print novels, offered a course at Penn State in nineteenth-century American realism. What those of us who signed up for that course expected, I suppose, was a reading list of the usual suspects—William Dean Howells and Henry James, Mark Twain and perhaps some Stephen Crane or Frank Norris thrown in. What we got instead were DeForest's Miss Ravenel's Conversion and Witching Times, as well as Albion Tourgée's Fool's Errand and Bricks without Straw, Hamlin Garland's Main-Travelled Roads, and several other more or less obscure (at least to me, at least at that time) authors and works. What I remember distinctly about those readings is that, although I found them all well worth reading for various reasons and in various ways, two stood out in my mind as superior fictions, Harold Frederic's Damnation of Theron Ware and Kate Chopin's The Awakening. The Awakening I found especially compelling, and I set out to learn whatever I could about this (to me) unknown author. I still keep the orange paperback edition of Chopin's novel that we used in that course, the one published by Capricorn books in 1964 with an introduction by Eble, crammed now with notes in the margins from the many times I used it to teach The Awakening before that novel achieved canonical status and began appearing in major anthologies, but I confess that I did not wonder at that time who else in all the graduate programs in the United States was reading that book or how Professor Rubin had come upon it and selected it for his course. Even Eble's introduction, with its brief (and sometimes incorrect) history of the critical neglect and misfortunes of this novel and its author, didn't register with me as it should have, and I had no idea then that I would soon be at work on an extended study of Kate Chopin's fiction.

I did not, indeed, settle on Kate Chopin as the subject of my dissertation for at least another year, not until the spring of 1969 when I was an instructor at Central Michigan University and, with my first year of full-time teaching almost under my belt, could turn seriously to the task of completing my PhD. That summer I visited the Missouri Historical Society (now the Missouri History Museum) in St. Louis and read for the first time some of Kate Chopin's fugitive pieces—I had borrowed from libraries or bought for a song at various used book shops copies of everything by her that had previously been in print in her books—and I remember particularly what a surprise and delight it was to read "The Storm. A Sequel to 'At the 'Cadian Ball'" in Kate's own handwriting. I had no idea that such a story existed, and as far as I knew at that time, neither did anybody else. I felt I knew something now about her that no one else knew, a secret we shared about at least one work of her fiction that was even more daring than The Awakening. Seeing the story in print when it later appeared in Per Seyersted's Complete Works of Kate Chopin was gratifying but did not possess nearly the same charge as handling the actual paper and thinking that I might have been one of the few people to read it—or maybe, I fantasized, the only person—since Chopin herself last laid it aside.

At that time, I should note, I had no idea that I was following in Per Seyersted's footsteps, and the news of his critical biography of Kate Chopin soon to be forthcoming from LSU Press (1969) startled me, to say the least, and made me wonder whether my research and writing so far had been upstaged and rendered irrelevant. (I am sure everyone who has ever been engaged in writing a dissertation has experienced similar sinking moments.) I was soon put at ease by reading his book that there was plenty of room for what I was doing, and now, of course, I find it absurd to have imagined that any one reading, whether Seyersted's or mine and however accomplished, could have exhausted the possibilities of her fiction. But then it was not so, and I was simply concerned with trying to find space for my own ideas in what I considered the merest cracks and crevices left by the few previous other commentators on her writing (Eble and Arms). My space, as I then conceived of it, was to write about stories that no one else, or almost no one else, had written about before me and to try to tie them somehow to the handful of her stories and the remarkable novel that at least some readers already knew.

By then I also had published or already had accepted a few brief pieces on Chopin's short fiction (scarcely referred to or even noted any more by most modern scholars of Chopin), including one about "The Storm" that was slated for publication soon in the *Markham Review*. This was more an appreciation of a (to my mind) newly discovered piece than a thorough analysis of the story, following closely what I had written for my dissertation, and I sent Professor Seyersted a complimentary copy in typescript. In our only communication ever, he responded somewhat testily that he was surprised that the folks at the Missouri Historical Society had allowed me to see that story because he thought he had secured their promise to keep it and several of her other stories under tight wraps until his book and then his two-volume edition of all Chopin's fiction should see the light of day. I was in those days still reeling from the discovery that some of the established scholars I had most revered in graduate school, men such as Sherman Paul, who wrote so persuasively about Emerson and other transcendentalist authors, had turned out to be when I met them not at all politically in tune with the bravest of Emerson's words (these were the years of the anti–Vietnam War protests), and now I faced for the first time (but unfortunately not for the last) a scholar who seemed to believe that he had the right to sequester literary and historical manuscripts and other resources from public view until he had finished his own work on and with them. I am certain that others who have written on Chopin since my time have had much more positive experiences than I had with Professor Seyersted, but at the time I felt offended and not a little angry with his (I thought) ungenerous response, and I do not recall whether I answered his letter (I hope I did not because I am sure I would have been rude). A few years later, at any rate, after I had joined the faculty at the University of Cincinnati, I received a response from a reader at W. W. Norton to my proposal for a critical edition of The Awakening that neither the author nor the novel was sufficiently important to merit such treatment, and since I had already begun to establish myself in early American studies, I more or less abandoned Kate Chopin to concentrate in other areas. Thus I had no longer occasion to renew correspondence with the one person who did more for the first wave of Chopin studies than anyone else. I am sure if I had I would have learned what others in the area know and have told me, that my experience on this one occasion was not typical of the man.

At that time, I don't think I particularly wondered what it was that drew me to The Awakening and, from that novel, to the rest of Chopin's writing, and I probably would have said if anyone had asked that it was merely because I needed a dissertation topic and Chopin seemed to be available for the taking. That would have been the wrong answer, or at least an incomplete one, I now realize. The appeal of The Awakening for me, a male reader, and eventually of the story of the rest of Chopin's career, as I came to understand, was a good deal more complex and had nothing to do with gender. I believe, first of all, that it was the stunning beauty and lyricism of her novel that made it stand out in my mind, her style of mythic and poetic realism, and maybe, too, it was a bit of the Swinburnian decadence (though I did not recognize Swinburne's presence as such at the time) and the Whitmanian insouciance and symbolism. I do know, however, that reading that book for the first time was not for me, as it seems to have been for some of the other contributors to this volume, a life- or even a career-changing experience. Perhaps if I had pursued the idea of writing about Chopin when it first wandered into my mind, I might have anticipated Seyersted in print, and then, of course, I would have identified my scholarly and critical interests much more completely with Kate Chopin's fiction than I was ultimately to do. I feel, I should also say at this juncture, honored to be admitted as an interloper within the present community of contributors to this volume, not having until now, as I previously mentioned, published a line about Kate Chopin since 1975.

In those halcyon days before Barthes and other creators of our current sophisticated critical baggage, it is well to recall, we were not burdened or blessed by the theories and ideologies that have since come to dominate so much of our discourse. We, or at least I, did not enter into any literary text with some preset notion of proving that such and such an author had indeed anticipated or at least had prophetically demonstrated the ideas of some presently popular sociologist or psychiatrist or psychoanalytical theorist. Impossible as it seems now to contemplate, we knew not Lacan or Kristeva. If we aspired to anything at all as readers, we aspired to close reading, to be by our own lights true to the text, often without much regard for historical context, biographical data, or extratextual nuance; I recall being told by one graduate professor, indeed, that it was a waste of time to read biographies of an author because information about her or his life could only mess up your understanding of what her or his writing was really about. We were, in a phrase, still very much the inheritors of New Critical (and sometimes of formalist) thought, although in some universities' graduate programs (but not, I dare say, at Penn State at the time) those methodologies were starting to show signs of severe strain at the seams. So I did not approach Kate Chopin's stories (or, as they say nowadays, interrogate her fictions) as a feminist, or Marxist, or neo-historical reader, or anything else in particular, but simply tried to provide what I hoped would prove to be an intelligent and useful introduction to most of her work. Of course I missed many things that have since been recognized as important in her fiction, and I certainly did not sufficiently emphasize her feminism (some would say I did not emphasize it at all). Rereading my dissertation after all these years, despite what I previously said in this essay, has sometimes been a lesson in humility, discovering in many stories what I wish I had seen at the time, and I am particularly dissatisfied now with my reading of the novel that started it all for me, The Awakening, although I continue to feel that there is something about that novel that none of the commentators or critics that I have read seems to have gotten at, something more deeply disquieting and disturbing than I have yet seen acknowledged in print.

This is about the whole history of Kate Chopin and me to date. I leave out a few sneers when I first arrived at the University of Cincinnati from some colleagues, no longer whinnying with us, who regarded a dissertation on a writer of whom they had never heard as beneath contempt, and a woman writer at that. I should have expected no less because at Central Michigan I had once been a member of a search committee whose chairman routinely threw to one side dossiers on which he had read only the name, declaring by way of explanation, "These are women, and we already have too many goddamned women in this department." That experience itself, had there been no other intrinsic reason, would have ensured that I would include Chopin's fiction, especially *The Awakening*, in every appropriate undergraduate survey and period course I teach, often pairing that novel with *The Adventures of Huckleberry Finn* and *Daisy Miller* as two other works about freedom or the illusion of freedom and the vastly different forms that freedom can take in America for men and for women. Before the university established a women's studies program that all but excludes male faculty as a matter of sexual politics, I offered *The Awakening* as a culminating work in a course on American women writers before 1900, where it made, I thought, a perfect end piece to a tradition that had begun with Anne Bradstreet, and on several other occasions I have featured Chopin's writing in a course on late nineteenth-century American realism that included only women writers. So I guess one might say that she has influenced me more than I thought before I started writing this essay, despite my own self-imposed exile from Chopin studies for all these years. I like to think overall that my chief contribution to Chopin studies lies in my having introduced her work to young men and women quite a few years before it became fashionable and then absolutely indispensable to do so (along similar lines, I am proud of having directed the earliest dissertation, subsequently published, on the writings of Susanna Haswell Rowson).[2]

In trying to catch up over the past several months with four decades or so of what has been written about Kate Chopin since (to take an arbitrary but defensible date) 1969 or 1970, it has seemed to me that, while much of it has indeed served to make Chopin's writing accessible from an increasing number of critical perspectives, much of it still fails to establish her reputation on the basis of closely contextualized readings, with the result that her status and the true nature of her accomplishment remain contested and in question for many modern readers. Of course, the accumulated critical literature, especially the body of work dedicated to *The Awakening*, can offer many exceptions to this observation, but nonetheless this remains my strong overall impression from the critical literature I have seen, and I think I can detect a sense of the same feeling of unease as well in what others have written about her in other contexts. I take a

cue here from Thomas Bonner Jr., who in another essay in this volume
has confessed to entertaining some youthful doubts about whether Kate
Chopin was, in his words, "a major writer or a minor writer with a major
novel." That question, which seemed important enough back in those early
days to generate for Bonner an entire seminar paper, still seems to linger
in the minds of many, even of those who have had the most to do with
the Kate Chopin revival (though it seems clear from the rest of his essay
and his other work that Bonner has long since made up his mind about
the matter). Perhaps the problem in this instance lies less with the per-
ceived content or performance of her fiction—one bright undergraduate
from whom I expected better things told me not long ago that he didn't
like Chopin because she never seemed to deal with "big issues," just with
the woes and wishes of women—than with Bonner's distinction between
major and minor writers, which certainly hearkens back to the elitism that
was one of the most disturbing features of New Critical ideology and the
old-style classic American canon, as he certainly recognizes. That is, he
may have become entrapped in his youth within a false critical dilemma
and asked the wrong questions about Chopin's writing.

But Mary E. Papke, in another essay in this collection, points to a
different source (or to different sources) of continuing resistance even
amounting to indifference to Kate Chopin's fiction, arising from or at least
represented somewhat surprisingly by an anonymous modernist feminist
who concedes only that Chopin's writing is "interesting" (a word that generally means that the person who uses it is really not interested at all)
but, by implication, not first-rate or really worthy of one's full attention.
This is perhaps only to say that for this reader about whom Papke tells
us, anything written more than a century ago could not possibly have the
urgency or insight required of modern feminist fiction, if only because of
the compromising historical situation around the turn of the last century
that necessarily inhibited female thought and expression. Such patronizing of the past is, alas, an all too common component of the mind-set
of those who have latched on to the latest critical lingo and who seem
to consider that most creative writing that is not at least approximately
contemporary with the language currently being spoken in cool critical
discourse is probably not worth talking about at all, but Papke's retell-
ing of her encounter with another faculty member at the University of

Tennessee, even though she defuses it somewhat by remarking that this same critical "reader" admitted to not having read Chopin's fiction at all, suggests a doubt about, not to say a disdain for, Chopin's abilities in some quarters where one would not expect to find it.

We might illustrate this ambivalence about Kate Chopin's writing and status by considering one of her most highly admired short stories, "A Pair of Silk Stockings," which Barbara Ewell has described as a "small masterpiece"[3]—but doesn't the word "small" here betray the kind of doubts about which we have just been talking?—and which Bernard Koloski has identified as one of the finest short stories to emerge from turn-of-the-century American literature.[4] But when we look into the literature that has accumulated around this story from Per Seyersted (who says nothing at all significant about it in his critical biography) to my own remarks as published in 1975 to Emily Toth, we do not find much in the way of validation of such large claims, only a general appreciation of the story, a few paragraphs or so of plot summary, and a few comments about, for example, "the power of money to enhance self esteem"[5] or about Kate Chopin's sympathy for how the other half lives.[6] To accept Koloski's characterization of Chopin's story, with which I happen to agree, and match it with Ewell's or Toth's observations, we might observe that Stephen Crane's near contemporary short story "An Experiment in Misery" is also about the power of money and how the other half lives, but it has been shown by commentators over the years to be a complex, ironic, and significant work of fiction in a way that "A Pair of Silk Stockings" has not. Complex and rewarding readings have been advanced for The Awakening, to repeat my earlier exclusion of that novel from the general rule about the critical tradition that has grown up around Kate Chopin's fiction, but mostly not for Chopin's individual stories, and until such readings are persuasively and convincingly set forth—that is, until we quit reading these stories largely in terms of how they do or do not foreshadow The Awakening or how one story does or does not resemble another or the extent to which a piece may or may not depend upon her autobiography—we will be left after all this time and effort with the doubts that nagged at Thomas Bonner many years ago, false dilemma or not: Is Kate Chopin a major writer or a minor writer with a major novel?

In the few pages remaining, I want to use "A Pair of Silk Stockings" to try to answer that question, at least provisionally, hoping in this way to make another small and belated contribution to the ongoing study of this remarkable writer. To do so I want to revert, somewhat atavistically, to certain of the long-abandoned New Critical strategies of close reading, as if the tale were a self-contained and carefully crafted artifact (or well-wrought urn, in Brooks and Warren's deathless phrase), but to argue at the same time that the internal patterns of irony and language, of subtle insinuation, do not predominantly point inward toward an appreciation of the story as merely an aesthetic entity but outward toward the historical, social, and cultural contexts that surround it and that render it fully meaningful. In terms of Brooks and Warren's titular allusion to Keats's "Ode on a Grecian Urn," we might say that we are interested in detecting these patterns within the work of art as a means to reflect not upon the aesthetic isolation of the object or its sacrosanct status as something set apart from the loud and busy world but upon what verbal patterns may establish or lead us to think about (again to use Keats's case) British imperialism, or what a Grecian urn was doing in the British Museum in the first place and what tale it silently told in that regard about competing cultural claims to ownership of the past and present, as well as about the value of art and artifacts within a world of being and becoming and the "possession" of such artifacts as symbols of colonial outreach and power. Without an active and operating consciousness of or curiosity about the relevant external circumstances of a literary work, moreover, we might miss altogether the patterns of language at work and play within any given text and fail in our readings to take account of that text's full range of intertextual reference.

What, for example, within the lexicon of the historical moment, did Kate Chopin have in mind when she described "little Mrs. Sommers," after she has allowed the silk stockings in the story to "glide, serpent-like" through her fingers, as being within the grip "of some mechanical impulse that directed her actions and freed her of responsibility"?[7] Why, for that matter, might Chopin have chosen to refer to her protagonist, in such apparently patronizing language, as "little Mrs. Sommers"? To be sure, the simile of the serpent and the reference to being freed of responsibility somehow entangle this story with issues of fate and free will raised initially in Christian theology and scripture within the context of the Garden and the Fall, but what, if anything, might have been the contemporary resonance of this allusion or its full function within the story? For an answer we might return (at last) to Ernest Hemingway's emphasis on leaving out, or seeming to leave out, things that are still somehow insinuated into the text throughout the story and from there into the consciousness or at least into the subliminal awareness of the reader as well. That is to say, the things left out are not really absent from a Hemingway story but deliberately underplayed or understated, at first seemingly only a part of the surface of the narrative but functioning in fact also as a key or clue to the deepest implications of the actions and as a marker of the large world beyond the immediate text (the tip of Hemingway's famous iceberg), like the word "nothing" in "A Clean, Well-Lighted Place" or the swamp in "Now I Lay Me," "The Battler," and a number of other stories. Such absent things might, in fact, not be stated at all, as in the famous case of World War I as the essential but virtually invisible background of "Big, Two-Hearted River."

In Chopin's "A Pair of Silk Stockings," a deceptively simple account of one woman and mother's shopping trip to a downtown department store where she spends on herself money that she had intended to spend on her children, the figurative tip of the iceberg can be detected, I believe, in the principal setting of the story, the department store, and its immediate and commercially contrived and calculated surroundings (bookstore, restaurant, and theater), as well as in the silk stockings that the title deliberately foregrounds as a fetish of fashion and female sexuality. The themes that open outward from a historical appreciation of these sites of symbolic compression involve a number of personal and social transformations that were only then emerging into clarity in company with the culture of consumption at the end of the nineteenth century. These include the appropriation and manipulation of female desire by an increasingly aggressive and male-managed capitalist culture in an attempt to create and sustain an inexhaustible market for services and goods, especially for luxury goods; the increasing emphasis on performative identity and personality rather than on innate and inherited character, with a corresponding new sense of self based upon lower- and middle-class imitation of the wealthy through the agencies of fashion and taste; and the reshaping of the American society into a consuming rather than primarily a producing nation. What befalls Mrs. Sommers during her fateful excursion, in other words, is exactly what the male managerial system had intended should happen, not particularly to her as an individual but to her as a member of an invented class of people, female shoppers, within the world that May and Macy and Wannamaker were in the process of creating. It is a situation that Mrs. Sommers herself dimly senses (and that Kate Chopin explicitly identifies) when she believes herself under the control of some "mechanical power" that simultaneously urges her on to keep spending money while absolving her of guilt and responsibility for her actions or when she begins to feel, beneath the glow of the department store's special lighting, disconnected from herself: "Her foot and ankle looked very pretty. She could not realize that they belonged to her and were a part of herself."[8]

My reading thus far has closely tracked Allen F. Stein's, who in *Women and Autonomy in Kate Chopin's Short Fiction* notes in regard to Chopin's reference to the serpent-like stockings and Mrs. Sommers's fall that there has never been any "latitude for free choice in her [Mrs. Sommers's] dutiful daily life."[9] This is the longest and best commentary to date on "A Pair of Silk Stockings." But Stein's reading fails to accommodate several aspects of Kate Chopin's story, including a passage such as the one above in which a newly attired Mrs. Sommers contemplates herself with a sense of detachment and unreality, becomes, as it were, the object of her own spectatorial gaze, her old identity having been challenged and transformed, not to say entirely possessed, by the commodities with which, almost against her will, she has adorned herself but that, as adornments, have now become part of her social as well as her personal self.[10]

Also, in stressing only Mrs. Sommers's "blind, impulsive, utterly desperate submission to the dictates of a commercially driven consumer ethic that insists one's true worth is determined by the quality and worth of one's possessions and amusements,"[11] Stein sells Chopin's story short, overlooking, for one thing, the "new freedom from self-denial and . . . repression" that one historian, William R. Leach, has claimed helps to explain the acquiescence in and even fierce loyalty to the new consumer culture by the American masses[12] and that surely is one component of Mrs. Sommers's experience on her memorable day in the store. Her choices on that day, as numerous commentators have pointed out, favor the sensuous, the aesthetic, and the pleasurable, all of them antithetical to the repressive national culture that was in the process of fading into the past, though it would not ever entirely do so; they are to this degree quite liberating choices not available in her domestic environment or within her domestic identity. "The culture of consumption," to cite Leach once again, "was an urban and secular one of color and spectacle, of sensuous pleasure and dreams . . . [that] subverted, but never overturned, the older mentality of repression, practical utilitarianism, scarcity, and self-denial."[13] Although scarcely the paean to "the joy that accompanies the fruitful use of money" that Doris Davis makes it out to be,[14] then, "A Pair of Silk Stockings" is not the anticapitalist manifesto of Stein's reading either but a story whose poignancy derives in large measure from exactly those unresolved contradictions and contrasts between the established and the emerging culture that Leach has described. In her portrait of Mrs. Sommers, Kate Chopin has given us not only a story about a particular woman who is economically on the margins of society but also a story of that entire society, whether wealthy or poor, in a time of transition, attempting to estimate through the sum of individual experiences the true psychological and spiritual costs of the bargain it has made or been forced to make with modernity.

A sense of dissociation from the self, a hallmark of social and self-awareness for people living through the 1890s, is operative throughout most of the story, as Mrs. Sommers plays at being someone who she is not, not only when she performs her ritual of sales resistance and fastidious and fashionable good taste for the sake of the shoe clerk, pretending she has enough money to spend for extra style and quality if she so chooses,[15] but also upon her entrance into the restaurant, where she half suspects that the well-to-do people who truly belong there (but do they really, or are they, like her, merely temporarily visiting within a foreign space?) will look up and detect her masquerade despite the new stockings, shoes, and gloves that outside on the street "had given her a feeling of assurance, of belonging to the well-dressed multitude."[16] The historical double consciousness that Leach assigns to the era, in other words, plays out in Mrs. Sommers's personal life as a feeling that she belongs to the fashionable crowd by reason of the disguise of her dress as against the knowledge that she does not. She tips the waiter, who bows before her (also performing in his turn, of course) "as before a princess of royal blood,"[17] displaying on the one hand and receiving on the other the deference that was so indispensable to the working of consumer culture. Then she is ready for the theater, where she transforms herself to all appearances and only for a time into one of the "brilliantly dressed women who had gone there to kill time and eat candy and display their gaudy attire."[18] She shares their manufactured emotions over different scenes in the drama and even partakes of some chocolates with one of the brilliant and gaudy women nearby. Afterward, she exits, waits for and boards the cable car, where her sense of alienation from herself deepens into a blank gaze and a melancholy fantasy about the car's going on and on with her forever. Which is now revealed to be the fictitious and the true identity, that of the mother who was preoccupied with questions of "investment" and "speculation" and worried about the welfare of her brood for days before her momentous trip downtown, contemplating the performance of traditionally male financial responsibilities in an ironically outsized economic vocabulary, or the one who indulged in earthly delights, satisfying her senses rather than following her common sense? The story suggests that both identities are equally true and equally false, or even more radically that neither is true at all but both are merely constructions that not only women but women especially are compelled to inhabit in various ways and at various times. In a world increasingly absorbed by image and display, the performative self, creature of social and economic (and sometimes biological) contingency, is all there is.

The young shoe clerk who waits on Mrs. Sommers but who "could not make her out"[19] would seem to share the lady's own bewilderment about her true identity, but his inability to interpret her character does not partake of any of her sense of tragic inner division or contemporary cultural complexity; rather, his is the bafflement appropriate to a society in which images of the self, constructed out of taste and fashion, are mistaken for substance as primary sources of information in our desire for knowledge about other people: "he could not reconcile her shoes with her stockings."[20] Another similarly impercipient male "reader" is the "man with keen eyes" who studies Mrs. Sommers on her cable car ride home but is unable to "decipher what he saw there."[21] His gaze is, ironically, described as penetrating, even predatory; possibly he is assessing whether this woman, an unchaperoned female in a public conveyance, might be available for sexual conquest as easily as she has made herself available for his scrutiny. As was the case with the shoe clerk, her attire doesn't help him to any understanding. If we imagine such characters as surrogates for male readers in general—for someone such as the husband of "Her Letters" obsessively perusing this tale in the same way that he searches in the margins of his dead wife's books for any clues to her erotic life, or someone such as Léonce Pontellier, with his insistence that Edna take care of her domestic chores before nurturing her artistic self and his commitment to keeping up appearances, reading this story out of an idle curiosity to see what women are up to nowadays—we recognize how Chopin has anticipated and provided for, perhaps even deliberately encouraged, a complete misreading (or let us say more generously a completely alternative reading) of "A Pair of Silk Stockings" from an exclusively male point of view.

This reading, which no one that I know of has previously commented on, would simply reinforce what it is that men believe they know about the opposite gender—that they have no head for figures, for "investment" and "speculation," that they cannot be trusted to manage money, that they are creatures of impulse rather than of reason, and so on and on—and would thereby ironically seem to validate the patronizing "little" before the name of Mrs. Sommers, as a man might call his wife "the little woman." As a professional writer, Kate Chopin surely knew that once a text had seen the light of print, the author could no longer maintain control of its meanings, but in the nuanced ironies involved with her economic vocabulary, in her own use of the word "little" in such a way as to render ambiguous its pejorative power, and especially in the two nonplussed male "readers" within the story, she has done her best to defend her story against such a misreading by exposing its errors within the text itself (she would not be so lucky later with The Awakening).

Mrs. Sommers herself is another reader written into the text, picking up and carefully opening a few fashionable magazines—it is tempting to think that one of them may have been Vogue—and reading the stories therein over lunch in a manner that serves almost as an ideal prescription for the pace and purpose of leisurely female reading: "She tasted a bite, and she read a word or two, and she sipped the amber wine and wiggled her toes in the silk stockings."[22] To this degree, she becomes a character within her own story, a metatextual element within the narrative as well as another device of self-distancing. More than that, she stands in for the reader of Vogue, "a dignified authentic journal of society, fashion, and the ceremonial side of life, that is to be, for the present, mainly pictorial" with "special attention . . . asked for the quality and character of the advertisements," representing the "leading merchants" in New York and "a class of trade of the highest order."[23] That is, as envisioned by the publisher, Arthur B. Turnure, Vogue was to be justified principally as an investment and an advertising medium, not as an outlet for extraordinary fiction, whatever the editor Josephine Redding may have thought,[24] and this promise is more than borne out by the pages and pages illustrating the latest or finest in luxury goods. By this logic, stories served mainly to sell both the magazine and the commodities advertised in it and as items to be consumed by the reader exactly as Mrs. Sommers consumes her luncheon and wine or as those having the means purchase the clothing, the silver, the carriages, and the rest of the stuff in the pages of Vogue. The habitual Vogue reader, like some modern critics, might sympathize with Mrs. Sommers or maybe even, like her husband, shake her head in dismay over Mrs. Sommers's foolishness and self-indulgence, but she would not be likely to detect the critique and exposure of the same consumer society in which she was daily immersed. The fashionable female reader, that is to say, is, like Mrs. Sommers, "hooked on images" (to use Rachel Bowlby's apt phrase) that she takes for her own identity "but does not recognize as not of her own making."[25]

The range and reach of implications in Kate Chopin's "A Pair of Silk Stockings" are thus far wider and deeper than previous readers seem to have suspected, in part because the kinds of approaches still most commonly taken to her fiction, and especially to her short fiction, are not necessarily compatible with or conducive to the kind of close historical and textual reading that I believe her writing demands. If, in the pages preceding, I have departed from the format of most of the other essays in this volume, and if any apology can be made for that aberration, it must be that, as stated before, my career as a scholar of Chopin has lasted far fewer years than the careers of the other contributors—that, and my conviction that her work is still being underread and hence undervalued by too many of her readers. So some of the things I still wanted to say about her writing I took the opportunity to say in this forum. The shape of the scholarly history that has grown up around her writing is what it is at the moment, but if readers will regard my self-indulgence in revisiting "A Pair of Silk Stockings" in the detail that I have pursued as merely a call for the coming generation of critics to secure and extend Chopin's reputation as one of the best American writers in the short story form, they will have encountered my essay in the spirit in which it is written.

NOTES

1. Kate Chopin, The Complete Works of Kate Chopin, ed. Per Seyersted (Baton Rouge: Louisiana State UP, 1969) 950.

2. Dorothy Weil, In Defense of Women: Susanna Rowson (1762–1824) (University Park: Pennsylvania State UP, 1976).

3. Barbara C. Ewell, Kate Chopin (New York: Ungar, 1986) 118.

4. Bernard Koloski, Kate Chopin: A Study of the Short Fiction (New York: Twayne, 1996) 73.

5. Ewell, Kate Chopin 119.

6. Emily Toth, Kate Chopin (New York: Morrow, 1990) 281. Other commentary is not significantly more useful than the passages I have quoted. For example, in "Kate Chopin Thinks Back through Her Mothers: Three Stories by Kate Chopin," 15–25, in Kate Chopin Reconsidered: Beyond the Bayou, ed. Lynda S. Boren and Sara deSaussure Davis (Baton Rouge: Louisiana State UP, 1992), Emily Toth says only that "A Pair of Silk Stockings" is one of several stories by Chopin in which a woman refuses to sacrifice herself for others (23), and Peggy Skaggs concludes her brief account of the story by remarking that the text contains "no hint of censure" for Mrs. Sommers's alleged "selfishness" (Kate Chopin [Boston: Twayne, 1985] 59–60), as if selfishness were the important theme (it might be if the story had been written by a man or by some more fully domesticated, less recalcitrant a woman than Kate Chopin).

7. Chopin, Complete Works 816, 818.

8. Chopin, Complete Works 818.

9. Allen F. Stein, Women and Autonomy in Kate Chopin's Short Fiction (New York: Peter Lang, 2005) 67.

10. In Just Looking: Consumer Culture in Dreiser, Gissing, and Zola (New York: Methuen, 1985), Rachel Bowlby writes what amounts to an excellent description of Mrs. Sommers's situation as she first allows the silk stockings to glide through her fingers—her ability to touch the sinuous merchandise is a key element of marketing strategy, as is the wide variety of sizes and colors—and later contemplates her newly adorned feet and ankles as objects of her own anatomy that nevertheless seem to have become alien to her: "The dominant ideology of feminine subjectivity in the late nineteenth century perfectly fitted woman to receive the advances of the seductive commodity offering to enhance her womanly attractions. Seducer and seduced, possessor and possessed of one another, women

and commodities flaunt their images at one another in an amorous regard which both extends and reinforces the classical picture of the young girl gazing into the mirror in love with herself. . . . 'Just looking': the conventional apology for hesitation before a purchase in the shop expresses also the suspended moment of contemplation before the object for sale—the pause for reflection in which it is looked at in terms of how it would look on the looker" (32).

11. Stein 70.

12. William R. Leach, "Transformations in a Culture of Consumption: Women and Department Stores, 1890–1925," *Journal of American History* 71 (1984): 320.

13. Leach 320.

14. Doris Davis, "*The Awakening*: The Economics of Tension," *Kate Chopin Reconsidered: Beyond the Bayou*, ed. Lynda S. Boren and Sara deSaussure Davis (Baton Rouge: Louisiana State UP, 1992) 148.

15. Chopin, *Complete Works* 818.

16. Chopin, *Complete Works* 818.

17. Chopin, *Complete Works* 820.

18. Chopin, *Complete Works* 818.

19. Chopin, *Complete Works* 818.

20. Chopin, *Complete Works* 820.

21. Chopin, *Complete Works* 819–20.

22. Chopin, *Complete Works* 820.

23. See the publisher's "Statement" in the inaugural issue of *Vogue*, December 1892: 8.

24. Emily Toth has a slightly different take than mine on Josephine Redding's editorial instrumentality in furthering Kate Chopin's career as a writer of short fiction. It is true that *Vogue* published a significant number of Chopin's short stories in the last decade of the nineteenth century and on into the twentieth, including some of her best, but even the eccentric editor Redding would have been constrained in her selection of stories for print by the broader and entirely commercial policies of the publisher. Had *Vogue's* "Statement" insisted that one of the functions of the magazine would be to publish the best-quality fiction it could find, perhaps Redding would have had better material overall with which to work, but the fact is that most of the stories that share *Vogue's* pages with Chopin's work are quite conventional and undistinguished, scarcely the sort of fictions that a crusading feminist editor would pick if she had real options (whether or not she wore her hat to bed). See *Unveiling Kate Chopin* (Jackson: UP of Mississippi, 1999) 171–72.

25. Bowlby 30.

8

The Death of Edna Pontellier
and the Card Catalog

MARLENE SPRINGER

IN 1976 MY BIBLIOGRAPHY of Kate Chopin's writings was published
by G. K. Hall as part of Joseph Katz's Reference Guides in Literature. The
volume, Edith Wharton and Kate Chopin: A Reference Guide, was largely devoted to Edith Wharton, since there was not enough scholarship focusing
on Kate Chopin to merit a volume about her alone; that the times have
changed so much is a credit to the fine literary critics who have dedicated themselves to the Chopin "discovery" and a testimony to the writer
herself. That the section of Chopin's writings appeared at all in my book
is emblematic of the personal and professional merging that so often
takes place in our profession: Joseph Katz, the series editor, was a graduate school friend; I was a young assistant professor looking for a route to
tenure that would satisfy my own interests in American literature while
being realistic enough to know that I had to have a manageable project.
But as I note in the preface to my volume, the course of Chopin criticism
has been extremely uneven:

> After her initial acceptance and then public rejection, Chopin's life and her
> work settled into obscurity until Daniel Rankin published his biography
> in 1932. Kenneth Eble's edition of The Awakening in 1964 further enhanced
> her reputation, but not until 1969, with Per Seyersted's publication of The
> Complete Works of Kate Chopin, were her works readily accessible for critical
> scrutiny. Her reputation has been steadily growing, due in large part to an
> increased interest in women novelists and feminist novels. Initially, however,
> she was lauded as a local colorist (though ironically the turn-of-the-century
> books on Southern writers do not mention her, and subsequent ones, in the

20's and 30's only give her passing mention), and long before she was adopted as a symbol of feminine rebellion she was discovered by critics dealing with the portrayal of Blacks in literature. Such ironies are emblematic of both her career and her critical treatment. She left the Church, yet her biography was first written by a priest. She was an American author, who owes much of her modern status to a Frenchman, Cyrille Arnavon, and a Norwegian, Per Seyersted. Primarily a short story writer, she is assured a place in literary history by her novel. And finally, though early praised for her simplicity and her unlettered approach, her subtleties and her sources are now major critical interests; studies of her imagery, her debt to Whitman and Maupassant, her impressionism, and perhaps appropriately enough, her ambiguity, abound. Kate Chopin was recognized by her contemporaries as being twenty years before her time; when the times caught up, she was forgotten. Only with the last fifteen years have critics begun to realize the contradiction between what her reputation ought to be and what it has been. Recorded here are both the neglect and the awakening.[1]

Chopin criticism was not brand new: Daniel S. Rankin's dissertation for the University of Pennsylvania, Kate Chopin and Her Creole Stories, appeared in 1932. But no other dissertations were written until Robert Arner's Music from a Farther Room: A Study of the Fiction of Kate Chopin in 1972, followed soon by the studies of Bernard Koloski, Emily Toth, and Thomas Bonner. The doors of perception to Chopin's work thus opened, from 1983 to 2008 sixty-five dissertations discussing Chopin's work were written (a significant increase from the twenty-six that were completed between 1932 and 1983). As the attention to Chopin grew, there was an obvious need to compile and categorize the scholarship and create a resource for scholars who would otherwise have a difficult time discovering what had already been said about a body of work that in itself was just gaining attention. The methodology for the volume was straightforward:

> The bibliography contains annotated items of scholarship, criticism, reviews, and miscellaneous commentary, published between 1890 and 1973 on Chopin and her works. Though I again include many items not listed in previous bibliographies, I do not attempt to be definitive. I have, however, included the discussions of Chopin found in literary histories and in several biographical dictionaries, even if brief, simply because a mention of a writer now recog-

nized as unjustly neglected is critically salient. I have for Chopin also included newspaper reviews from more minor newspapers and journals than for Wharton, primarily because Chopin's early recognition was largely regional. Here too I have often quoted to give the flavor of Chopin's reception.[2]

In 1981, I was asked to supplement the Chopin volume with an article in *Resources for American Literary Study.*[3] Abashedly, I still have the correspondence relating to the article: stamps were 15 cents. After that article, I devoted my time to reading and teaching Chopin, rather than searching for others' work, which was a nice change.

But it seems that no good scholarly project is without its modicum of drama. When the book finally arrived, there was joy—as only holding your first book in your hands can bring—then dismay. I opened the volume to find that nearly ten pages in the middle were blank. Printer's error on the advanced author's copy? Or did the entire run have the flaw? I was in Rio de Janeiro at the time, with no real way to contact the publisher to explain the problem: fax machines were not yet widely available. Fortunately, friends again stepped in: very likely the first letter explaining a problem in literary scholarship publication was dispatched via U.S. consulate pouch, and the press had time to correct the error. The U.S. government had met Kate Chopin.

In retrospect, the road to completing the bibliography seems straightforward. Distance has blurred the endless hours tracking down the sources, scouring the MLA *Bibliography,* eagerly awaiting the next volume of *Dissertation Abstracts* and the union catalogs—the list seems endless, and it was. Once sources were identified, there was then the time-consuming task of gathering the references: trips to the St. Louis Historical Society (fortunately, I was then located in Kansas City); correspondence with scholars (most of whom were helpful, some of whom were not); visiting major libraries around the country to find the rarer texts; talking with many helpful librarians who led me to references. The search was enjoyable, though frustrating at times. I had signed my contract with G. K. Hall in 1973—the book was three years in the making, which enhanced my sympathy for young scholars when, as a college president, I made tenure decisions.

Since this bibliography was compiled (from 1973 to 1976), much has changed for scholars. I moved diligently forward without the benefit of

James Harner's On Compiling an Annotated Bibliography. Had I had the luxury of that volume, his helpful hints would have saved me much work, though it possibly would have shattered my naïveté to the extent that I may not have had the nerve to continue. Harner outlines some major questions that one must answer before taking on such a project:

(1) Is there a need for this bibliography?
(2) Do I have the temperament and qualifications for the work?
(3) Do I have the necessary resources to complete . . . the project?[4]

The answer to question one was affirmative: necessary, and overdue. The answer to question two was more complicated: qualifications, yes; temperament, decidedly dependent on the day—and teaching, and family demands, and time. The answer to question number three was uncertain, for it is difficult to determine ahead of time just how many trips to archives, libraries, and other collections will be required. Thus the answer really depended on the commitment of personal finances that one was willing to make. Again, naïveté was a saving grace.

While my inexperience might have been helpful for beginning this project, confidence was, too. The dangers of undertaking such a task are formidable. As Harner has since noted, some bibliographies can be "models of their kind: intelligent, accurate, thorough, efficiently organized works that foster scholarship by guiding readers through accumulated studies as well as implicitly or explicitly isolating dominant scholarly concerns, identifying topics that have been overworked, and suggesting needed research."[5] Conversely, such a collection, like any scholarly work, can be seriously flawed, either in execution or in basic conception. To the uninitiated, the project can seem simple—the perils of trying to track down sources in a pre-Internet age often go unrecognized. I would like to think that my book falls in the former category, but I am not that arrogant. I hope it falls near the "intelligent, accurate" category, and its subsequent use by scholars supports that assessment. However, I also acknowledge that there were inevitable omissions—lost cards, or untraceable sources that could be found now with the click of a mouse.

Nonetheless, when I was working on the book in 1974, the MLA Bibliography was the Bible of the times, and it too has gone through several metamorphoses:

For example, before 1956 the Bibliography nominally included works by American scholars only. Although it became "international" in 1956, it is still not exhaustive in its coverage. The taxonomy and indexing procedures have also changed, most radically with the Bibliography for 1981, which introduced a sophisticated classification and indexing system. In searching the MLA International Bibliography, you would, of course, examine the entries in the subject-author section (and, for post-1980 volumes, the subject-author listings in the comprehensive subject index). In addition, you would have to search (1) the General heading and relevant genre headings in appropriate period sections (in the 1981 Bibliography and after, you cannot follow this procedure because general studies of a theme or genre in a single national literature are listed according to chronological span covered—e.g., a study of the English lyric from 1300 to 1900 would be listed under "English Literature/1300–1899" and would appear near the beginning of the English section of volume 1); (2) The English I (General and Miscellaneous) and English III (Themes, Types, and Special Topics) sections or the American I (General and Miscellaneous) section; (3) possibly all of the following sections, depending on the year of the Bibliography: General I (Esthetics), General II (Literary Criticism and Literary Theory), General III (Literature, General and Comparative), General IV (Themes and Types), General V (Bibliographical), and General VI (Miscellaneous).[6]

Nor was MLA content to let the matter rest there. In the 1981 Bibliography and subsequently, the General headings of volume 1 were replaced by a fourth volume with nine separate divisions, such as General Literature, Literary Theory and Criticisms, and so on. Also eliminated were cross references, so it also became necessary to check all topics important to your research in the comprehensive subject index.[7]

This byzantine process, so taken for granted by early scholars, is becoming increasingly dated—but in the 1970s the process was a godsend, as was the 3" × 5" card. Though I saved all the correspondence concerning the volume, I did not save the 3" × 5"s. (I'm proud of myself for that; cards for my dissertation are another matter.) First, the references must be located and examined. Fortunately, the academic calendar allows time for such searches, and the task is at least definable and divisional. However, the bibliographer must learn to function with Keats's "Negative Capability" (as defined in his 21 December 1817 letter to his brothers George and

Thomas)—the capability of "being in uncertainties, mysteries, doubts, without any irritable reaching after fact and reason"—until the actual reference is located or determined to be lost forever. Once located and read, each reference must be summarized. When one is faced with well over five hundred cards, color-coded by subject, type of reference, author, and so on, the prospect of annotating them seems overwhelming and can be very subjective: the entries must be consistent, clear, and, especially important, concise. Here, at least, the computer has not taken over, and human talent, thankfully, maintains some relevance.

The same can be said for indexing, which was a daunting task in the 1970s and remains so today, as a good index is a necessity (I now boycott all books without them, unless they are rare or biblical). Organizing an index is deceptively simple, but deciding which subjects to include, how to list citations, which personal titles to use, what themes to include—these are all decisions that must be made early and decisively. Starting over with a new theme or subject after you are 300 cards through is not pleasant. Putting the cards in alphabetical order is the least formidable task and one I assigned to my seven-year-old (her sister, at age three, was still too young, but she was assigned for the next book), and I had to smile when I overheard her proudly sigh to a friend, "I can't play right now; I have to help index my mother's book." A family cottage industry had begun.

Owing to expanded technology, however, research methodology has changed radically, though several of the challenges remain the same. With the explosion of information access, the question for the bibliographer now becomes not what can one find but when to stop looking. For example, in 1996 there were 10,000 scholarly databases online; now there are more than 18,000. The Web itself now has more than 100 million sites.[8]

Indeed, scholars are challenged just to keep up with the advances in the online research catalogs. In 1995, when Charles Hildreth wrote his detailed history of the online public access catalog (OPAC) for the Council on Library Resources,[9] he questioned even then whether catalog designers were moving in the right direction. In the previous fifteen years, two access models shaped the design of the first OPAC: one emulated the good old card catalog; the second adopted a different model familiar to commercial search series. System developers were challenged to merge the two approaches. The second generation of OPAC was a vast improvement, providing more browsing options, multiple catalog arrangements in a single source, better search results, remote access, materials status and availability information, access to the resources of other libraries, increased utilization of library resources, and, perhaps most important to scholars, greater enjoyment and satisfaction with the results.

Succeeding generations of OPAC continued to expand the searches' boundaries, as Hildreth further notes: "The enabling technology of the online catalog makes it possible to *expand* the scope of the library catalog, and, joined with telecommunications technologies, to *extend* its range. With the online catalog, it is again feasible to expand the catalog's coverage over, and to deepen access to, all the information materials in the library's collection."[10]

Interlibrary loans also became much more efficient as databases enabled bibliographers to determine the locations and availability of obscure references. Information displays also required sophisticated design techniques, and the full-text transfer of articles became the delight of researchers and students alike. As Hildreth's article continues:

> Effective bibliographic displays are influenced by both content and presentation factors. The design goal is to facilitate user comprehension and decision making. Key decisions involved in the bibliographic search process include accurate identification of a work, suitability of a retrieved work for a particular need, and the desirability of modifying a search strategy or expanding a search. The data content of the records in the database is often out of the hands of the system designer. The designer must use the available tools to present information in the most useful way contemplated.[11]

After 1995, OPAC expanded exponentially, and the term OPAC became synonymous with a variety of databases as the science of searching exploded. It is little wonder that the scholar can often feel lost in a morass of information. Fortunately, search designers are constantly improving the process. For example, "the syntax and mechanics of entering subject searches have been simplified, and the task of precise search statement query formulation has largely been delegated to the system software,"[12] a consummation always welcomed by the researcher.

It is breathtaking to contemplate the speed and scope of improvements to the tools available to bibliographers and literary critics only in the past forty years. Certainly the old "drive and search" method of gathering references seems as quaint as a horse-drawn carriage. But something has been lost: the adventure of visiting a new library; the camaraderie of meeting new librarians; the excitement of finding an obscure review; even the fun of having your children learn to index.

There is also a human loss for librarians in this "galloping technology." Librarians, who previously had been seen as fellow scholars and colleagues, are now increasingly separated from the actual practice of student learning and scholarly research. Instead of engaging in conversation about the latest history publication, for example, they are now forced to contend with learning to master the latest computer catalog and are concerned with how fast a transmission can go. Instead of joining colleagues to search for and select new books to buy, they must argue for more upgrading of their machines—an endless and useful process but distancing nonetheless.[13] As the library is transformed, the librarian is being redefined. Librarians' training now focuses more on the technical skills required for specified programs and databases than on the development of interpersonal skills. Deanna Marcum says it best:

> The point of all this is that librarians are more than processors of information. If we continue to focus on how to make machines work in our libraries, we fundamentally change the nature of what we do, but we also become members of a different community. No longer are we allies of scholars; no longer are we active researchers ourselves into the substance of an academic discipline; no longer are we the experts on our collections. Instead of seeing us in the stacks, our users will find us bent over a CD-ROM player trying to repair it or connecting it to the printer so students can find the information they want and leave quickly. Students begin to think of us as the technicians who will change the paper, not the experts who will help them think through the substance of important questions.[14]

We as scholars are losing something too. Roaming through the stacks has always been a pleasant, though admittedly inefficient, experience. The pleasure of reading a book that has little to do with one's topic is restricted if one's computer screen demands search-specific input. We have achieved information literacy too often at the expense of intellectual curiosity—a loss we increasingly see in our students as well.

It is somewhat sad to realize that compiling a hard-cover bibliography is essentially a dying art, and such volumes are also victims of technology, going the way of rotary phones, mimeograph machines, and ditto paper (though few will miss that purple monstrosity). A bibliography such as mine would be out of date long before it was published and now is relevant only for historical purposes, to inform Chopin scholars about what was available at the time it was compiled. As active scholars now realize, it is imperative to rely on technicians, whose profession requires a different set of skills than the literary critics'.

Given all the resources now available to Chopin critics, it is difficult to even speculate about the future of Chopin studies. The focus has evolved radically over the years, through local colorist, to short story writer, novelist, feminist, radical, conservative. Yet the abiding theme remains: Edna Pontellier and her fellow characters are as intriguing today as they were in the nineteenth century, and the human dilemmas they confronted, the love and sorrow they experienced, the fatal solutions they sometimes sought are eternally relevant. Such universal topics are limited only by the human imagination, which in itself is unlimited and incredible. It is that exploration of the human condition, I suspect, that keeps scholars and students alike returning to the study of Chopin and readers the world over turning to her stories. I am glad to be a part of the early history of the Chopin revival, and I admittedly stand in awe of the subsequent explosion of scholarship that followed. Maybe if Edna could have had a brief glimpse of the future, she would not have walked into the water.

NOTES

1. Marlene Springer, Edith Wharton and Kate Chopin: A Reference Guide (Boston: Hall, 1976) xii.

2. Springer, Edith Wharton and Kate Chopin xi.

3. Marlene Springer, "Kate Chopin: A Reference Guide Updated," Resources for American Literary Study 11 (1981): 280–303.

4. James L. Harner, On Compiling an Annotated Bibliography, 2nd ed. (New York: Modern Language Association, 2000) 4–5.

5. Harner 1.

6. Harner 19–20.

7. Harner 20.

8. Andrea L Foster, "Information Navigation 101," *Chronicle of Higher Education* 9 Mar. 2007: A38.

9. Charles R. Hildreth, "Online Catalog Design Models: Are We Moving in the Right Direction?" Myweb@C.W.Post, C. W. Post Office of Information Technology, 27 Mar. 2000. Web, 2 Jan. 2009.

10. Hildreth.

11. Hildreth.

12. Hildreth.

13. Deanna B. Marcum, "Librarians or Technicians? Which Shall We Be?" *Information for a New Age: Redefining the Librarian*, comp. Library Instruction Round Table (American Library Association) (Englewood: Libraries Unlimited, 1995) 11.

14. Marcum 13.

I wish to thank Professor Lisa Holland and especially Dr. Lia Kudless for their research assistance for this article.

9

Romantic Overtures

LYNDA S. BOREN

KATE CHOPIN ENTERED MY LIFE more than twenty years ago when I inherited a Women in Fiction course at Tulane. It had been a popular class, and as the departing instructor handed me her syllabus, she pointed to one writer in particular on the list. "You will love teaching Kate Chopin's *The Awakening*. It is a gem. Your students will love it too; it is set in Louisiana." There was a slight wistfulness to her look and her voice, betraying mixed emotions at moving on.

The experience of teaching Chopin's novel in its unique romantic setting, under the spell of live oaks festooned with Spanish moss and the distant rumble of streetcars up and down St. Charles Avenue, proved irresistible. I was hooked. Throughout the ensuing years, *The Awakening* followed me from one teaching position to another. In snowbound Vermont, my colleague and department chairman at Middlebury expressed a fervent wish that I offer the novel to students in my American literature survey course. As I reflect back on this, I was perhaps seen as a golden opportunity to have Chopin taught by someone who was herself a native of Louisiana, whose heritage stretched back for generations into not only the culture of New Orleans but the lesser known region of gentle pine-covered slopes within miles of Natchitoches and the Cane River.

Eventually, Chopin led me back to the place of my own birth, and I found myself rediscovering sights and sounds, sensations from my childhood that evoked memories long buried. It was then that I realized the essential romantic quality of my relationship to Chopin's work. In an uncanny way, she was instrumental in my own awakening.

In Natchitoches I helped to organize the Kate Chopin International Conference at Northwestern State University and chaired a special session on Chopin at the MLA convention in New Orleans. Out of this grew an edition of essays on Chopin, a manuscript still in progress when I made my way to Thailand as a Fulbright professor in Bangkok. I had brought Chopin to Thailand, or had she brought me?

Contemplating once again the pleasure of reassessing Chopin, I realize that the enduring appeal and essential power of her masterpiece that were so far beyond the abilities of her critics to appreciate draw upon those classical elements of romanticism that have resonated for centuries with readers: the alienated hero or heroine defying convention in search of self-fulfillment, the glorification of imagination and creativity over the mundane, and the often tragic consequences that preempt happy endings.

Within this romantic context lies a range of writers from Rousseau to Anne Rice and beyond. The mysterious, the gothic, the ambiguous, the strange and hypnotic draw us into the narrative, where defiant souls struggle for self-realization. This is the Chopin that now speaks to me most clearly after many years of teaching and whose masterpiece, The Awakening, invites us to accompany its heroine on her romantic voyage of self-discovery.

Where does one begin to map the romantic journey? What is the starting point? Historically, we might claim that it began with the Crusades, with Malory's Morte d'Arthur, or with those moments in history and romance that elevate our symbolic heroes above reason, beyond established codes of social behavior, into spiritual realms of self-realization—no matter the cost. Spiritually, it has its beginnings, as one well-known critic reminds us, in ancient thought and themes.[1] Philosophically, the romantic impulse, in its questioning of reason or rational behavior as a guide to moral governance and law, severs the obligation to deny ego, self, or desire in the preservation of a so-called social good. But it goes without saying that society cannot remain a static, absolute entity. The social good itself changes as a direct result of those very individuals who find themselves most at odds with it. At the heart of romanticism lies this obvious paradox: the ethos of individualism, which eventually leads to social change and acceptance, inevitably isolates and punishes those courageous enough to undertake such a quest.

For Edna Pontellier in Chopin's *The Awakening*, the beginnings of her
journey reside in submerged childhood memories, in impulses that com-
pel her to flee the confining and suffocating forces that deny her a much
desired freedom. These memories are triggered by her growing unhappiness in marriage to a man who has no appreciation for her emotional
needs, who reproaches Edna with "her habitual neglect of the children. If
it was not a mother's place to look after children, whose on earth was it?"[2]
Edna escapes from her husband's bed into the solitude of the night: "she
slipped her bare feet into a pair of satin mules at the foot of the bed and
went out on the porch."[3] Once alone, she gives vent to her deep unhappiness in a cathartic stream of tears. Chopin's narrative voice, which blends
so harmoniously with the portrait of Edna as to vocalize her heroine's
emotional turmoil and yet remain somehow serenely removed from it,
reveals the source of Edna's distress:

> An indescribable oppression, which seemed to generate in some unfamiliar
> part of her consciousness, filled her whole being with a vague anguish. It
> was like a shadow, like a mist passing across her soul's summer day. It was
> strange and unfamiliar; it was a mood. She did not sit there inwardly upbraid-
> ing her husband, lamenting at Fate, which had directed her footsteps to the
> path which they had taken. She was just having a good cry all to herself. The
> mosquitoes made merry over her, biting her firm, round arms and nipping
> at her bare insteps.[4]

Chopin's choice of words conveys Edna's powerful need for emotional
fulfillment; the experience itself is satisfying to Edna because it offers a
much needed release, "a good cry all to herself." The tone of Chopin's narrative voice offers an overlay of wisdom, suggesting that while her heroine
"could not have told you why she was crying" it is readily apparent to our
narrator not only why but that it is a good thing, a positive experience.
Chopin's sympathetic tone and subtlety of narration lead us step by step
into the corridors of an interior romantic landscape, the exploration of
which begins in the shadows and mists of suppressed memories and desires, while the discovery of which is permissible only under the cloak of
darkness, the secrecy of night.

Rousseau's *Confessions* would seem to inform the essential nature of
Edna's dilemma. Abandoning himself without shame, indeed, even with

self-indulgent pleasure, as he "sighed and wept like a child" along the shores of Lake Geneva, Rousseau was, nevertheless, compelled to share these private moments in confession. Solitude and night heighten Rousseau's sensuous awareness of natural beauty, much as the "voice of the sea" both invokes and reflects Edna's suppressed longings: "At night I lay in the open air, and, stretched on the ground or on a bench, slept as calmly as upon a bed of roses. . . . I spent a delightful night outside the city, on a road which ran by the side of the Rhone or Saone. . . . I walked on in a kind of ecstasy, abandoning my heart and senses to the enjoyment of all, only regretting, with a sigh, that I was obliged to enjoy it alone."[5]

Romantic solitude allows reflection, heightens awareness, and prompts such universal insights as Emerson's feelings of transcendence in the presence of natural beauty. Paradoxically, as Rousseau and Edna realize, there is also a human need to share such experiences with others, a sometimes tragically impossible need that can never be fully realized. And thus the romantic quest remains inviolable, isolating and, ironically, in its transcendence, more supernatural than natural, more unique than communal, as it plays itself out in lives of its participants.

Edna's need for a confidante reflects the duality of her own romantic awakening. Her "inward life which questions" clashes so disturbingly with that "outward existence which conforms"[6] that Edna seeks validation through confession or sharing of her intimate thoughts with Adele Ratignolle. With her eyes gazing steadfastly on the sea, Edna's entire being is transformed by her self-absorption, as though the sea itself had "seized and fixed every feature into a statuesque repose." In response to Adele's query as to her thoughts, Edna retraces the images and associations that had so transfixed her, and here I might add, so elevated her in her statuesque description from mere mortal to something bordering on the mythic. Edna's response signifies not only her ability to lose herself in contemplation but also her boundless capacity for creative, imaginative experience: "the sight of the water stretching so far away, those motionless sails against the blue sky, made a delicious picture that I just wanted to sit and look at."[7] The hot wind against Edna's face triggers a vivid memory from childhood, when, as a "very little girl," our heroine walked diagonally through the tall grass, beating it back with extended arms "as one strikes out in the water." These crystallizations of Edna's insights, goaded by sensations and memory, are highly romantic, defining moments in Edna's development, epiphanies that cast a luminous glow over Chopin's narrative. For not only does Edna make the connection between ocean and grass, swimming and walking, she also allows herself to entertain the possibility of her own seemingly innate need for independence: "Likely as not it was Sunday . . . and I was running away from prayers, from the Presbyterian service, read in a spirit of gloom by my father that chills me yet to think of." Edna quickly responds to Adele's playful "have you been running away from prayers ever since, ma chère?" with the revelation that religion was not the issue, that, indeed, since the age of twelve religion had taken "a firm hold upon [her]."[8] Edna's passivity in the grips of such experiences— her transfixion in the presence of a natural or physical beauty that renders her immobile as a statue, her description of religion as something that descends and seizes one's very soul—adds an otherworldly, spiritual dimension to her character, gracing it as well with a delicate supernatural resonance.[9]

Edna's openness to such experiences becomes the avenue through which heightened imaginative feelings and impressions make their way, so much so that Edna's desire for a fulfilling "inward life" takes on a compulsive, fatalistic air. Her senses lead her on, drawing her farther and farther away from the natural, imperfect environs of the physical as we know it into a landscape reserved for exalted or, as one might claim, idealized or supernatural inhabitants. Even when she was a small child, Edna's view, as she confessed, was obstructed by her bonnet, yet she felt compelled to continue her journey across the big field: "I felt as if I must walk on forever, without coming to the end of it."[10] This note of compulsion, combined with the linking of Edna's statuesque, Greek-like appearance to realms more pagan than Christian, has led at least one critic to identify a mythology of addiction in Chopin's work. Sara Davis "would argue that the recurrence of sleep, night, and death as a mythic triad among the Vocation stories suggests Chopin's knowledge that these ancient Greek deities—Hypnos, Nyx, and Thanatos—all wore wreaths of poppy, the source of opium and its derivatives." As Davis argues, Edna's trancelike, hypnotic experiences describe altered states of mind, which enable her to escape the unbearable pressures of wifedom and motherhood in a loveless marriage. "In these altered states, generated by a force over which the character exercises little or no control, the character moves out of the ordinary world, out of the historical moment, and into a mythic world within reach of wisdom."[11] I might also suggest that such transcendent states, whether addictive or the product of an innate artistic sensibility, clearly link Chopin with the romantic movement—both here and abroad—a romantic movement that attendant to its origins in the joyous adoration of the natural world yet also encouraged exploration of dreams, visions, fantasy, and the unknown, without condemnation and without distinguishing clearly the origins of such experiences, whether heaven-sent or demon-driven, imaginative or drug-induced. We have only to witness Coleridge's "Rime of the Ancient Mariner," "Kubla Khan," and "Cristabel," Wordsworth's "intimations of immortality," or Keats's "Lamia" to acknowledge that the seeds for later gothic fiction and such memorable classics as Wuthering Heights were early sown when the boundaries between the real and the imaginary, the hallucinatory and the actual, vanished in what Coleridge called a "willing suspension of disbelief."[12] The very essence of Hawthorne's romance narratives rests on the supposition that when the subject of one's art is the human soul or heart the ostensibly "real" as we know it ceases to exist. New worlds are created, landscapes become dim or illuminated, as the journey moves ever forward with remarkable ambiguity.

Nor should we ignore the power such artistry has over its readers, a power evident in Chopin's narrative. In my own experience teaching the Romantics, I have often shared with my colleagues the delight that comes with students' enthusiastic responses to the genre and have come to acknowledge the universal appeal that timeless classics such as the film Dead Poets Society hold for even the most cynical of our youth.[13] Atara Stein's commentary on her own teaching experiences attests to this phenomenon:

> The Byronic hero, with his ambition, aspiration, aggressive individualism, and "Promethean spark," is alive and flourishing in the latter half of the 20th century. Although they may not know it, my students see him again and again on their television screens and in movie theaters. For me, one of the particular interests in teaching the Romantic period is that, in some respects, I believe it has never ended. And the interest in the Romantic poets themselves is a continuing motif in popular culture.... While I discuss these connections in my undergraduate classes, I also created a graduate seminar on the subject,

"The Development of the Byronic Hero." It is a topic which engages student interest and provokes some of the most thoughtful and original papers I read each semester, papers which further the work of exploring the dynamic inter-action between Byron's works and the dark heroes of contemporary popular culture.[14]

Considering the elements above that define and give life to the various subgenres of romanticism, we might agree that many of those same ele-ments speak to us from the pages of Chopin's masterpiece. Key passages and descriptions in The Awakening suggest irrational modes of thinking and feeling beyond the compass of realism. As I reconsider these passages, I am reminded that my initial fascination with Henry James began with The Turn of the Screw and eventually led to a dissertation and a book on, among other things, James's depiction of human consciousness and the power such consciousness exerted over his characters. I am also reminded that a large part of my fascination with James was due to the somewhat terrifying possibility suggested by James that consciousness creates re-alities for good or ill, as it does in the case of the governess in The Turn of the Screw. The psychological frissons depicted in the governess's own words and her altercations with what are manifested as evil spirits intent on possessing the innocents under her charge result in a narrative style that partakes of the gothic while remaining grounded in the real. And it is just this balancing feat that links James's art to Hawthorne's ambiguity, to Poe's host of unforgettable narrators, and to Chopin's narrative voice in The Awakening. His is a style that has led more than one critic to see portrayed in James a type of spiritual vampirism that often threatens to, if not in actuality does, devastate his principal characters.[15] Instances of such vampirism in Chopin's masterpiece occur when Edna is seemingly seduced into what Adele Ratignolle regards as dangerous territory.

One such instance records Edna's memorable night swim in the Gulf, a swim suggested by Robert Lebrun "at that mystic hour and under that mystic moon": "She turned her face seaward to gather in an impression of space and solitude, which the vast expanse of water, meeting and melt-ing with the moonlit sky, conveyed to her excited fancy. As she swam she seemed to be reaching out for the unlimited in which to lose herself."[16]

As Edna turns to regard the distance between herself and the shore, she is suddenly smitten with fear: "A quick vision of death smote her soul, and for a second time appalled and enfeebled her senses. But by an effort she rallied her staggering faculties and managed to regain the land."[17] Clearly, Edna's physical swim transforms in Chopin's narrative to symbolic movement; her heroine is "reaching out for the unlimited in which to lose herself," another example of transcendence. Sharing her exultation with Robert, Edna muses, "I wonder if any night on earth will ever again be like this one. It is like a night in a dream. The people about me are like some uncanny, half-human beings. There must be spirits abroad to-night."[18] The prelude to Edna's transforming swim in the Gulf is the musical wizardry of Mademoiselle Reisz, which so overwhelms her that she is moved to tears:

> The very first chords which Mademoiselle Reisz struck upon the piano sent a keen tremor down Mrs. Pontellier's spinal column. . . . Perhaps it was the first time she was ready, perhaps the first time her being was tempered to take an impress of the abiding truth. . . .
>
> [T]he very passions themselves were aroused within her soul, swaying it, lashing it, as the waves daily beat upon her splendid body. She trembled, she was choking, and the tears blinded her.[19]

As if to give bodily form to these combined forces, to the "spirits" of Edna's enchanting night, Robert entices her further with his tale of a lonely spirit in search of his soul mate:

> On the twenty-eighth of August, at the hour of midnight, and if the moon is shining—the moon must be shining—a spirit that has haunted these shores for ages rises up from the Gulf. With its own penetrating vision the spirit seeks some one mortal worthy to hold him company, worthy of being exalted for a few hours into realms of the semi-celestials. His search has always hitherto been fruitless, and he has sunk back, disheartened, into the sea. But to-night he found Mrs. Pontellier. Perhaps he will never wholly release her from the spell. Perhaps she will never again suffer a poor, unworthy earthling to walk in the shadow of her divine presence.[20]

The implications of this lonely, ghostly lover and the connections drawn between the spiritual and the sea, the physical and the shore, offer obvious multiple parallels with Whitman and Twain. Huck's escape down the Mississippi is a truly romantic quest, the river itself providing a spiritual haven from the vices on shore. The fact that Edna looks back at the shore, that she appears at the conclusion of *The Awakening* to be drawn to her death by thoughts of her obligations on the shore, suggests to Barbara Ewell that "unlike the orphaned, unrelated Huck, she cannot abandon or even deny her relations and responsibilities on shore: her children."[21] However, as Ewell also acknowledges, the ending is ambivalent; perhaps, she suggests, we can also interpret Edna's death as a victory, a victory in achieving selfhood. I would like to reinforce Edna's choice to swim into the Gulf, as she does, naked and without fear, as symbolizing much the same romantic decision made by Huck. Huck has gone too far in his rejection of the shore to ever return to what it represents; he decides to head for the unknown and to remain true to himself, much in the same way that Edna fiercely reflects in her final swim that "[Léonce and the children] need not have thought that they could possess her, body and soul."[22] If one considers that Chopin's original title for her book was "A Solitary Soul" and given the symbolic burden demonstrated in this story by the sea and all that exerts an oppositional force to it, the message is consistent and lucid. Tragedy lies outside of and yet encircles both Huck and Edna; they cannot return to what they escaped from, and yet they do come full circle back to their own spiritual origins. If their journeys assume the configuration of a tragic circle, it is only because that society represented by the shore lags far behind them in courage and conviction. Yes, they are left in the end utterly alone but, otherwise, in total possession of self, their essential integrity intact.

Such isolation is what defines and sets apart all such portraits in romantic literature: Hester Prynne in *The Scarlet Letter*, Heathcliff in *Wuthering Heights*, and even the forlorn Louis of Anne Rice's *Interview with the Vampire*,[23] a work whose "unique fascination," according to Brian Frost, "lies in the way it minutely examines the vampire's innermost feelings, transforming a somewhat pedestrian plot into a tour de force."[24] Frost reminds us that the transformation of the vampire figure from one of loathing to that of the elegant, noble seducer of women was due to the influence of Byron's close associate, Polidori:

The story that did more than any other to establish this trend was Dr. John William Polidori's "The Vampyre" (1819), which was considered quite sensa-

tional in its day because its vampire-hero was a nobleman. . . . When Polidori
created his prototypal vampire, the misanthropic Lord Ruthven, he took as
his model a real-life nobleman, the flamboyant Lord Byron, whom Polidori
had ample opportunity to study as he was for a time his private secretary
and traveling companion. Like his factual equivalent, the vampiric Ruthven
takes a subtly perverse pleasure in tormenting those he loves; and it is this
particular trait that identifies him as one of the many incarnations of the
Fatal Man, the archetypal anti-hero created by the founders of the Romantic
school of literature. The Romantics were primarily obsessed with the affinity
between love and death and the way pain is sometimes linked with pleasure. Accordingly, they portrayed the vampire as an irresistible seducer, the
personification of darkness and forbidden desires. His choice of victims is
almost exclusively limited to innocent young women, whom he takes a delight in corrupting, robbing them not only of their blood but also their virtue.
Later, in the repressive Victorian era, when censorship and strict moral codes
deterred authors from dealing specifically with certain human impulses, vampire stories were increasingly invested with erotic symbolism. . . . Paradoxically, despite the Byronic vampire's forbidding appearance, his female victims
find him utterly irresistible. For though they may shrink instinctively from
his presence at first, the fatal seducer's magnetic personality and overpower-
ing sexual fascination overcomes their morbid fear of his ultimate objective.
Using the stratagem of a lover rather than a predator, the vampire's initial
amatory advances—feigned to lull his victim into a false sense of security—
give no hint of the terror to come.[25]

When one the considers the multiple instances of seduction in The
Awakening—the voice of the sea, Robert Lebrun's whispering tale of a
ghostly lover, Alcée Arobin's opportunistic maneuvers, not to mention
Mademoiselle Reisz's manipulation of Edna through her music—one is
struck by the sheer intensity of the theme. Its manifestations, however, are
possible only because of Edna's essential romantic nature, which opens itself to manifold experience, both physical and spiritual. While Mademoiselle Reisz's music releases Edna's deepest emotions, Arobin's advances
culminate only in Edna's submission to a purely physical relationship. Her
affair with Arobin has all the characteristics of vampirelike possession,
which interestingly enough begins with Arobin's revelation of a wound:

With ingenuous frankness he spoke of what a wicked, ill-disciplined boy he had been, and impulsively drew up his cuff to exhibit upon his wrist the scar from a saber cut which he had received in a duel outside of Paris when he was nineteen. She touched his hand as she scanned the red cicatrice on the inside of his white wrist. A quick impulse that was somewhat spasmodic impelled her fingers to close in a sort of clutch upon his hand. He felt the pressure of her pointed nails in the flesh of his palm.[26]

Edna's reaction to Arobin's scar—it "agitates and sickens" her— resonates with subtle allusiveness to the letting of blood, to the permanent and fatal stigma associated with outcasts, with vampires, and certainly with romantic antiheroes intent on provoking a duel. We notice in this passage, as we do in so many descriptions of Edna's behavior, something again operating beyond her rational control, drawing her to what appears to be a fatal contact with the forbidden. Her subconscious fear drives her to attempt to deny this fatality by covering up the stigma at the same time that she binds herself to it, flesh to flesh. When Arobin senses the duality of Edna's response, his seduction intensifies: "He stood close to her, and the effrontery in his eyes repelled the old, vanishing self in her, yet drew all her awakening sensuousness. . . . And he bent and pressed his lips upon her hand as if he wished never more to withdraw them."[27]

Chopin's narrative voice intervenes lest we mistakenly assume that Edna's seducer is sincere: "He cast one appealing glance at her, to which she made no response. Alcée Arobin's manner was so genuine that it often deceived even himself." Arobin's touch is fatal indeed, and once again we witness Edna's trancelike submission to the inevitable: "When she was alone she looked mechanically at the back of her hand which he had kissed so warmly. Then she leaned her head down on the mantelpiece. She felt somewhat like a woman who in a moment of passion is betrayed into an act of infidelity, and realizes the significance of the act without being wholly awakened from its glamour."[28] Her only concern at this moment is a vague sense of misgiving over what Robert, not her husband, would think. The implication here is that Edna in her need to meld body and soul in the consummation of her desires has somehow betrayed the integrity of her own soul through the realization of this purely physical act. This self-betrayal is transferred to Robert, the unattainable object of her soul's desire, and thus Edna's unresolved dilemma impels her ever onward in a romantic spiral that ultimately negates the physical as fiercely as it embraces the spiritual.

And yet Edna is powerless to reject Arobin's advances, lending credence to Sara Davis's uncovering of a theme of addiction prevalent in Chopin's writing. He "smoothed her hair with his soft, magnetic hand," and in spite of Edna's ostensible intention to bid him "good night," Arobin continues to "caress her. He did not say good night until she had become supple to his gentle, seductive entreaties."[29] It is only after Edna's affair with Alcée that she awakens into the troubled realization that she has somehow been untrue to her other self, that inner, spiritual self, whose desire remains unfulfilled. Without Robert, Edna's vision of a perfect love, an idealistic vision, if you will, remains incomplete. "'I love you,' she whispered, 'only you; no one but you. It was you who awoke me last summer out of a life-long, stupid dream.'"[30] And yet it is without Robert that she ventures out alone to embrace her destiny. His absence from her "little parlor" and thus from her life is conveyed with repetitive intensity: "He was nowhere at hand. The house was empty. He had scrawled on a piece of paper that lay in the lamplight: 'I love you. Good-by—because I love you.'"[31]

To those who would claim that Edna's apparent suicide following her abandonment by Robert suggests victimization or weakness, I would ask that they consider the merits of Barbara Ewell's reading of Edna's actions as a "victory in achieving selfhood." Chopin's beautifully crafted ending assumes not only the configuration of the mythic quest of the soul described by M. H. Abrams but also the aspects of divine apotheosis:

> When she was there beside the sea, absolutely alone, she cast the unpleasant, pricking garments from her, and for the first time in her life she stood naked in the open air, at the mercy of the sun, the breeze that beat upon her, and the waves that invited her.
>
> How strange and awful it seemed to stand naked under the sky! how delicious! She felt like some new-born creature, opening its eyes in a familiar world that it had never known.
>
> The foamy wavelets curled up to her white feet, and coiled like serpents about her ankles.[32]

Edna, like Huck, has never been untrue to her essential self. She has remained consistent in her nature, and in her romantic quest she returns, as all romantics do, to the innocence of a "new-born creature," perhaps, as Robert foretold, to dwell forever in the "realms of the semi-celestials."

NOTES

1. In his discussion "The Great Circle: Pagan and Christian Neoplatonism," M. H. Abrams retraces the concept of the spiritual voyage to Plotinus: "[In] the parable of an internal spiritual journey in quest of a lost home . . . Plotinus proposes an allegoric reading of Homer's epic narrative which was destined to have a long and prolific life in European thought." *Natural Supernaturalism: Tradition and Revolution in Romantic Literature* (1971; New York: Norton, 1973) 149.

2. Kate Chopin, *The Complete Works of Kate Chopin*, ed. Per Seyersted (Baton Rouge: Louisiana State UP, 1969) 885.

3. Chopin, *Complete Works* 886.

4. Chopin, *Complete Works* 886.

5. Jean Jacques Rousseau, *The Confessions of Jean Jacques Rousseau*, bk. IV, 1782. Project Gutenberg, 15 Aug. 2004. Web. 2 Jan. 2009.

6. Chopin, *Complete Works* 893.

7. Chopin, *Complete Works* 896. Thomas MacFarland in his study *Romanticism and the Heritage of Rousseau* points out that "romanticism was profoundly involved with dreams, reveries, twilight states of consciousness—all those 'petites perceptions' summoned by Leibniz against Locke" (Oxford: Clarendon, 1995) 290.

8. Chopin, *Complete Works* 896–97.

9. James Engell in his essay "The Soul, Highest Cast of Consciousness" claims that for the Romantics "the exploration of the soul means an exploration of human nature, of inner life and being as it confronts experience. To speak about the soul in this way engages what might be called Romantic humanism. When C. S. Lewis first read the Romantic poets, he noticed this undogmatic, spiritual sensibility, and later wrote in his autobiography *Surprised by Joy*: 'The only non-Christians who seemed to me really to know anything were the Romantics; and a good many of them were dangerously tinged with something like religion.'" *The Cast of Consciousness: Concepts of the Mind in British and American Romanticism*, ed. Beverly Taylor and Robert Bain (New York: Greenwood, 1987) 3–4.

10. Chopin, *Complete Works* 896.

11. Sara deSaussure Davis, "Chopin's Movement toward Universal Myth," *Kate Chopin Reconsidered: Beyond the Bayou*, ed. Lynda S. Boren and Sara deSaussure Davis (Baton Rouge: Louisiana State UP, 1992) 201.

12. *Biographia Literaria* chap. 14.

13. Dead Poets Society, dir. Peter Weir, perf. Robin Williams, Touchstone, 1989. Film.

14. Atara Stein, "Immortals and Vampires and Ghosts, Oh My! Byronic Heroes in Popular Culture." Romantic Circles. Ed. Neil Fraistat, Steven E. Jones, and Carl Stahmer. U of Maryland, 15 Feb. 2007. Web. 2 Jan. 2009.

15. See J. A. Ward, The Imagination of Disaster: Evil in the Fiction of Henry James (Lincoln: U of Nebraska P, 1961), and Dorothea Krook, The Ordeal of Consciousness in Henry James (Cambridge: Cambridge UP, 1962).

16. Chopin, Complete Works 908.

17. Chopin, Complete Works 908–9.

18. Chopin, Complete Works 909.

19. Chopin, Complete Works 906.

20. Chopin, Complete Works 909–10.

21. Barbara Ewell, "Kate Chopin and the Dream of Female Selfhood," Boren and Davis 164.

22. Chopin, Complete Works 1000.

23. Anne Rice, Interview with the Vampire (New York: Ballantine, 1976).

24. Brian J. Frost, The Monster with a Thousand Faces: Guises of the Vampire in Myth and Literature (Bowling Green: Bowling Green State U Popular P, 1989).

25. Frost 38–39.

26. Chopin, Complete Works 959.

27. Chopin, Complete Works 959–60.

28. Chopin, Complete Works 960.

29. Chopin, Complete Works 976.

30. Chopin, Complete Works 993.

31. Chopin, Complete Works 997.

32. Chopin, Complete Works 1000.

3

EXPANSIONS

10

Kate Chopin and the Future of Short Fiction Studies

SUSAN LOHAFER

SINCE LEARNING ABOUT THE PLAN to revisit Kate Chopin, I have been asking myself why an essay on this writer has appeared in each of my three books on short fiction theory even though I have never considered myself a Chopin scholar. Clearly, she has been useful to me for reasons I look forward to recovering, but I believe she has also influenced me—a genre theorist with no special interest in either feminist or regional literature—in ways that have affected my changing conception of the short story form. Getting back in touch with her stories shows me something else, too. She has something to say to those interested in the future of short fiction studies. In particular, she has something to offer those of us who are working in the boundary zone between genre theory and cognitive science.

Yes, of course, she has had her place as a regionalist; later, she was recognized as an early naturalist, and, as this volume will testify, she continues to be an inspiration to readers craving an honest portrayal of female experience. For a historian of the short story like Richard Fusco, she brought to the American tale the wry clarity and formal economy of the French conte, and surely it was this wired strength beneath the quaint surface that first attracted me in the late seventies.[1] She has often been the victim of a condescending accolade—that she is the mistress of an "artless art"—and perhaps it isn't surprising that I turned to her at about the time I was noticing, and deciding to resist, a similar condescension toward the genre itself. However, there was a simpler and more nostalgic reason for choosing to work with Chopin. Years earlier I had written my dissertation and first book on an unrelated topic, but under the guidance of

William M. Gibson, friend of an early Chopin scholar, George Arms. I am quite sure that I first encountered "Athénaïse" in my mentor's classroom at New York University.

In *Coming to Terms with the Short Story* (1983), I was interested in developing a genre-specific vocabulary for talking about short stories.[2] At the time, most theoretical discussions borrowed heavily from the study of poetry or the novel or from the general domain of narratology. I was then using available notions of spatiality and linearity, combined with stylistic analysis and my own closure-based model of narrative progression. Later in the book, I applied these terms and this model to selected short stories, including "Athénaïse." Provincial, sentimental, feminine, French—there were plenty of labels. What I found, however, was a story so rooted in the primacies of the genre that it could survive each wave of dismissal, holding its own—in my terms, at least—with honored entries in the canon. To prove it, I had placed "Athénaïse" alongside Hawthorne's "Roger Malvin's Burial" in a chapter on American classics.

At first glance, the pairing still looks absurd. Yet, if you will, let me expand a moment on that comparison, for the sake of perspective. In his gravely historical opening, Hawthorne reminds us of the warfare between the settlers and the "Indians."[3] After a battle, wandering alone in the forest, a fatally wounded old man urges his young companion and intended son-in-law, Reuben Bourne, to save himself. Reuben allows himself to be persuaded, promising to return and bury the old man's remains. Back home, tended by the grieving daughter, presumed by everyone to have witnessed the old man's death and faithfully interred him, Reuben does not have the moral courage to admit that he left the old man to die alone. Just as a slanted history of the battle serves the self-image of the white community, so the tweaked story of Reuben's retreat serves his self-image as hero and soon-to-be husband and father. Eventually, as he tries to save his sinking fortunes by heading westward into the forest, he accidentally kills his beloved son—near the very tree where he had long ago abandoned the boy's grandfather. This cruel irony marks the *true* tale (the one Hawthorne gives us) that counters, illuminates, and revokes—but *does not erase*—the false ones by which Reuben has lived. In Hawthorne's world, maturity means accepting the burden of the fall.

"Athénaïse" is another story about delayed maturation.[4] Although it, too, sets a moral crisis beneath a tree, we can hardly imagine a world farther from Hawthorne's. From rugged North to languid South; from soldier's grit to girlish pique. William Gibson did say that Chopin is concerned with "the truths of the human heart in the vein of Hawthorne and Faulkner," but the same might be said of many a writer.[5] My interest at the time was in moving away from thematic interpretations and toward an analysis based on the movement from threshold to closure.

There are two linear progressions within the story, as each of the central characters—Cazeau and Athénaïse—evolves in his or her new role as a marital partner. Athénaïse, indulged by a carefree childhood, remains a girl, annoyed by the household responsibilities and physical importunities of her new estate. The older Cazeau, though genuinely in love, remains a plantation owner whose latest acquisition is not what he expected. His young wife flees to her mother's house, is retrieved by Cazeau, and then, with her brother's connivance, escapes to New Orleans. Ensconced in a genteel boardinghouse, she becomes friendly with a man of the world whose code prevents him from abusing her innocence. His company is delightful, her freedom is heady, and the amenities of the city beguile her. Soon, though, she is fretful and homesick. It is the landlady who reveals to her that she is pregnant. Touched by the wand of maternity, Athénaïse blooms instantly into womanhood, ready and eager for the role—and the passion—of a wife.

And what of Cazeau? He had pursued her on that first retreat to her childhood home, forcing her to return with him. Chagrined and defiant, she had galloped ahead. Following her, he had passed an old oak tree that triggered, suddenly, a memory from his past. His father, herding a recaptured slave past this very spot, had stopped to allow the black man to rest. The mental picture disturbs Cazeau. While he does not make a conscious connection between his wife and the slave, this is his moment of transformation. It is a scene of moral reckoning, triggered (as, in part, was Reuben Bourne's) by an overlap of past and present beneath the canopy of nature. Thereafter, and throughout his wife's absence in New Orleans, Cazeau will refrain from imposing his will. When she does return to him, he, too, has evolved. He no longer confuses "husband" with "master."

It is easy to see the his-and-her trajectories. In crisscrossing so neatly, they create a spatial design that firms and compresses the narrative within the boundaries of the "short" genre. As I look back, though, it is easier for me to see that formality is not the point. Balance is. Focusing too exclusively on Athénaïse encourages a reading of the story prejudicial to the emancipation of women. Such a reading emphasizes the biological determinism—romantic in a warm light; naturalistic in a cool one—that makes a woman of Athénaïse only when, *and only because*, she fulfills the procreative role. On the surface, it is the most conventional and conservative of endings, turning the girl's defiance into the womb's victory. Focusing on both of the narrative arcs throws more emphasis on the fluctuations of power, on the shifting loci of authority. Legal duty, male desire, marital custom—these are Cazeau's guides before his enlightenment. Sensitivity, love, and decency—these are the promptings of his finer nature, and in listening to them, he becomes a better man and, therefore, a better husband.

Cazeau is shamed into respecting his wife's free will. His growth attests to his moral capacity. Athénaïse finds her identity through the ripening of her body. Her growth attests to her healthy hormones. If this story is a problem for feminists, if its cozy ending disappoints when compared with the edgy irony of "The Story of an Hour" or the wry amorality of "The Storm" (not to mention the potent drama of *The Awakening*), then it is perhaps useful to look a little more closely at the design of the story, as I was doing in the late seventies. And when we do, the pairing of trajectories says less about sexism than about Chopin's evenhandedness. She enjoys Athénaïse; she admires Cazeau. Perhaps, for her, there was no privileging of the ethical over the instinctual. The body and its needs often have something like a moral force in the world of her fiction, exerting as powerful a guiding force, and exacting as stiff a penalty for suppression, as the gnawing sins of the Puritan. What strikes me now is that the ending of Chopin's story, a woman's ear attuned to an infant's cry, seems as neat as Reuben's melted heart. But it is not. It is just a point of intersection. The narrative does, indeed, link sexual awakening with conventional marriage, but with this story—unlike Hawthorne's—there is no reason to assume that the path of experience has traced a full circle, a period for all eternity. Unlike the sin-and-redemption cycle, the phases of a marriage are many. The wheel will turn again. In Chopin's world, maturity means accepting life's vagaries.

That perspective, which seems truer to the underlying humor of Chopin's vision, is even more relevant to the second story I'll revisit. "Aunt Lympy's Interference" came to my aid twice, first in a chapter of my coedited collection Short Story Theory at a Crossroads (1989), and then again—in a reduced and slightly changed version of the earlier essay—in my latest book, Reading for Storyness (2003), which points more decidedly toward empirical and cognitive study.[6] In the late eighties, still interested in finding methodologies and concepts uniquely suited to the study of short stories, I became interested in the text-processing experiments of cognitive psychologists. The alien yet elegant work of textual linguists and story grammarians convinced me of the genre's primal roots in the cognitive scenarios (a sort of neural hardwiring) by which humans make sense of their experience in short narrative bundles—that is, short stories.

According to some psychologists, children learn to recognize, tell, and process stories in about their fifth year. Before then, they are able to reel off strings of events, to tell "what happened," but a certain maturation of mind and exposure to the storytelling of elders are necessary before children develop true "story competence"—that is, the ability to select and order a series of events to make a point or send a message.[7] By the time these children morph into the young adults in my classroom, they are adepts at this basic mode of storing cultural information, mediating their emotions, and holding the attention of others. The least gifted, the least experienced of these readers has an innate sense of storyness that is rich in the DNA of literary history. Accessing it is the challenge.

Whereas I had conceived of whole-storyness as the movement of a text toward closure, I was now thinking of it as a cognitive strategy for chunking experience into tellable units and, in turn, for processing narratives that presented such chunks as readable "stories." The breakthrough came when I realized I could, in a limited way, isolate the capacity for recognizing storyness without divorcing it from the "normal" reading of a particular story. I could trigger that built-in capacity, watch it in action, and use it to shed light on the texts I was interested in and on the genre of the short story in general.

All of this was achieved by the simplest of experiments. I gave a group of readers a short story text and asked them to identify every point where they felt the story could end before it actually did. These sentences— preclosure points, I called them—told me where each reader's internal story meter had beeped, registering the completion of a viable tale. What I did with these data would vary from experiment to experiment, but I would always identify the most frequently chosen preclosure points. Because I could never predict these results with any certainty, and because I could never guess the choices of any particular reader, the findings had an aura of objectivity. However, as soon as I began to analyze the preclosure points, I would reclaim my subjectivity, my interests and habits as a literary critic, my focus as a genre theorist. And thus Chopin's amusing, romantic bagatelle became my "demo," the foundational expression of an evolving theory about the pre-oral roots of the short story *as a genre*.

As it happens, I had in this case the largest pool of readers I have ever been able to muster, including the widest cross section of educational levels: 90 high school students and 90 other readers who were mostly college age, with the addition of several teachers and a doctoral student. With 180 subjects, I felt some confidence in my findings. Why had *these* sentences, in particular, been chosen? Many of them came at the end of a paragraph, and in future experiments, I would remove indentations, white spaces, or other indications of section breaks to cancel the effect of merely visual cues. I was looking for other kinds of signals in these "end"-marked sentences. Eventually, I would develop a system for tracking the (pre)closure signals I discovered in these richly charged units of text, and I refer those interested to the published analyses. Here I'll just say that Chopin's little story flowered under the lens of preclosure study.

It is a minor story you may not remember. I chose it for its slightness (still nudging the critics who belittle the genre), for its cultural remove from my late-eighties students, and for its capacity (like "Athénaïse") to tempt and then frustrate ideological readings. The main character of "Aunt Lympy's Interference" is a young girl, Melitte, whose parents have apparently died and who is still living in her childhood home under the protection now of her brother and his wife. Down the road, the son of the neighboring landowner has returned from his travels and assumed his birthright. Melitte sees him at his work every day as she walks to the local school where she teaches. What is wrong with this picture? According to the traditions of her culture, Melitte is thrice displaced: no longer a daughter, she is not yet a wife, and, as a teacher, she is only a surrogate mother—and for hire, too!

The social stigma registers keenly on Aunt Lympy, a former family servant who feels responsible for Melitte's welfare. In regal sorrow, she visits Melitte, ostensibly to find out whether the awful rumor is true but really to urge the girl to think better of her choices. Melitte, affectionately amused but determined, stands her ground, and we soon learn that she takes pride in her small salary. To her, it represents not a social embarrassment but a personal achievement. Independence. Work she loves. In the character of Aunt Lympy the stereotype of the officious but loving black mammy is somewhat offset by the humor of the old woman's "interference." Behind Melitte's back, she writes to the girl's well-to-do uncle in New Orleans, painting a vivid picture of disgrace. Soon a letter comes for Melitte from her penitent uncle, opening his home to her, offering her a life of glamour and ease.

Whereas Athénaïse is a young bride who needs to grow into the role she nominally inhabits, Melitte must decide between three possible futures: as self-supporting teacher, as urban socialite, or as Victor's wife. The last option is, of course, not fully present until the end of the story, when Victor asks her to stay. And even though it is Victor who precipitates Melitte's "choice" to become his wife, that outcome is shaped by forces stronger than Aunt Lympy: the warm, fertile season; the girl's young, healthy body; Victor's proximity; Melitte's fondness for children. In the end, her concession to Victor may seem as old-fashioned and preordained as Athénaïse's maternal instinct.

Several of the preclosure points occurred within the body of the story, usually coinciding with a change of scene and a leaning toward one future or another. For example, Aunt Lympy's departure was considered by some readers as a possible ending to the story, at a moment when Melitte is happily and firmly committed to her life as a teacher. Another possible ending occurs when Melitte's eyes fill with tears after she petulantly cries, "Oh, I'll go," conceding to pressure to accept her good fortune.[8] Yet another possible ending comes when, under pressure from Victor, she tells him she'd consider staying if he asked her to do so. In that admission is the seed of the last option, her marriage to Victor. Interestingly, another group of preclosure points falls within the epilogue. There the authorial voice reasserts itself in a wry summary of the reactions to Melitte's choice. What is worth restating here is that the preclosure points reemphasize the serialized presentation of the alternate futures, but also the larger perspective, unseen by Melitte, that shades all her options with humor and irony. The authorial commentary takes a dig at the elders who've forgotten what it is like to be young and suggests that Aunt Lympy may have lost the battle yet won her campaign: Melitte has been saved from a sin against her class.

Whatever *we* may think of Melitte's fate—and I suspect our opinions, too, would be subject to Chopin's wit—the upshot of the preclosure experiment was to highlight the structural importance of Melitte's three options for adulthood. At the time, I was interested in the demographics of the reading population, correlating preclosure choices with such variables as the respondents' gender, level of schooling, and experience with creative writing vis-à-vis training in critical analysis. As I mentioned earlier, I reworked the material slightly for inclusion in my most recent book, Reading for Storyness. However, I did not update it completely, did not bring to bear upon it the later developments of preclosure theory. That is what I would like to do now.

For my study of individual preclosure points, I had developed a system for identifying and coding preclosure signals. These included local markers, such as the repetition of letters, words, phrases, and so on, or the syntactic inversion of subject and verb, or the presence of inherently closural words such as "last" or "end" or "final" or of keywords with special meaning in the story. There were also global markers, suggestions within a given sentence that a larger arc was ending there. In naming these global shapes, I relied on standard notions of resolution, in particular the work of John Gerlach, who had studied the kinds of closure often found in American short stories.[9] These included, among others, the resolution of a problem; natural terminations like sleep, death, or sunset; antithesis (or paradox); and moral encapsulation.

So I had been in the habit of looking at portions of the text retrospectively from the vantage point of each preclosure point. After analyzing the local features, I would shift to a global perspective. For example, consider sentence #163. Melitte, having had her hand seized through the schoolroom window and having confessed that she would stay if Victor asked her, adds, "Oh—never mind my hand; don't you see I must shut the window?"[10] Even though Melitte is pettishly struggling to get back her hand (and her schoolroom), the question of her future is resolved. Why? Because her deepest need has been fulfilled: to be loved where she resides. The play of local resistance against global concession gives the sentence its charm, humor, and sly subversiveness. Other preclosure sentences offered their own freight of meaning when viewed as the terminus of a shorter short story.

It was a small methodological step to grant these embedded spans of text their own status and viability. It proved, however, to be a large theoretical shift in the practice of preclosure study. Here is how it works. After the favored preclosure points have been analyzed on their own, our attention can move to the narratives they complete. These embedded units are "putative stories." Each, of course, includes the earlier one(s) within itself, until actual closure arrives and the "actual story" is complete. The more I thought about these putative stories, the more interesting they became. They resulted from—and, indeed, concretized—that faculty I'd been calling the recognition of storyness. Often, these putative stories looked familiar. That is, they aligned themselves with familiar types of short narratives. There were love stories, parables, fairy tales, revenge plots, slice-of-life stories—the possibilities were as endless as the history of story making. What happens when you fold out a text into a series of putative stories, each with a resonance within the history of the short story?

The existence of these inner texts is derived from the evidence of preclosure experiments. Inner texts are not foreign to narratology. But who or what authorizes the labeling of these units as a type of story, and what is gained by so doing? Those are questions I addressed in Reading for Storyness, and will glance at again in the following discussion. Now is the time to say, as forcefully as possible, that we are in the realm of judgment here, not fact. Preclosure study is truly a marriage of science and art. If I were to do the original experiment again with a different group of 180 readers—or even the same group of 180 readers—the favored preclosure points would be different. Were another scholar to label those different putative stories—or even the same putative stories I have isolated—his or her terms would differ from mine. In other words, the collection of preclosure points and the labeling of putative stories are not repeatable in the scientific sense. The results can't be duplicated. Yet both activities are endlessly and fruitfully repeatable in another sense. Each experiment, each set of preclosure points, says something real and true about the story and its readers. Each labeling of the putative stories says something informative about the story's structure (and hence its meaning), but also something about the taste and experience of the investigator, the person whose vision is reflected in the exercise. Isn't that one definition of scholarship in the humanities?

When I was asked to revisit my relationship to Chopin, I knew I had unfinished business with "Aunt Lympy's Interference." Previously, I had discussed the favored preclosure points, even talked about the way each brought to a close one phase of Melitte's struggle to define herself. However, my work with the story predated the concept of "putative stories" and the role they can play in literary criticism. I am grateful for the chance to carry that work forward, but my aim isn't really to elucidate a story. I would like to illustrate an approach and, by doing so, place Chopin at the center of a minority report on recent trends in criticism. Most of all, I would like to suggest where short fiction theory may be heading in the future.

The original experiment netted at least nine preclosure points, but I will focus on only six here. Clearly, this is an arbitrary decision. On another occasion, three might serve the purpose. I will take each of the six sentences in order and talk about the putative story they conclude. Percentages refer to the number of readers who chose each preclosure point.

Sentence #107: The familiar road was a brown and green blur, for the tears in her eyes. (p. 515) [17%]

> Melitte has received the offer to live with her uncle, and is feeling hurt that no one at home has urged her to stay. She is now on her way to the school where she teaches, telling herself "Oh, I'll go! I will go!" to New Orleans.

When Melitte says, "Oh, I'll go!" and tears blur the road ahead of her, she is at a low point in her self-estimation. Half willfully, and mostly—as Chopin wisely points out—to give herself an excuse for an emotionality whose source is hidden from her, Melitte has convinced herself that nobody loves her enough to ask her to stay home. Whatever the deeper reasons, the effective dynamic here is submission to the expectations of others. Everybody thinks she should jump at the chance to be pampered by her uncle. Nobody admires her independence as a self-supporting teacher. The story that ends here is about social pressure. I would call it a tribal parable. This term emphasizes the portrait of group pressure, but also an underlying model of human experience. Survival of a class, a region, a culture, a way of life, depends upon just such conservative patterns as patrimony and matrimony: Victor's return to his father's estate; Melitte's co-option by that neighboring family. Melitte's tears are a girlish and transitory price to pay for the continuance of the Annibelles' world.

Sentence #162: "I believe I would, Victor." (p. 517) [19%]

> Victor has accosted her on the way to school, she has reacted petulantly to his assumption that she will be leaving, and he has confessed that he "can't bear to have [her] go"—the very response she has longed for. He has waited outside the school until closing time and has now asked if she'd stay if he begged her.

Earlier, when Melitte had asked Victor if he'd been planning to let her leave without saying good-bye, he had replied, "I believe I was." Now, when she responds to his indirect proposal by saying "I believe I would," she is not only reciprocating his love but echoing his language. What is that but the marriage plot in miniature, a love story with the usual goal of "I do's." Or, at least, "I believe's." Victor and Melitte are testing a commitment to a future together.

Sentence #163: "Oh—never mind my hand; don't you see I must shut the window?" (p. 517) [20%]

> As noted earlier, this is Melitte's mock impatience with Victor's importunity, but also a link back to the story's initial image of an open window through which Victor's house is visible and the scent of flowers sensuously fills the air.

Woman's hand is captured; man stakes his claim ("I reckon it's instinct fo' a man to fight fo' his happiness just as he would fight fo' his life").[11] Woman outwardly resists but is inwardly fulfilled. As I've already suggested, there are ambiguities in this sentence that enrich its simplicity and complicate its conservatism. Victor has made an indirect marriage proposal, Melitte has indicated her acceptance, they are on the brink of a new life together—and yet—and yet this sentence is about withdrawing the hand, about shutting the window. Victor is (still) on the outside and Melitte is (still) on the inside—of her school, of her life as a teacher. Is this simply prim coquettishness, or is it a signal—patent to the reader, liminal for Melitte—that the marital option, or, indeed, the marriage plot itself, is no "happily ever after"? Between one sentence and the next, one putative story and the next, a window sash has dropped. Were the story to end with this image, the love story might be skewed ever so slightly toward a cautionary tale. Melitte is not ready.

Sentence #164: So after all Melitte did not go to the city to become a grande dame. (p. 517) [23%]

> This is the beginning of the epilogue in which an expository, authorial voice takes over and summarizes reactions to Melitte's decision (presumably) to stay home and marry Victor.

The line is crawling with preclosure. "So" implies logical summary; "after" implies temporal shift; "all" is an absolute; "grande dame" is a keyword identifying one of Melitte's three optional identities; "did not go" states an antithesis or reversal that (given all the pressures on Melitte to go) has the strongest closural force of all. That leaves the keyword "city." It refers to New Orleans, but it also resonates with a long history of linked opposition to "country." The story opens with a vision of rural Louisiana, where men are working in the cotton fields and the scent of flowers and fertile soil is intoxicating. On her way to work each day, Melitte trips daintily along a country road. When the parish priest comes to visit, he, assuming like everyone else that Melitte should go to New Orleans, nevertheless warns her, in principle, of "the perils and fascinations of 'the city's' life."[12] So might the local curé speak to a young man of the provinces about to seek his fortune in Paris. The paradigm is familiar. Yet Melitte never does leave the blooming fields, never does trade the rural simplicity for the urban excitement. By not going to "the city," she has opted for the village idyll.

[Sentence #165: Why?] Sentence #166: Simply because Victor Annibelle asked her not to. (p. 517) [21%]

> The authorial voice continues, underscoring the point that Melitte had wanted someone to confirm that she was needed and loved in her familiar world.

Three paths in a wood. Three wishes. Three gifts. Such patterning of experience is common in folklore. There is something magical about a desire neatly fulfilled, a wish brought to life. Melitte desperately wants someone to say, "I can't bear to have you go."[13] That yearning, that power of wishful thinking, has efficacy in her world. Her heart's desire materializes in the form of the blushing young man who, on cue, says, "I can't bear to have you go."[14] Why didn't she go? "Simply because" the hero came through for her. There is a good deal of psychological realism in Chopin's story, but there is also an echo of wish fulfillment, a suggestion of the domesticated fairy tale.

Sentence #168: Some of the younger ones thought she was right, and many of them believed she was wrong to sacrifice so brilliant an opportunity to shine and become a woman of fashion. (p. 517) [24%]

> Having noted the reaction of the "old people," the author now comments on the split opinions of "the younger ones," suggesting that most think Melitte should have chosen the more worldly and glamorous option.

Here ends the last of the putative stories I'll discuss. The "city," along with its temptations, has resurfaced. It is the option many of Melitte's contemporaries would have chosen. Chopin, with typical neutrality, is reminding us of the fluidity and diversity of public opinion. Perhaps she is also reminding us that there are two sides to every story. We've already met a woman of Melitte's class—Athénaïse—who chose the city over the country, freedom over marriage, for a brief span of time. Whether such choices are "right" or "wrong" depends upon the point of view, upon the season in a life, upon the needs that are uppermost. The expository coda of this story might seem an artistic blemish if it were not so important for us to realize that Melitte's fait is not accompli. By leaving us in the court of local opinion, by showing us that its judgment is split, Chopin takes us back to the dilemma. We know what Melitte chose, but what if . . . ? What if Melitte had really shut that window, packed up her pencils, and headed for New Orleans? What if she marries Victor and then wishes she hadn't? A story that keeps us thinking, that raises complicated issues, is a problem narrative.

Preclosure analysis always leads us, eventually, to the "real" end. As noted earlier, the story concludes with the wry suggestion that Aunt Lympy won after all. She "felt that her interference had not been wholly in vain."[15] Melitte has been reabsorbed into respectable society. Why isn't Aunt Lympy happier? It's worth recalling that her "interference" was not only for Melitte's sake. Her real goal is family solidarity. We know, too, that the priest would have been "happy to see the end of a family estrangement."[16] (No details are given, but as the beneficent uncle is on the maternal side, and as Aunt Lympy implied a guilty obligation to his dead sister, we can imagine a possible scenario: Melitte's mother may have left her New Orleans home, against her family's wishes, in order to marry into the community where Melitte decides to stay. The decision to marry Victor would thus be, from Aunt Lympy's perspective, a replay of the past, a second disappointment, a second-best victor-y. What volumes of familial and social irony lie within this delightful little story of a girl who gets her man.)

Preclosure study pries open the folds of apparent simplicity. Analyzing the preclosure points, sentence by sentence, is the first step. Identifying the putative stories, tale by tale, is the next phase of critical inquiry. But it isn't the last. In *Reading for Storyness*, I began looking at the progression of the putative stories. Because they were serially and overlappingly embedded in the actual text, they offered yet another form of metanarrative structure, yet another way of talking about the much meaning within the little compass of the short story. What do we see when we look at the following progression: *tribal parable—love story—cautionary tale—village idyll—domesticated fairy tale—problem narrative*? We see Chopin's versatility, but we also find a metanarrative. In the first two putative stories, a self-regulating social order is confirmed. The third offers a minor countermovement, a check on the optimism of the first two. The fourth and fifth are again confirmatory, though the domain is more fragile; idylls and fairy tales are always poised over grief, holding it at bay or mediating its terms. Finally, the sixth putative story picks up the note of caution, deepening it to a wise neutrality.

Perused in a beeline from first word to last, this is a story with a "happy ending." Read recursively, read with an eye to the putative stories embedded within it, this is a story about the coexistence of options. Read alone, this is a story about a girl who gets to stay home, to marry her sweetheart, to have babies of her own, as adorable as that "little tot of a nephew who wabbled in" to announce Aunt Lympy's arrival.[17] Read in company with "Athénaïse," this is a story about a girl who briefly chose a role other than wife. Focusing on the putative stories allows us to see that, like those embedded texts, the alternative life choices are rejected but not removed. Like the cover stories in "Roger Malvin's Burial," the once-real options in Chopin's world never really go away, though their costs are seen differently. Will Athénaïse never yearn for those charming little dinners with Gouvernail? Will Melitte never wish that the money in her purse were her own?

These are, of course, the scenarios for other stories, any of which Chopin could have written, and some of which she did. Chopin's vision of the world, her tolerance for erratic desire, makes her stories unusually receptive to the kind of analysis I've performed. Where her texts may appear "artless" in form, or conversely, too neatly wrapped up; where they may appear more sentimental than in her more famous work; where they seem more sketchy and regional than rooted in the global history of storying—even there, *especially* there, we find richer work by looking for preclosure points and following their lead.

Perhaps that is why I have circled back to this author so often. Surely we do not need preclosure experiments to show us the undercurrents in Chopin's stories, although casual readers might miss them. My contention is simply that we get deeper faster, initially more objectively, and with more grist for our mill if we give ourselves the benefit of this analysis. What we are bringing to our aid is not only the powerful engine of our cognitive capacities for storying—a gift shared by humankind and of surprising interest to the best and the weakest of our students—but also our training and experience as the closest of readers and as genre specialists.

If this sounds like formalism-by-the-back-door, it is. But I would also suggest that it is a handy side entrance to the exciting arena of empirical research in cognitive poetics. I would argue that it is a path around the preemptive deployment of fashionable ideology. At the same time, preclosure study helps us identify the cultural issues that derive from (rather than precondition) a word-by-word experience of the text. Interpretive bias is still present. It just comes into play later, with a greater chance of being turned to account as the freshness of approach we value in a critic. Looking back on Chopin, I see also my graduate mentor, whose age at the time of his death was not so far from mine now. Retrospectives can be sobering, as any Hawthorne plot reveals, but fables are rechargeable, as any preclosure point will demonstrate. There is always more to the story, as Bill Gibson knew. I would want him to know, too, that there is more to the project of short fiction theory.

We are being told that the world is, after all, "flat."[18] There is no language more global than Microsoft, but there is a layer of understanding more profound, and it is encoded in our sense of storyness. If we are going to learn something new about literature and how it functions cross-culturally, the answers will be coming from empirical research. We will need a working relationship between those who read stories and those who read neurons. We can use Chopin's help.

NOTES

1. Richard Fusco, *Maupassant and the American Short Story: The Influence of Form at the Turn of the Century* (University Park: Pennsylvania State UP, 1994).

2. Susan Lohafer, *Coming to Terms with the Short Story* (1983; Baton Rouge: Louisiana State UP, 1985).

3. Nathaniel Hawthorne, "Roger Malvin's Burial," *Nathaniel Hawthorne's Tales*, ed. James McIntosh (New York: Norton, 1987).

4. Kate Chopin, *The Complete Works of Kate Chopin*, ed. Per Seyersted (Baton Rouge: Louisiana State UP, 1969) 426–54.

5. William M. Gibson, "Love in Louisiana: Kate Chopin, a Forgotten Southern Novelist," rev. of *Kate Chopin: A Critical Biography*, by Per Seyersted, and *The Complete Works of Kate Chopin*, ed. Seyersted, *Times Literary Supplement* [London] 9 Oct. 1970: 1163.

6. Susan Lohafer and Jo Ellyn Clarey, eds., *Short Story Theory at a Crossroads* (Baton Rouge: Louisiana State UP, 1989). See also Susan Lohafer, *Reading for Storyness: Preclosure Theory, Empirical Poetics, and Culture in the Short Story* (Baltimore: Johns Hopkins UP, 2003).

7. Margaret S. Benson, "The Structure of Four- and Five-Year-Olds' Narratives in Pretend Play and Storytelling," *First Language* 13 (1993): 203–23.

8. Chopin, *Complete Works* 515.

9. John Gerlach, *Toward the End: Closure and Structure in the American Short Story* (Tuscaloosa: U of Alabama P, 1985).

10. Chopin, *Complete Works* 517.

11. Chopin, *Complete Works* 517.

12. Chopin, *Complete Works* 514.

13. Chopin, *Complete Works* 515.

14. Chopin, *Complete Works* 516.

15. Chopin, *Complete Works* 517.

16. Chopin, *Complete Works* 514.

17. Chopin, *Complete Works* 523.

18. Thomas L. Friedman, *The World Is Flat: A Brief History of the Twenty-first Century*, updated ed. (New York: Farrar, 2006).

11

Reckoning with Race in *The Awakening*

ANNA SHANNON ELFENBEIN

WHEN I WAS IN HIGH SCHOOL and college in the 1960s, no one I knew
had ever heard of Kate Chopin. She first came to my attention in 1973,
when I was a graduate student in English at the University of Nebraska–
Lincoln. It was a sign of the times that my introduction to Chopin took
place, not in an American literature course, but in a women's restroom
in the university's English Department, where I happened to overhear
a sotto voce conversation about "The Storm." Curious as to what all the
fuss was about, I went straight to the library and found Per Seyersted's
recently published edition of her complete works.[1] Because of the honesty
and artistry of her novels and stories, discovering this volume was, for
me, an electrifying experience. It was also a life-altering one inasmuch
as Chopin's works sparked my interest in feminism, awakened me to the
need for primary research that would serve to excavate our lost tradition
of women writers, inspired me to do such research myself, and eventually
determined the course of my academic career.

At the time of my serendipitous introduction to Chopin, I was not yet
a feminist critic or even a feminist and did not yet understand that some
of what I was encountering in my courses and my reading was the result
of sexual politics. Thus, when I wept at the plight of Catherine Sloper in
Henry James's *Washington Square*, I did so because her yearning for her
father's love remains unfulfilled and not, as I do now, because she is a
woman in a patriarchal society whose opportunities for self-expression
and fulfillment are perforce few.[2] By the same token, I was not yet aware
that the syllabi in my English courses were biased in favor of male authors; nor was I yet familiar with the female authors who were being un-

justly neglected. It was my reading of Chopin's works that gave rise to the realization there were women writers who deserved to be included in the first rank of American authors but had been excluded from the canon because they were women and had written from a woman's perspective. And it was the interaction between that reading and certain aspects of my personal life that produced a shift in my consciousness and set me on the path to becoming a feminist and a feminist critic.

In 1973, of course, women's writing did not yet enjoy the prestige we now take for granted. This was evident, for example, in the graduate course I had taken on American literary realism, which had given me and my fellow students the impression that an author had to be male in order to be a realist worthy of being read. The course had exposed me to the fiction of George Washington Cable, a contemporary of Chopin's who wrote, as she did, about life in New Orleans, and had prompted me to think about issues of race and class in ways that would later inform my work on Chopin. But it had left me in the dark about Chopin and about the other women authors who could and should have been on the syllabus. So normative was the male bias of the Nebraska curriculum in the early 1970s that even Willa Cather, now venerated as the tutelary icon of the university's Center for Great Plains Studies, was then stigmatized among many of the faculty members and graduate students in Lincoln as a "regional" author of marginal importance.

The revolution was not long in coming, however. By the end of the decade, thanks in part to the transformation of literary studies catalyzed by the rediscovery of The Awakening, faculty members teaching American realism had begun to assign works by Chopin, and scholars at the University of Nebraska–Lincoln had begun to take pride in Cather. Today it is not uncommon for undergraduates to tell me that they are interested in Chopin because they had read her stories in high school. Such comments remind me of how far the discipline has come since I was in college.

The work that eventually culminated in my own modest contributions to Chopin scholarship commenced in 1976, when I decided to write a dissertation on the ways in which racial issues are treated in her fiction and that of George Cable. While I was discussing my dissertation topic with Linda Ray Pratt, one of the few women faculty members in Nebraska's English Department at the time, she told me about a recent dissertation by

James R. Frisby Jr. on the depiction of black characters in the fiction of five white southerners writing in the period 1870–1900.[3] After reading Frisby's discussion and discovering, to my relief, that he had not preempted the topics of interest to me, I began to explore the issues of race, gender, and social class as they impinged upon the mixed-race women characters in postbellum Louisiana fiction. As Frisby had done, I employed techniques of close reading, but I restricted myself to three of the five New Orleans authors considered by him: Chopin, Cable, and Grace King. My selection of them was grounded in a belief that their contrasting accounts of their racially stratified society might yield new insights into the ideologies of oppression.

Cable and Chopin challenged the nostalgic, romanticized view of the Old South purveyed by such plantation-school authors as Thomas Nelson Page and Joel Chandler Harris but did so in different ways. Cable's principal objective was to launch an attack upon racial injustice and hypocrisy. His searing depiction in *The Grandissimes* of the internecine racism of New Orleans at the time of the Louisiana Purchase exposed facts white southerners like myself were often inclined to deny, even to themselves: that their families extended into black communities and that racism and racial discrimination therefore violated their most basic human obligations.[4] Cable sometimes diluted the effectiveness of his realistic portrayal of racial prejudice, however, by incorporating into his narratives sentimental and didactic stories of love between chivalrous white men and beautiful near-white women. In addition, he was less enlightened on the woman question than on the issue of race.

Chopin, in contrast, grappled courageously and insightfully with sexual issues that Cable and the authors of the plantation school had been unable to confront in their fiction. She asked her readers to reflect upon the destructive power of sexual passion by presenting them with unflinchingly realistic accounts of the plight of exploited women on both sides of the color line. The purpose of fiction, Chopin once said, was to depict "human existence in its subtle, complex, true meaning, stripped of the veil with which ethical and conventional standards have draped it."[5] In my dissertation I tried to demonstrate that one of the hallmarks of her own fiction is the consistency with which it subverts convention and reveals the truth about women's sexual nature.

The research I did for the dissertation consisted of a close examination of the women of color and ambiguous race who appear in stories by Cable, King, and Chopin that are explicitly about racial issues. Spotting the appearances and reappearances of these characters, tracing their trajectories, analyzing the ways in which white characters interact with them, and reflecting upon their functions in the narratives yielded insights, some of which were surprising, into the nexus of gender, class, and race in the fictional worlds they inhabit.

I completed my dissertation and received my PhD in 1979. After entering the academic job market in that same year, I discovered that my dissertation topic was affecting my search for a teaching position in an unexpected way. At the time there was an acute shortage of openings for new graduates of doctoral programs in English, and I was therefore surprised when I received about twenty invitations to interview with hiring committees at the convention of the Modern Language Association. During the interviews I quickly learned that the title of my dissertation, "Women on the Color Line," had caused most of the interviewers to presume, incorrectly, that I must be a woman of color myself and hence someone who could help their departments to meet their affirmative-action goals. Had I yielded to the temptation to try to pass myself off as an African American job candidate, I might by now be well schooled in the frustrations of being the lone black professor in a large, lily-white department. My African American colleague Ethel Morgan Smith describes what it is like to be in that position in a humorous essay, which includes an account of the nonce attention and the many speaking invitations she receives every year around the time of Black History Month.[6]

While revising the dissertation in 1986, I submitted to *Southern Studies* a short essay that summarized my views of *The Awakening*. Entitled "Kate Chopin's *The Awakening*: An Assault on American Racial and Sexual Mythology," this article carries a publication date of 1987 but because of problems at the journal did not actually appear until two years later.[7] In 1994 Margo Culley reprinted the piece in the Norton Critical Edition of *The Awakening*.[8] The University Press of Virginia published an expanded and revised version of the dissertation in 1989 under the title *Women on the Color Line: Evolving Stereotypes and the Writings of George Washington*

Cable, Grace King, Kate Chopin.[9] Chopin's works are discussed in one of the book's chapters.[10]

In the early stages of my research on Chopin, it appeared to me that *The Awakening*, which is not centrally concerned with racial issues, had little relevance to my dissertation topic. While revising the dissertation for publication, however, I gave further thought to the novel and discovered that in fact race does play a major role in creating the no-exit situation faced by Edna Pontellier, Chopin's white, upper-class heroine. For by committing adultery, Edna violates the code of sexual conduct applied by her patriarchal, racist society to women of her race and class and engages in behavior deemed by that society to be appropriate only for women of color and of the lower class. And it is her transgression of this racial and class norm, together with her inability to free herself from the constraints of convention, that causes her to take her own life.

The gradual process by which I arrived at these conclusions about *The Awakening* began with my analysis in the dissertation of "Désirée's Baby," the most famous of Chopin's stories. In my discussion of the story, I examined the one woman of mixed race who appears in it and the ways in which she affects Désirée Aubigny, its central character, and that examination later helped me to find the key to understanding the function of the many "dark" women in the novel. The woman on the color line in "Désirée's Baby" is the mysterious La Blanche, a light-skinned slave owned by Désirée's planter husband, Armand. Instead of allowing La Blanche to appear or speak in the story, Chopin presents a series of incidents that reveal telling bits of information about her. In one such incident Désirée says that Armand can hear his infant son crying as far away as La Blanche's cabin; in another Désirée reacts with horror when she sees La Blanche's son and her own together. Thus, through the absent presence of La Blanche, Chopin provides her readers with provocative clues that invite them to speculate about certain unanswered questions such as whether Armand has had a sexual relationship with La Blanche since his marriage to Désirée and the birth of their child and whether Désirée perceives a family resemblance between La Blanche's boy and her own. From these clues and the inferences they support, readers can construct their own interpretations of the story.

I first noticed the subtle way in which Chopin had employed the character of La Blanche to illuminate Désirée's plight in the late 1970s. It was not until several years later, however, that it occurred to me to investigate whether women characters of mixed or ambiguous race perform a similar function in The Awakening. My discovery that such characters do in fact shed light on the psychology and the plight of Edna Pontellier formed the basis for the critical essays I subsequently published on the novel.

One of the influences that guided me as I was seeking to gain insight into the pernicious effects of Edna's socialization as a privileged white woman was the powerful critique of white feminism constructed by Alice Walker and other black feminists in the late 1970s and early 1980s. Addressing the convention of the National Women's Studies Association in 1979, Walker said that her efforts to inform Patricia Meyer Spacks, her white feminist colleague at Princeton University and the author of The Female Imagination, of the literary achievements of women of color had made her feel as if she were hitting a brick wall.[11] When Walker pointed out that The Female Imagination, a study of the themes and tropes to be found in the writings of British and American women, does not consider a single black author, I was immediately struck by the validity of her protest. Reflecting upon Walker's remarks, I recognized that they applied to my own research as well inasmuch as my dissertation examined in some detail the works of three white authors who had written about racially marginalized women but considered the perspectives of black authors only cursorily. I then attempted to correct my error by reading Zora Neale Hurston, Nella Larsen, Charles Waddell Chesnutt, and other African American authors whose works were relevant to my subject and by adding citations to them to the dissertation. This transformation of my critical perspective and practice alerted me to the possibility that race is a more significant aspect of The Awakening than I had originally thought.

Reading Ain't I a Woman: Black Women and Feminism by bell hooks, another African American critic, forced me to confront the fact that I had been guilty, albeit unconsciously, of another type of racial bias when writing the dissertation.[12] In the text I had made frequent use of the phrase "blacks and women" without realizing that it is often employed by white writers who understand "blacks" to refer exclusively to black men and "women" to refer exclusively to white women. In her analysis of the phrase, hooks points out that its use in any discussion has the effect of leaving black women out of account. Embarrassed by the discovery that I had engaged in the same kind of unconscious verbal exclusion I had been urging my students to avoid by shunning the generic pronouns he and him, I immediately deleted this offensive expression from my manuscript.

In addition to prompting me to restore women of color to my text by deleting references to "blacks and women," Walker, hooks, and other African American feminist critics inspired me to take notice of the black and mixed-race women who inhabit *The Awakening* and to appreciate the crucial role they play in the novel. By making a careful study of their interactions with Edna, I was able to gain a deeper understanding of the novel's protagonist than would otherwise have been possible. The interaction between Edna and her maid in the scene in which Edna breaks a vase and throws down her wedding ring, and the maid picks up the ring and hands it back to her, illustrates the way in which such women shed new light upon Edna's "awakening."

In my initial reading of this key scene, I had noticed that it echoes an earlier scene in which Edna's husband, Léonce, drops her rings into her hand, and I had interpreted the maid's action as a reinforcement of patriarchal power. Thanks to the insight I had derived from the black-feminist critique, I came to see that here the maid performs a far more important function than that of surrogate for Edna's husband. For by entering the room while Edna is throwing her tantrum and by cleaning up her employer's mess, the maid motivates Chopin's demonstration of Edna's self-centered presumption of privilege and her lack of consideration of other people. Once I could see Edna from the implied perspective of the maid, I looked for other indications of her narcissism and found that she fails repeatedly to concern herself with the interests of the women whose labor enables her to keep up appearances without lifting a finger.

Before swimming to her death, for example, Edna instructs Mariequita, a woman of color and one of the last people to see her alive, to order fish for a supper she does not intend to eat. Thus, to Edna's way of thinking, it is better to make needless work for Mariequita than to permit the truth about her suicide to be known. Edna's failure to take any interest in the plight of women like her maid and Mariequita is one manifestation of her inability to escape from the conventional constraints placed upon white, upper-class women by a racist, classist, and patriarchal society, and her suicide is another manifestation of that same inability.

As a consequence of my analysis of Edna's interactions with her maid, Mariequita, and other women on the color line, I came to appreciate how much Chopin had achieved by giving her readers a perceptive account of the way in which her protagonist's class- and race-bound perspective impairs her own awakening, the developmental process that commences when she begins, early in the novel, "to realize her position in the universe as a human being, and to recognize her relations as an individual to the world within and about her."[13] The effect of this insight into Edna's "white solipsism" on me and my interpretation of The Awakening was profound.[14] Although I had once identified with Edna, I came to realize that I had been as blind as she is to the costs her presumption of privilege imposes upon other women. And although I had once regarded her as an exemplary figure, I came to see her as a cautionary one whose conventional, class-bound attitudes not only harm other women but also circumscribe her sense of herself, causing her to think that, having committed adultery, she has no choice but to take her own life. In addition, I came to regard Edna's suicide, which I had once valorized as a testament to her refusal to be someone she is not, as evidence of the woman she is, a woman whose sexual behavior breaks with convention but whose thinking does not.

While reconsidering the scenes in which Edna interacts with the women who serve her, I also discovered that Chopin had represented realistically the alienation of these women from the tasks they must perform and, by extension, from the system that exacts their labor. In the wedding-ring scene, for example, Chopin has the maid sweep up the broken glass in defiance of Edna's explicit request that she postpone the chore until the following day and thus depicts her as behaving with passive aggression toward her heedless employer. Such scenes seemed to me to constitute evidence that Chopin had transcended the racist self-flattery to which most of the other white southern authors of her day had resorted by populating their fiction with black characters who are happy despite the subservience and backbreaking work that are their lot.

When I published my analyses of Chopin's treatment of race in The Awakening, I had not yet had the benefit of reading any extended discussions of the topic by other scholars. After I had completed my article and book, Helen Taylor published Gender, Race, and Region in the Writings of Grace King, Ruth McEnery Stuart, and Kate Chopin, in which she argued that "Chopin's racism is a central element in her writing," that Chopin had populated her fiction with "stereotypical black characters," and that she had "appropriated" the suffering of black people in order to dramatize the oppression of white women.[15] Subsequently, Elizabeth Ammons indicted Chopin for filling The Awakening with images of blacks that are "stereotypic and demeaning" and for purveying a fantasy of female liberation that is "purchased on the backs of black women."[16]

While writing about The Awakening myself, I was unable to address these provocative interpretations of the novel because they were not yet available to me. When they appeared, I found them to be difficult to reconcile with my own interpretation. For in my own reading of The Awakening, I had been struck by the fact that Chopin's depiction of black and mixed-race characters, albeit it sketchy and in some respects stereotypical by the standards of our own time, was enlightened relative to the manner in which her white southern contemporaries had portrayed such characters inasmuch as it refuted the myth of contented servitude by realistically rendering their alienation from their work and their employers. Despite my disagreement with Taylor and Ammons, however, I published no commentary on their interpretations of The Awakening because, by the time of their appearance, I had turned my attention away from Chopin and was focusing upon other subjects.

Notwithstanding our different interpretations of The Awakening, Ammons, Taylor, and I share the view that the way in which Chopin represented characters of color and ambiguous race in its pages is a topic worthy of study. In the first edition of the Norton Critical Edition of the novel, its editor, Margo Culley, did not reprint any essays on Chopin's treatment of race, presumably because no such criticism was available by the time of its publication in 1976.[17] Culley's decision to incorporate into the second incarnation of her critical edition not only my essay on the racial aspect of The Awakening but also excerpts from the books by Taylor and Ammons in which they comment on Chopin's dark characters testifies to the growing interest in this subject. Several of the scholars who have produced books or articles on the novel since Ammons, Taylor, and I published our discussions and since Norton's second edition appeared

have examined the subject as well.[18] Whatever they may think of my interpretation of The Awakening, I can derive some satisfaction from the fact
that a number of recent critics have concurred in my judgment that this
aspect of the novel deserves to be considered.

The question of whether I have succeeded in persuading other critics of the validity of my interpretation of The Awakening's representation
of race is difficult for me to answer because I have not been in touch
with many Chopin scholars since publishing my essays on her fiction. In
their published commentary on the novel, several critics have been kind
enough to acknowledge that they have been influenced by my reading of
it.[19] It is impossible for me to gauge, however, the extent to which their
views are typical of those held by the critical community in general. The
inclusion of my interpretation of The Awakening in the Norton edition of
the novel means, at the very least, that it has been and will continue to be
readily available to a great many of the college and high-school teachers
and students who have read or will read Chopin's masterpiece in their
English courses. I can only hope that some of them have also found or
will also find the essay to be illuminating.

In my work on The Awakening, I set out to demonstrate that the representations of characters of color and ambiguous race in the novel enrich
its social texture and enhance its characterization of the tragic false consciousness of Edna Pontellier. I tried to show that, far from being a blot
on this great novel, these representations are evidence of Chopin's genius
as a literary realist. Some other critics have implicitly rejected this argument because they regard her portrayals of characters on the color line as
evidence, not of her genius, but of her racism. The question of whether
one of these opposed interpretations is more persuasive than the other is
still a controversial one. It is my hope that as readers in the twenty-first
century ponder this issue and others raised by The Awakening, they will be
awakened, as I was more than three decades ago, to the richness and complexity of Edna's world and that some of them will also find, as I did, that
reading and reflecting upon the novel have altered their understanding of
themselves in fundamental ways.

NOTES

1. Kate Chopin, *The Complete Works of Kate Chopin*, ed. Per Seyersted (Baton Rouge: Louisiana State UP, 1969).

2. Henry James, *Washington Square* (New York, 1881).

3. James R. Frisby Jr., "New Orleans Writers and the Negro: George Washington Cable, Grace King, Ruth McEnery Stuart, Kate Chopin, and Lafcadio Hearn, 1870–1900," diss., Emory U, 1972.

4. George W. Cable, *The Grandissimes: A Story of Creole Life* (New York, 1880).

5. Chopin, *Complete Works* 691.

6. Ethel Morgan Smith, "Come and Be Black for Me," *Honey, Hush! An Anthology of African American Women's Humor*, ed. Daryl Cumber Dance (New York: Norton, 1998) 532–38.

7. Anna Shannon Elfenbein, "Kate Chopin's *The Awakening*: An Assault on American Racial and Sexual Mythology," *Southern Studies* 26 (1987): 304–12, rpt in Kate Chopin, "*The Awakening*": An Authoritative Text, Biographical and Historical Contexts, Criticism, ed. Margo Culley, 2nd ed. (New York: Norton, 1994) 292–99.

8. Chopin, "*The Awakening*," ed. Culley, 2nd ed. 292–99.

9. Anna Shannon Elfenbein, *Women on the Color Line: Evolving Stereotypes and the Writings of George Washington Cable, Grace King, Kate Chopin* (Charlottesville: UP of Virginia, 1989).

10. Elfenbein, *Women on the Color Line* 117–57.

11. Patricia Meyer Spacks, *The Female Imagination* (New York: Knopf, 1975).

12. bell hooks, *Ain't I a Woman: Black Women and Feminism* (Boston: South End, 1981).

13. Chopin, *Complete Works* 893.

14. For a discussion of white solipsism, see Adrienne Rich, "Disloyal to Civilization: Feminism, Racism, Gynephobia," *On Lies, Secrets, and Silence: Selected Prose, 1966–1978* (New York: Norton, 1979) 299.

15. Helen Taylor, *Gender, Race, and Region in the Writings of Grace King, Ruth McEnery Stuart, and Kate Chopin* (Baton Rouge: Louisiana State UP, 1989) 156, 157.

16. Elizabeth Ammons, *Conflicting Stories: American Women Writers at the Turn into the Twentieth Century* (New York: Oxford UP, 1991) 75.

17. Kate Chopin, "*The Awakening*": An Authoritative Text, Contexts, Criticism, ed. Margaret Culley (New York: Norton, 1976).

18. For examples of such criticism, see Michele A. Birnbaum, "'Alien Hands': Kate Chopin and the Colonization of Race," *American Literature* 66 (1994): 301–23, and Kate Mc-Cullough, *Regions of Identity: The Construction of America in Women's Fiction, 1885–1914* (Stanford: Stanford UP, 1999) 185–226.

19. See, for example, Mary E. Papke, *Verging on the Abyss: The Social Fiction of Kate Chopin and Edith Wharton* (Westport: Greenwood, 1990) 29; Rebecca Aanerud, "Fictions of Whiteness: Speaking the Names of Whiteness in U.S. Literature," *Displacing Whiteness: Essays in Social and Cultural Criticism*, ed. Ruth Frankenberg (Durham: Duke UP, 1997) 42; and McCullough 210, 319 n. 23.

12

Feeling the Countercurrent

BERNARD KOLOSKI

THE UNDERTOW IN KATE CHOPIN'S FICTION has absorbed me for thirty years. Chopin's best-known stories speak of women's struggles for better lives—for independence, fulfillment, integrity, intimacy, joy. But deep in some of those works and in much of her other fiction runs a countercurrent telling of other things—of economic, social, racial, and religious forces, of tension between freedom and security, of a deep-seated optimism about life, and of roots in the language and culture of France. *The Awakening* and stories like "Désirée's Baby," "The Story of an Hour," or "A Pair of Silk Stockings" end in death, despair, or poverty. But *At Fault* and stories like "A No-Account Creole," "Athénaïse," or "The Storm" point toward growth, fulfillment, or happiness.

In the 1970s I wrote not about feminist themes but about how Chopin's characters—her men and her children as well as her women—search for freedom from a community as well as freedom within a community. I probed the place of the Swinburne passage in *The Awakening* and outlined the structure of *At Fault*. In the 1980s I sought to make the Modern Language Association's *Approaches to Teaching Chopin's "The Awakening"* all inclusive, inviting essays from experienced and beginning scholars on the full range of ideas they proposed, many of them feminist, many of them not. Later I wrote about Chopin's short stories and edited paperback editions of *Bayou Folk*, *A Night in Acadie*, and *At Fault*.

Over the years I've come to understand Chopin's work in the context of the bilingualism and biculturalism that make her what she is: that rare nineteenth-century writer in the United States who sees beyond American values, who is post-Christian, at ease with true diversity of thought and action, comfortable with her sexuality, and shaped as much by European as by American influences—in the final analysis, not so much an American writer as a French-American writer.

I certainly didn't grasp all this when I first came across Kate Chopin in August 1970 as I was seeking a subject for a PhD dissertation. Per Seyersted's *Complete Works* and *Critical Biography* had just appeared on the shelves of the library where I spent my days, and I had been overwhelmed by the power of *The Awakening* and fascinated by some of Chopin's short stories. I could not have articulated just what I was responding to, but no other American author spoke to me as Kate Chopin did.

My adviser had not read Chopin and was not pleased with my proposing to write about her. "You're making a bad choice," he said. "If this woman isn't known, it's because she's not very good, and you'll be hurting your career working on her. You won't find anyone to publish what you write." We went back and forth on the subject for weeks—me insisting that I could do something with Kate Chopin, him countering that I should work on F. Scott Fitzgerald.

In desperation, I approached him on a Friday afternoon and handed him George Arms's little orange edition of *The Awakening*. "Look," I pleaded, "would you please take this novel home with you over the weekend and read it? If you tell me on Monday morning that Chopin is not worth writing about, I'll begin on Fitzgerald in the afternoon."

That Monday will stick in my mind forever. I found my adviser sitting in his chair behind a walnut desk that had only that orange paperback on its glossy surface. He looked up at me and held my gaze for what felt like minutes, as if he were struggling with his emotions—then leaned forward, slid the paperback across the table toward me, and said, "Do it."

"It's a beautiful book," he added. "I can't understand how we missed it. It deserves to be known. You're right. So get to work."

It was the ending of *The Awakening* that had caught my attention when I first read Kate Chopin, but it was the beginning of Chopin's career that I focused on in the fall of 1970, and that focus established the direction I would follow for the decades afterward.

It's not easy today to read Kate Chopin as you could forty years ago. In twenty-first-century America, readers almost always see what's feminist about her work because, I suppose, we read the past through what we know in the present. But in the 1970s, we Chopin-obsessed graduate students didn't know very much. We had Daniel Rankin's 1932 biography, Per Seyersted's *Complete Works of Kate Chopin* and his Chopin biography, and pieces by George Arms, Larzer Ziff, Lewis Leary, Edmund Wilson, and a few others. I remember that, except for the Seyersted and Rankin volumes, my entire collection of Chopin scholarship fit neatly in the cardboard box that came with my new boots.

We could not know what was to be published. Neither Seyersted nor other early critics carried the ecstasy of Sandra Gilbert's introduction to the widely used Penguin Classics *Awakening*, which presents Edna Pontellier as Aphrodite rising from the sea. None of the scholars we read offered the powerful feminist background readings and critical approaches in Margo Culley's ever popular Norton Critical Edition of the novel. Nobody knew about Chopin's life what Emily Toth would describe in her two biographies. And nothing in print even hinted at the rainbow of approaches contained in the hundreds of Kate Chopin entries indexed in the current MLA international bibliography. We worked with what we had.

I was determined, as Bob Arner, Barbara Ewell, and others were, to look at all Chopin's fiction. It would not have occurred to me to select only stories that establish what some later readers would understand as Chopin's feminist credentials. Yet select I did, using what my instincts told me were her best works, her most true-to-life works, her most beautifully written works, the works whose language pushed the Beatles' "Let It Be" out of my head that autumn as I walked among the olive trees to the university library, where I studied the stories, spread out my papers, and drafted my dissertation.

I at once was attracted to some of Chopin's daring, energetic women— not just to Edna and Calixta and Mrs. Mallard but to Euphrasie in "A No-Account Creole" and Athénaïse and Charlie, among others. And I was struck by the sensitive strength of some of Chopin's men—Wallace Offdean in "A No-Account Creole," David Hosmer in *At Fault*, Gouvernail in "Athénaïse" and "A Respectable Woman," and even the much maligned Cazeau in "Athénaïse."

These characters were my contemporaries. They were struggling with the same issues I had struggled with, was struggling with—marriage, divorce, work, money, children. And they were yearning for what I yearned for—freedom, integrity, security, hope. They wanted, as I wanted, a richer life, a more fulfilling life, a life of balance.

As I saw it, "A No-Account Creole," Chopin's first story, and At Fault, her early novel, set out the basic thematic language of her fiction. Euphrasie Manton in "A No-Account Creole," has, as I later phrased it, a "deeply socialized disposition toward a life of rich possibilities."[1] Euphrasie cannot articulate her needs, but she knows when she meets Wallace Offdean, the businessman from New Orleans, that she wants more than her lifelong friendship with her fiancé, Placide Santien, more than her simple life with her father, and more than the duplicate of that life she will have when she marries Placide. Euphrasie has seen better days, having been raised by wealthy neighbors after her mother died. She had not, like Calixta in "The Storm," spent passionate moments with the man she loves—she has only recently met Offdean—but her eyes are "intense with the unnatural light that glowed in them" when she is around him.[2]

Offdean embodied for me the sort of man so rare in Chopin's later stories. He has "healthy instincts," he comes from "good society," and he wants "a life that, imposing bodily activity, admits the intellectual repose in which thought unfolds."[3] Chopin's further description of his intended trajectory in life verified for me precisely why, unlike some of my friends in MBA programs, I was working in the humanities. "He would keep clear," Chopin writes, "of the maelstroms of sordid work and senseless pleasure in which the average American businessman may be said alternately to exist, and which reduce him, naturally, to a rather ragged condition of soul."[4] The words seem as prescient to me in 2009 as they did when I first read them decades ago.

Offdean and Euphrasie, I understood, will build together a life that Chopin's later, better-known characters find beyond their reach. "A No-Account Creole" was appealing for me not because it was romantic, in the popular sense of that word, and not because it presented a sugar-coated view of the world, but because it established for me what was on Chopin's mind as she began her writing career. It gave me a position from which I could view the rest of her fiction.

At Fault, I discovered, worked out the philosophical underpinnings that "A No-Account Creole" hinted at. Critics have not thought much of Chopin's early novel, complaining about sentimental coloring and clumsy, contrived plotting. Per Seyersted saw it as a thesis novel, and most critics since him think of it as an apprentice piece, a way for Chopin to polish her craft. But for me At Fault was important as a critical text that illuminates The Awakening.

Both of Kate Chopin's novels are about a woman seeking to balance her private needs with her public responsibilities. But while The Awakening speaks to us though incident and imagery and metaphor, At Fault addresses the subject directly through philosophical discussions among characters about what French novelist George Sand, whom Chopin had read, called the "social right" and the "human right." Arguments about "rights," religion, and "natural adjustment" make explicit the dilemma at the heart of the novel—widowed Thérèse Lafirme's struggle to overcome her Catholic-inspired prejudice toward divorce and to accept the love of divorced businessman David Hosmer.[5]

Thérèse is older than Euphrasie Manton and had once known happiness and security in her marriage. She has now at her fingertips the rich future that Euphrasie yearns for, but, like Edna Pontellier, she has trouble balancing her "outward existence" with her "inward life." Edna's problem, as readers fully understand, is inside her, is the consequence of her abrupt awakening to herself in relation to the social world, the cultural milieu that so restricts her options. That world is fixed, static—or at least Edna sees it that way. It's why she feels so trapped, why she sees no hope for her future.

Thérèse Lafirme's problem is quite different. It is she, not her society, that is static. She cannot deal with the idea of divorce. "With the prejudices of her Catholic education coloring her sentiment," Chopin says of her, "she instinctively shrank when the theme confronted her as one having even a remote reference to her own clean existence."[6] Thérèse is fixed in her opinions and her beliefs.

But her world is dynamic, changing as the influence of the postbellum North makes itself felt in rural Louisiana in the form of a new railroad and the arrival of David Hosmer, the businessman from St. Louis who has persuaded Thérèse to let him cut timber and erect a sawmill on her land. Her physical world, too, is in flux. The powerful Cane River beats at her levees and sweeps away parcels of her land.

Yet, despite her intransigence, it is Thérèse herself who sets in motion the events that bring closure to the novel. In the manner of a George Sand sentimental heroine, she actively provokes a crisis by insisting that the man she loves return to the wife he divorced—and that he bring his former wife into her presence.

Decades later, in the introduction to the Penguin Classics edition of the novel, I wrote that "At Fault is Kate Chopin's novel of hope," that it is "a powerful love story that points the way to The Awakening." I have seen it that way since I assembled my dissertation. Edna Pontellier dies because she is without hope. Thérèse Lafirme lives because, in spite of herself, she is forced to reconcile her convictions with the changes taking place in the world around her. Her story is an expression of what seems to me unmistakable in Kate Chopin's fiction—an essential belief that, "in spite of everything," as I phrased it in my introduction, "people have a decent chance to find happiness."[7]

Between my dissertation and the MLA Approaches volume, I went off to Poland as a Fulbrighter—and the experience solidified and expanded my view of Chopin's work. The Polish government declared martial law shortly after I arrived in 1981 because the Solidarity trade union was taking to the streets and initiating what turned out to be the death throes of Soviet-style communism. Student protests had already shut down most of the Polish universities, and with the coming of martial law the government closed the rest of them—for several months, actually—so the situation of university professors, including visiting scholars, was tenuous, and Americans were not eager to submit themselves and their families to such uncertainty. I ended up being a Fulbrighter in the country for a very unusual three years.

I discovered that The Awakening had been translated into Polish and tracked down the translator in Warsaw, who entertained me with stories about her troubles in finding Polish equivalents for Chopin's dialectal expressions. But I discovered that my students at both universities where I taught had little sympathy for Edna Pontellier's plight.

"The trouble with Edna," one bright young woman insisted (virtually all my Polish students were bright; English was a highly competitive and a prestige major under communist rule because it opened opportunities in the West and gave students access to BBC and Voice of America accounts about was happening in their country)—"The trouble with Edna," my student argued, "is that she does not need to stand in line to buy bread!"

I had viewed Chopin through several lenses, but economics was not one of them.[8] Yet the cost of living, the shortage of nearly all consumer goods, and the political inability to bring about change were near obsessions for my Polish students. Westerners like Kate Chopin, as these students saw it, could concentrate on gender inequalities or on emotional differences between marriage partners because Western economic and political systems were functioning—not equally well for everyone, as I again and again pointed out, but well enough for people to turn their attention to other things.

"I cannot even imagine what it would be like to be Edna Pontellier," another young woman said. She, like almost all my students, was living in a cramped apartment with her parents—and her husband had moved in, too. Like so many others, she had married young because only married people could apply to the government for an apartment, and the wait could take ten years. "To live in my own house," she added, "to have someone to care for my child, to sit on the beach or paint pictures or go to horse races or throw dinner parties. . . . And to have a husband who earns enough to pay the bills, let alone to send me bon bons! I simply can't imagine it."

Years later, when I taught for a semester in postcommunist Russia, I found that the situation had changed. Things were still tough in 1999, but the worst of Soviet economic pressures seemed to have melted away for most of my university students. They struggled, but they could identify with the concerns of a woman like Edna Pontellier.

I had contracted to edit the Modern Language Association's *Approaches to Teaching Chopin's "The Awakening"* before I left for Poland, thinking my stay there would be short. I was, in fact, surprised to receive that contract. The staff at MLA—concerned, I assume, about a male editing the volume—had asked me to suggest a woman who could serve as coeditor of the book. I sent along a list of women I would be happy to work with. But in their letters of support for the project, Caroline Heilbrun, celebrated feminist and former president of MLA, and Peggy Skaggs, author of an early Chopin study, persuaded the staff that I knew what I was doing and that they should let me alone.

In part because of my experience in Poland I was convinced that teachers working with *The Awakening* ought to have available a full spectrum of possible readings of the novel. I tried with the MLA *Approaches* volume to offer that. I had a wealth of proposals to choose from, and to include as many ideas as possible in the space I had to work with, I solicited essays from twenty-one scholars but held everyone to tight word limits.

The book is as inclusive as I could make it at the time, but its focus is on women's experience. It charts Kate Chopin's entry into the literary canons through the interest of feminists in the 1970s. It makes clear why Chopin's most popular work remains that which emphasizes how intelligent, sensitive women are damaged, sometimes destroyed, by patriarchal society. *The Awakening* touched a nerve when it became known precisely because it embodies that line of thought. As I wrote in the *Approaches* preface, the novel "helped satisfy Americans' suddenly discovered hunger for a classic woman writer who addresses some of contemporary women's concerns."[9]

Editing the MLA volume was a heady experience, but I quickly returned to what my Fulbright years in Poland had shown me—the importance of economic conditions in people's lives. As I reread Chopin's short stories, I was struck by how her focus on people striving to build more fulfilling lives, better-balanced lives, must have been influenced by her youth in St. Louis during the privations of the Civil War and by her fourteen years in Louisiana among people whose previous way of life had been annihilated. The per capita wealth in Louisiana when Chopin arrived there had plunged from one of the highest in the United States to one of the lowest. The war had wiped out about a third of the state's prewar wealth and destroyed its slave-based agricultural economy. Plantations were in ruins, and plantation houses were half dismantled, with dilapidated galleries and leaking roofs.

Many of Chopin's characters are desperately poor, clothed in rags, living in shacks, surviving from day to day. One little girl unknowingly sells a priceless violin to feed her sick siblings. Another drives a load of cotton to the river landing for fear her lazy father will lose his job. A former slave collects scraps of leftovers at the French market and delivers them to the dying, poverty-stricken woman who was once the mistress of the plantation where he lived. Two children walk home barefoot carrying their first pair of shoes so they don't get them dirty. And a young woman attends a 'Cadian ball in old shoes that she has covered over with pieces of her first-communion veil.

You would not be aware of such poverty in Chopin's works if you knew only The Awakening, "The Storm," "The Story of an Hour," or "Désirée's Baby." You can sense it in "A Pair of Silk Stockings," but the truth is that even today few readers think of Kate Chopin as a writer especially focused on poor people. Yet if you read Bayou Folk and A Night in Acadie, the two anthologies Chopin published between At Fault and The Awakening, it seems to me the reality is unavoidable.

Some of the poverty is tied to race, and some critics have complained about Chopin's treatment of race in her fiction; Anna Elfenbein discusses the matter at length in this volume. It is, of course, true that Kate Chopin's family had slaves in the house when Chopin was a child and that her husband joined the notorious White League in New Orleans. And it is true that characters in some of her works see life in racist terms and use racial expressions that are offensive to the ears of twenty-first-century readers, although such expressions were employed widely by both white people and people of color at the time. Chopin carried within her characteristics of other white, nineteenth-century, southern, American women, characteristics of what Toni Morrison calls a "wholly racialized" way of life.[10]

But Chopin carried, too, characteristics of nineteenth-century French women because she was bilingual and bicultural from birth, used French at home and at school, visited France on her honeymoon, read French literature in its original, translated Guy de Maupassant short stories into English, knew French music and opera, and interacted with both English- and French-speaking communities in St. Louis and Louisiana. She was not naive; she would have been aware that nineteenth-century French people struggled with racial issues of their own, but different ones than those of Americans.

She always understands more than her characters understand, and she sees life from far broader perspectives than they do. Her attitudes toward race—like her attitudes toward love, sex, and so many other matters—are complex, reflecting nineteenth-century European (particularly French), as well as American, ways of thinking. She treats her African Americans as she treats her Acadians, her Creoles, her Native Americans, her "Americans," and others—her adults and her children—with tenderness and acceptance. And her *Bayou Folk* story "Désirée's Baby," her best-known work through the first seven decades of the twentieth century, condemns in stunning, withering terms white fantasies of racial superiority.

The *Night in Acadie* story "Athénaïse" struck me in the 1970s as one of Chopin's most beautiful works, and I was delighted years later when Susan Lohafer described it as a nineteenth-century classic. But the story has not been popular with some readers because, after running away from her country home and her husband, Cazeau, and meeting an attractive stranger in New Orleans, the strong-willed Athénaïse realizes she is pregnant and immediately returns to the country and to her husband, her body now awakened with passion for him.

Athénaïse is not a woman whom readers of *The Awakening* or "The Storm" may be expecting to find in Chopin's fiction. She has left Cazeau because she is miserable, disillusioned, and frustrated, because marriage is not what she thought it might be, because she cannot deal with sex. She doesn't hate her husband, she says. "It's jus' being married that I detes' an' despise. I hate being Mrs. Cazeau, an' would want to be Athénaïse Miché again."[11] She is glad for the option her brother offers her of a secret hiding place in the city.

Chopin is sympathetic to her plight but details the limitations of her character. Athénaïse is, as Gouvernail, the journalist she meets in New Orleans, realizes, "self-willed, impulsive, innocent, ignorant, unsatisfied, dissatisfied."[12] Yet Gouvernail himself has problems, as does Cazeau. The story has no flawless characters. Nobody is triumphant at the end. Nobody wins.

Gouvernail is one of Kate Chopin's most fascinating men, modeled, I assume, on some of the sophisticated journalists Chopin knew in St. Louis as she was writing her stories. When Athénaïse turns to him for help in mailing letters, he senses her loneliness and, in spite of his initial assessment of her, befriends her, coming slowly to realize just how beautiful she is, coming slowly to fall in love with her. When she throws herself in his arms for comfort, he knows that he is a substitute for her brother and does not seek her lips, although he yearns to.

Her being married, Chopin writes, "made no particle of difference" to Gouvernail. "He could not conceive or dream of it making a difference. When the time came that she wanted him,—as he hoped and believed it would come,—he felt he would have a right to her. So long as she did not want him, he had no right to her,—no more than her husband had."[13]

Gouvernail was, it seemed to me in the 1970s, a remarkable nineteenth-century character, and his role in "A Respectable Woman" and in the party scene late in *The Awakening* reinforced that impression for me. And Athénaïse's husband, Cazeau, was equally impressive for me. He is, it's true, imperious, short tempered, too sure of himself, and contemptuous of Athénaïse's brother, but he has what Barbara Ewell calls "a blunt integrity."[14] He has lived alone for ten years since his former wife died and has, as he sees it, responded to advances from Athénaïse in proposing marriage to her. In one memorable scene near a live oak, he is horrified when it occurs to him that he may be treating his wife as his father once treated a runaway slave.

He is at least as depressed as Athénaïse over the state of their marriage, having lost, he is convinced, his last chance for happiness. He will not search her out in her hiding place, he tells her in a letter, but will wait patiently for her, hoping she will not come back unless she can in some way "return affection and respect for the love which he continued and would always continue to feel for her."[15] He cannot imagine loving another woman, and he cannot believe his wife will ever love him.

Athénaïse does not return to Cazeau because she is trapped by her pregnancy but because the child within her has awakened her to the richness that life with Cazeau can offer her. She is deliriously happy, is "steeped in a wave of ecstasy," and the "first purely sensuous tremor of her life" sweeps over her.[16] Like Euphrasie Manton and Thérèse Lafirme, she reaches for her best option. Of course, Athénaïse has grown. But Cazeau has grown, too. As Susan Lohafer phrases it in this volume, "legal duty, male desire, marital custom—these are Cazeau's guides before his enlightenment. Sensitivity, love, and decency—these are the promptings of his finer nature, and in listening to them, he becomes a better man and, therefore, a better husband." Together in their newly fulfilling married life, Athénaïse and Cazeau find possibilities that they could not find separately.

Bayou Folk and A Night in Acadie have a character of their own, as does A Vocation and a Voice, which did not appear as a separate volume until Emily Toth published it as a Penguin Classics edition in 1991.[17] Chopin clearly intended the three volumes to be distinct, and she selected carefully the stories she wanted included in each. The works she apparently intended for A Vocation and a Voice are of a different nature—darker, less focused on life in Louisiana—than that of the ones she included in A Night in Acadie, even though she wrote them at roughly the same time.

If the French influence on Kate Chopin is felt in At Fault, in her two anthologies of stories, and in The Awakening, it is made explicit in A Vocation and a Voice. Throughout her fiction, Edmund Wilson argues in the foreword to Seyersted's Complete Works, Chopin's style combines "French limpidity with Irish grace."[18] But it's more than style; it's the direct presence of France that Chopin turned to in the anthology she hoped would appear after The Awakening. The volume's title story, "A Vocation and a Voice," prepares the way. It features a woman who once sang in the chorus of an opera, apparently a French opera by Ferdinand Hérold.[19] And the story "Lilacs" is set in France and, it seems to me, is inspired by the great nineteenth-century French stage performer Sarah Bernhardt.

Chopin may well have seen Bernhardt in St. Louis or New Orleans during one of the player's grand tours of the United States in the 1880s and 1890s. But whether she saw Bernhardt or not, Kate Chopin would certainly have known of the flamboyant woman's professional and private life because newspapers and magazines gave her broad coverage. Adrienne Farival in "Lilacs," as I describe elsewhere, is Chopin's Sarah Bernhardt, a talented, celebrated stage artist with lovers eating out of her hand and a servant rushing to meet her every need.[20] But, as with so many Kate Chopin characters, what Adrienne needs most is balance—a temporary retreat from her wild Parisian life, a place where she can at times find "the intellectual repose in which thought unfolds," as Chopin phrases it in "A No-Account Creole."

That place for Adrienne is the convent where she studied as a young girl and where she escapes to for two weeks each spring. "Lilacs" is the story of her last excursion to the convent, and it is remarkable how similar the piece is to Chopin's other stories. The setting is urban France, not rural Louisiana. The landscape is "smiling," not depressed. And Adrienne is rich, sophisticated, adventurous, independent. She is free to do whatever she chooses. Her life is brimming with almost limitless possibilities—ones beyond those that even Edna Pontellier might imagine. But for Chopin, all that is beside the point. When Adrienne is refused entry to the convent, she "leaned her forehead against the heavy oaken panel of the door and wept with the abandonment of a little child." Cut off from the "haven of peace" that makes the sometime "despondency" and "heaviness of heart" of her life in Paris bearable, banished from the escape that gives balance to her life, she is devastated.[21]

Chopin had read many classic and contemporary writers, including French writers, and from time to time she mentions them in her work. There is a reference to Émile Zola in "Lilacs," a reminder of what Kate Chopin thinks of as imperative for a writer. Chopin had reviewed Zola's 1894 novel *Lourdes*, and critics generally conclude that she disliked his work because she finds fault with the book. But it is instructive to see how she begins her review:

> I once heard a devotee of impressionism admit, in looking at a picture by Monet, that, while he himself had never seen in nature the peculiar yellows and reds therein depicted, he was convinced that Monet had painted them because he saw them and because they were true. With something of a kindred faith in the sincerity of Mons. Zola's work, I am yet not at all times ready to admit its truth, which is only equivalent to saying that our points of view differ, that truth rests upon a shifting basis and is apt to be kaleidoscopic.[22]

This is the essence of Chopinism, the heart, the soul, of what it seems to me Kate Chopin offers us. There is nothing, in her mind, more important than striving to tell the truth. It is what she so admired in the French writers she read, Zola and Guy de Maupassant, in particular, and, I assume, what she responded to in Walt Whitman, as well. It is what she so courageously set out to do in writing "The Storm."

If we can judge by its appearance in anthologies and by usage data from the KateChopin.org Web site, "The Storm" is today one of Kate Chopin's most popular works—along with *The Awakening*, "The Story of an Hour," and "Désirée's Baby."[23] "The Storm" fully captures Chopin's notion of truth's "shifting basis," its "kaleidoscopic" quality. I loved it when I came across it decades ago, and I think I have been right in arguing that it is America's first great twentieth-century short story.

Its prequel, "At the 'Cadian Ball," demonstrates how Calixta and Alcée are hemmed in by their responsibilities to others, to their respective Acadian and Creole families and communities. It is not surprising that in the few minutes the two spend together in the darkness outside the ball, they are interrupted three times or that when Clarisse makes her cultural claim to marriage with Alcée, Calixta accepts the hand of Bobinôt. The two respond to what others demand of them. They accept offers of security and stability. The needs of their groups, the story suggests, are primary.

But "The Storm" posits that what others need, what others think—at least at this moment—is irrelevant. The idea is not new for Kate Chopin. Her early novel At Fault makes clear that the personal demands of Thérèse Lafirme and David Hosmer must take precedence over the wishes, the customs of the Creole community. The marriage of Thérèse and Hosmer is the subject of gossip even two months after it takes place, but Thérèse has grown. "I have seen myself at fault in following what seemed like the only right," she concludes near the end the book. "I feel as if there were no way to turn for the truth. Old supports appear to be giving way beneath me. They were so secure before."[24]

Hosmer counters that we are not given to know "the truth in its entirety," and "The Storm" makes no claim to tell the entire truth. What Chopin describes in the story is Calixta's and Alcée's truth—at this place, at this time. The two have been yearning for each other for at least six years, since the summer before the 'Cadian ball, the summer when they stirred up "a breath of scandal" in Assumption Parish. Then, as later at the ball, the pressures of their communities, the norms of their communities, intervened. In Assumption, Alcée would kiss Calixta and kiss her and kiss her—and then "to save her he would resort to a desperate flight. If she was not an immaculate dove in those days, she was still inviolate; a passionate creature whose very defenselessness had made her defense, against which his honor forbade him to prevail."[25]

Now everything is different. Now Calixta, too, is sexually experienced, and now it is safe for the two of them to finally make love, to revel for the first time in their "birthright," as Chopin phrases it.[26] They have for five years met their responsibilities to their families and their communities, and nothing in the story suggests that they will not continue to do so. But for now, for the duration of the storm, it is they themselves that matter, their needs, their passions, their individuality, their personhood. "The Storm" is a joyful work, a hopeful work, a contemporary work, a French-American work—Kate Chopin at her best.

I have come over the years to think of Chopin as poised between her two internationally known contemporaries: Mark Twain, who tugged American fiction toward rural, inland speech while mocking European values and extolling the superiority of American ways, and Henry James, who invented a cosmopolitan language for sensitivity while contrasting Europe's values with America's and finding both wanting.

Chopin embraces rural American speech as much as Twain—the famous little note to the reader at the start of Huckleberry Finn could as well be placed at the start of Bayou Folk—but glories in the continental origins that make it unique. And she knows European ways—or at least French ways—better than James, knows them from birth, from the inside rather than the outside, and she has no need to compare or contrast because she has integrated both cultures into herself and into the lives of her characters.

That's what I've sought to argue as I've worked alongside my feminist colleagues these past three decades, doing what I can to promote their scholarship while hoping that at least a few will come to see a little of what I've been responding to.

When all is said and done, it seems to me, it's the undertow in her works that sets Kate Chopin apart from other writers focused on women's concerns, the undertow that makes her so complex, so deliciously ambiguous, so wonderfully resonant today. It's that countercurrent of external forces and internal tensions, of French language and culture and American optimism and hope, that makes her the extraordinary writer we know her to be.

NOTES

1. Bernard Koloski, Kate Chopin: A Study of the Short Fiction (New York: Twayne, 1996) 15.

2. Kate Chopin, The Complete Works of Kate Chopin, ed. Per Seyersted (Baton Rouge: Louisiana State UP, 1969) 94.

3. Chopin, Complete Works 81, 97.

4. Chopin, Complete Works 81.

5. Bernard Koloski, introduction, At Fault, by Kate Chopin (New York: Penguin, 2002) xii–xv.

6. Chopin, Complete Works 764.

7. Koloski, introduction, At Fault viii, xxi.

8. See John Carlos Rowe, "The Economics of the Body in Kate Chopin's The Awakening," Kate Chopin Reconsidered: Beyond the Bayou, ed. Lynda S. Boren and Sara deSaussure Davis (Baton Rouge: Louisiana State UP, 1992) 117–42.

9. Bernard Koloski, ed., Approaches to Teaching Chopin's "The Awakening" (New York: Modern Language Association, 1988) ix.

10. Toni Morrison, Playing in the Dark: Whiteness and the Literary Imagination (Cambridge: Harvard UP, 1992) xii.

11. Chopin, Complete Works 431.

12. Chopin, Complete Works 446.

13. Chopin, Complete Works 450.

14. Barbara C. Ewell, Kate Chopin (New York: Ungar, 1986) 112.

15. Chopin, Complete Works 439.

16. Chopin, Complete Works 451.

17. Sandra Gilbert's Kate Chopin: Complete Novels and Stories includes a note arguing that it's not possible to know which stories, exactly, Kate Chopin meant to include in Vocation and a Voice (New York: Library of America, 2002) 1058–59.

18. Edmund Wilson, foreword, Chopin, Complete Works 14.

19. Koloski, Short Fiction 54–58.

20. Koloski, Short Fiction 58–61.

21. Chopin, Complete Works 357, 365, 357–58.

22. Chopin, Complete Works 697.

23. Usage data shows that site visitors are consistently most interested in Chopin biography and these works. KateChopin.org, Kate Chopin International Society, 2 Jan. 2009. Web. 2 Jan. 2009.

24. Chopin, Complete Works 872.

25. Chopin, Complete Works 872, 219, 594.

26. Chopin, Complete Works 595.

BIBLIOGRAPHY

Unless noted as Web or Film, all entries refer to printed materials.

Aanerud, Rebecca. "Fictions of Whiteness: Speaking the Names of Whiteness in U.S. Literature." Displacing Whiteness: Essays in Social and Cultural Criticism. Ed. Ruth Frankenberg. Durham: Duke UP, 1997. 35–59.

Aaron, Daniel. "Per Seyersted: Kate Chopin. A Critical Biography." Edda: Scandinavian Journal of Literary Research 71 (1971): 341–49.

Abrams, M. H. Natural Supernaturalism: Tradition and Revolution in Romantic Literature. 1971. New York: Norton, 1973.

Ammons, Elizabeth. Conflicting Stories: American Women Writers at the Turn into the Twentieth Century. New York: Oxford UP, 1991.

Ammons, Elizabeth, and Valerie Rohy, eds. American Local Color Writing, 1880–1920. New York: Penguin, 1998.

Arnavon, Cyrille, trans. Edna. By Kate Chopin. Paris: Club Bibliophile de France, 1953.

Arner, Robert D. "Kate Chopin." Special issue of Louisiana Studies 14 (1975): 11–139.

Bardot, Jean. "Kate Chopin: Her Actual Birth Date." Xavier Review 7 (1987): 70–72.

Bayou Folk. Advertisement. Publishers' Weekly 17 Mar. 1894: 450.

Beer, Janet, ed. The Cambridge Companion to Kate Chopin. Cambridge: Cambridge UP, 2008.

Beer, Janet, and Elizabeth Nolan, eds. Kate Chopin's "The Awakening": A Sourcebook. London: Routledge, 2004.

Benfey, Christopher. Degas in New Orleans: Encounters in the Creole World of Kate Chopin and George Washington Cable. Berkeley: U of California P, 1997.

Benson, Margaret S. "The Structure of Four- and Five-Year-Olds' Narratives in Pretend Play and Storytelling." First Language 13 (1993): 203–23.

Birnbaum, Michele A. "'Alien Hands': Kate Chopin and the Colonization of Race." American Literature 66 (1994): 301–23.

Bloom, Harold, ed. Kate Chopin. New York: Chelsea, 1987.

Bonner, Thomas, Jr. The Kate Chopin Companion: With Chopin's Translations from French Fiction. New York: Greenwood, 1988.

Boren, Lynda S., and Sara deSaussure Davis, eds. Kate Chopin Reconsidered: Beyond the Bayou. Baton Rouge: Louisiana State UP, 1992.

Bowlby, Rachel. Just Looking: Consumer Culture in Dreiser, Gissing, and Zola. New York: Methuen, 1985.

Brockmeier, Kevin. The Brief History of the Dead. New York: Pantheon, 2006.

Cable, George W. The Grandissimes: A Story of Creole Life. New York, 1880.

Chopin, Kate. At Fault. Ed. Bernard Koloski. New York: Penguin, 2002.

———. The Awakening. New York: Capricorn, 1964.

———. "The Awakening": An Authoritative Text, Biographical and Historical Contexts, Criticism. Ed. Margo Culley. 2nd ed. New York: Norton, 1994.

———. "The Awakening": An Authoritative Text, Contexts, Criticism. Ed. Margaret Culley. New York: Norton, 1976.

———. "The Awakening" and Selected Stories of Kate Chopin. Ed. Barbara H. Solomon. New York: New American Library, 1976.

———. "The Awakening" and Selected Stories. Ed. Sandra M. Gilbert. New York: Penguin, 1984.

———. Bayou Folk and A Night in Acadie. Ed. Bernard Koloski. New York: Penguin, 1999.

———. "Commonplace Book." Toth, Seyersted, and Bonnell 9–122.

———. The Complete Works of Kate Chopin. Ed. Per Seyersted. Baton Rouge: Louisiana State UP, 1969.

———. Kate Chopin: Complete Novels and Stories. Ed. Sandra M. Gilbert. New York: Library of America, 2002.

———. Portraits: Short Stories Selected and Introduced by Helen Taylor. London: Women's Press, 1979.

———. A Vocation and a Voice: Stories. Ed. Emily Toth. New York: Penguin, 1991.

Davis, Doris. "The Awakening: The Economics of Tension." Boren and Davis 143–53.

Davis, Sara deSaussure. "Chopin's Movement toward Universal Myth." Boren and Davis 199–206.

Dead Poets Society. Dir. Peter Weir. Perf. Robin Williams. Touchstone Pictures, 1989. Film.

Despain, Max, and Thomas Bonner Jr. "Shoulders to Wings: The Provenance of Winged Imagery from Kate Chopin's Juvenilia through The Awakening." Xavier Review 25 (2005): 49–64.

Donovan, Josephine. *New England Local Color Literature: A Women's Tradition.* New York: Ungar, 1983.

——. *Sarah Orne Jewett.* New York: Ungar, 1980.

Dyer, Joyce. *"The Awakening": A Novel of Beginnings.* New York: Twayne, 1993.

Eble, Kenneth. "A Forgotten Novel: Kate Chopin's The Awakening." *Western Humanities Review* 10 (1956): 261–69.

Elfenbein, Anna Shannon. "Kate Chopin's The Awakening: An Assault on American Racial and Sexual Mythology." *Southern Studies* 26 (1987): 304–12. Rpt. in Chopin, *The Awakening.* Ed. Culley. 2nd ed. 292–99.

——. *Women on the Color Line: Evolving Stereotypes and the Writings of George Washington Cable, Grace King, Kate Chopin.* Charlottesville: UP of Virginia, 1989.

Eliade, Mircea. *The Sacred and the Profane: The Nature of Religion.* Trans. Willard R. Trask. New York: Harcourt, Brace, 1959.

Engell, James. "The Soul, Highest Cast of Consciousness." *The Cast of Consciousness: Concepts of the Mind in British and American Romanticism.* Ed. Beverly Taylor and Robert Bain. New York: Greenwood, 1987. 3–19.

Ewell, Barbara C. *Kate Chopin.* New York: Ungar, 1986.

——. "Kate Chopin and the Dream of Female Selfhood." *Boren and Davis.* 157–65.

Ewell, Barbara C., and Pamela Glenn Menke, eds. *Southern Local Color: Stories of Region, Race, and Gender.* Athens: U of Georgia P, 2002.

Fetterley, Judith, ed. *Provisions: A Reader from 19th-Century American Women.* Bloomington: Indiana UP, 1985.

Foster, Andrea L. "Information Navigation 101." *Chronicle of Higher Education* 9 Mar. 2007: A38–40.

Friedman, Thomas L. *The World Is Flat: A Brief History of the Twenty-first Century.* Updated ed. New York: Farrar, 2006.

Frisby, James R., Jr. "New Orleans Writers and the Negro: George Washington Cable, Grace King, Ruth McEnery Stuart, Kate Chopin, and Lafcadio Hearn, 1870–1900." Diss. Emory U, 1972.

Frost, Brian J. *The Monster with a Thousand Faces: Guises of the Vampire in Myth and Literature.* Bowling Green: Bowling Green State U Popular P, 1989.

Fusco, Richard. *Maupassant and the American Short Story: The Influence of Form at the Turn of the Century.* University Park: Pennsylvania State UP, 1994.

Gardner, Sarah E. *Blood and Irony: Southern White Women's Narratives of the Civil War, 1861–1937.* Chapel Hill: U of North Carolina P, 2004.

Gerlach, John. *Toward the End: Closure and Structure in the American Short Story.* Tuscaloosa: U of Alabama P, 1985.

Gibson, William M. "Love in Louisiana: Kate Chopin, a Forgotten Southern Novelist." Rev. of *Kate Chopin: A Critical Biography*, by Per Seyersted, and *The Complete Works of Kate Chopin*, ed. Seyersted. *Times Literary Supplement* [London] 9 Oct. 1970: 1163.

Gilbert, Sandra M., and Susan Gubar. *The Madwoman in the Attic: The Woman Writer and the Nineteenth-Century Literary Imagination*. New Haven: Yale UP, 1979.

Harner, James L. *On Compiling an Annotated Bibliography*. 2nd ed. New York: Modern Language Association, 2000.

Hart, James D. *The Oxford Companion to American Literature*. 4th ed. New York: Oxford UP, 1965.

Hawthorne, Nathaniel. *Nathaniel Hawthorne's Tales*. Ed. James McIntosh. New York: Norton, 1987.

Heidari, Melissa Walker, ed. *To Find My Own Peace: Grace King in Her Journals, 1886–1910*. Athens: U of Georgia P, 2004.

Herzberg, Max J., and the Staff of the Thomas Y. Crowell Company. *The Reader's Encyclopedia of American Literature*. New York: Thomas Y. Crowell Co., 1962.

Hildreth, Charles R. "Online Catalog Design Models: Are We Moving in the Right Direction?" *Myweb@C.W.Post*. C. W. Post Office of Information Technology, 27 Mar. 2000. Web. 2 Jan. 2009.

hooks, bell. *Ain't I a Woman: Black Women and Feminism*. Boston: South End, 1981.

James, Henry. *Washington Square*. New York, 1881.

Jones, Anne Goodwyn. *Tomorrow Is Another Day: The Woman Writer in the South, 1859–1936*. Baton Rouge: Louisiana State UP, 1981.

KateChopin.org. Kate Chopin International Society, 2 Jan. 2009. Web. 2 Jan. 2009.

Koloski, Bernard. "The Anthologized Chopin: Kate Chopin's Short Stories in Yesterday's and Today's Anthologies." *Louisiana Literature* 11 (1994): 18–30.

———, ed. *Approaches to Teaching Chopin's "The Awakening."* New York: Modern Language Association, 1988.

———. "The Awakening: The First 100 Years." Beer 161–73.

———. Introduction. Chopin, *At Fault* vii–xxii.

———. *Kate Chopin: A Study of the Short Fiction*. New York: Twayne, 1996.

Kristeva, Julia. *Possessions: A Novel*. Trans. Barbara Bray. New York: Columbia UP, 1998.

Krook, Dorothea. *The Ordeal of Consciousness in Henry James*. Cambridge: Cambridge UP, 1962.

Leach, William R. "Transformations in a Culture of Consumption: Women and Department Stores, 1890–1925." *Journal of American History* 71 (1984): 319–42.

Lewis, C. S. Surprised by Joy: The Shape of My Early Life. New York: Harcourt, 1956.

Lohafer, Susan. Coming to Terms with the Short Story. 1983. Baton Rouge: Louisiana State UP, 1985.

———. Reading for Storyness: Preclosure Theory, Empirical Poetics, and Culture in the Short Story. Baltimore: Johns Hopkins UP, 2003.

Lohafer, Susan, and Jo Ellyn Clarey, eds. Short Story Theory at a Crossroads. Baton Rouge: Louisiana State UP, 1989.

Long, Alecia P. The Great Southern Babylon: Sex, Race, and Respectability in New Orleans, 1865–1920. Baton Rouge: Louisiana State UP, 2004.

Marcum, Deanna B. "Librarians or Technicians? Which Shall We Be?" Information for a New Age: Redefining the Librarian. Comp. Library Instruction Round Table (American Library Association). Englewood: Libraries Unlimited, 1995. 11–14.

Martin, Wendy, ed. New Essays on "The Awakening." New York: Cambridge UP, 1988.

May, John R. "Local Color in The Awakening." Southern Review 6 (1970): 1031–40.

McCullough, Kate. Regions of Identity: The Construction of America in Women's Fiction, 1885–1914. Stanford: Stanford UP, 1999.

McFarland, Thomas. Romanticism and the Heritage of Rousseau. Oxford: Clarendon, 1995.

McPherson, Tara. Reconstructing Dixie: Race, Gender, and Nostalgia in the Imagined South. Durham: Duke UP, 2003.

Moers, Ellen. Literary Women. Garden City: Doubleday, 1976.

Morrison, Toni. Playing in the Dark: Whiteness and the Literary Imagination. Cambridge: Harvard UP, 1992.

Papke, Mary E. "Chopin's Stories of Awakening." Koloski, Approaches 73–79.

———. Verging on the Abyss: The Social Fiction of Kate Chopin and Edith Wharton. Westport: Greenwood, 1990.

Pattee, Fred Lewis. The Development of the American Short Story: An Historical Survey. New York: Harper, 1923.

"Per Seyersted." Wikipedia Den frie encyklopedi. Wikipedia, 14 Jan. 2008. Web. 2 Jan. 2009.

Rankin, Daniel S. Kate Chopin and Her Creole Stories. Philadelphia: U of Pennsylvania P, 1932.

Reilly, Joseph J. Of Books and Men. New York: Julian Messner, 1942.

Rice, Anne. Interview with the Vampire. New York: Ballantine, 1976.

Rich, Adrienne. "Disloyal to Civilization: Feminism, Racism, Gynephobia." On Lies, Secrets, and Silence: Selected Prose, 1966–1978. New York: Norton, 1979. 275–310.

Roberts, Diane. *The Myth of Aunt Jemima: Representations of Race and Region*. London: Routledge, 1994.

Rousseau, Jean Jacques. *The Confessions of Jean Jacques Rousseau*. Bk. IV. 1782. Project Gutenberg, 15 Aug. 2004. Web. 2 Jan. 2009.

Rowe, John Carlos. "The Economics of the Body in Kate Chopin's *The Awakening*." Boren and Davis 117–42.

Sandberg, Elisabeth. Personal interview by Emily Toth. May–July 2008.

Scott, Anne Firor. *The Southern Lady: From Pedestal to Politics, 1830–1930*. Chicago: U of Chicago P, 1970.

Seyersted, Per. *Kate Chopin: A Critical Biography*. Baton Rouge: Louisiana State UP, 1969.

Seyersted, Per, and Emily Toth, eds. *A Kate Chopin Miscellany*. Natchitoches: Northwestern State UP, 1979.

Shaker, Bonnie James. *Coloring Locals: Racial Formation in Kate Chopin's "Youth's Companion" Stories*. Iowa City: U of Iowa P, 2003.

Showalter, Elaine. *A Literature of Their Own: British Women Novelists from Brontë to Lessing*. Princeton: Princeton UP, 1977.

Skaggs, Peggy. *Kate Chopin*. Boston: Twayne, 1985.

Smith, Ethel Morgan. "Come and Be Black for Me." *Honey, Hush! An Anthology of African American Women's Humor*. Ed. Daryl Cumber Dance. New York: Norton, 1998. 532–38.

Spacks, Patricia Meyer. *The Female Imagination*. New York: Knopf, 1975.

Spiller, Robert E., Willard Thorp, Thomas H. Johnson, Henry Seidel Canby, and Richard M. Ludwig, eds. *Literary History of the United States*. 3rd ed. New York: Macmillan, 1963.

Springer, Marlene. *Edith Wharton and Kate Chopin: A Reference Guide*. Boston: Hall, 1976.

———. "Kate Chopin: A Reference Guide Updated." *Resources for American Literary Study* 11 (1981): 280–303.

Stein, Allen F. *Women and Autonomy in Kate Chopin's Short Fiction*. New York: Peter Lang, 2005.

Stein, Atara. "Immortals and Vampires and Ghosts, Oh My! Byronic Heroes in Popular Culture." *Romantic Circles*. Ed. Neil Fraistat, Steven E. Jones, and Carl Stahmer. U of Maryland, 15 Feb 2007. Web. 2 Jan. 2009.

Stern, Milton R., and Seymour L. Gross, eds. *American Literature Survey: Nation and Region, 1860–1900*. 3rd ed. New York: Viking, 1975.

Taylor, Helen. *Gender, Race, and Region in the Writings of Grace King, Ruth McEnery Stuart, and Kate Chopin*. Baton Rouge: Louisiana State UP, 1989.

———. "Paris and New Orleans: The Transatlantic Cultural Legacy of Prostitution." *Transatlantic Exchanges: The American South in Europe—Europe in the American South.* Ed. Richard Gray and Waldemar Zacharasiewicz. Vienna: Verlag der Österreichischen Akademie der Wissenschaften, 2007. 309–34.

———. "'The Perfume of the Past': Kate Chopin and Post-Colonial New Orleans." Beer 147–60.

———. "Walking through New Orleans: Kate Chopin and the Female Flâneur." *Southern Quarterly* 37.3–4 (1999): 21–29.

Thomas, Heather Kirk. "'A Vocation and a Voice': A Documentary Life of Kate Chopin." Diss. U of Missouri–Columbia, 1988.

Timmermans, Stefan. *Postmortem: How Medical Examiners Explain Suspicious Deaths.* Chicago: U of Chicago P, 2006.

Toth, Emily. Introduction. Chopin, *Vocation* vii–xxvi.

———. *Kate Chopin: A Life of the Author of "The Awakening."* New York: Morrow, 1990.

———. "Kate Chopin Thinks Back through Her Mothers: Three Stories by Kate Chopin." Boren and Davis 15–25.

———. *Unveiling Kate Chopin.* Jackson: UP of Mississippi, 1999.

———. "What We Do and Don't Know about Kate Chopin's Life." Beer 13–26.

Toth, Emily, Per Seyersted, and Cheyenne Bonnell, eds. *Kate Chopin's Private Papers.* Bloomington: Indiana UP, 1998.

Trilling, Diana. Letter to Barbara H. Solomon. 23 Feb. 1975.

Turnure, Arthur B. "Statement." *Vogue* Dec. 1892: 8.

Walker, Nancy A. *Kate Chopin: A Literary Life.* New York: Palgrave, 2001.

Ward, J. A. *The Imagination of Disaster: Evil in the Fiction of Henry James.* Lincoln: U of Nebraska P, 1961.

Weil, Dorothy. *In Defense of Women: Susanna Rowson (1762–1824).* University Park: Pennsylvania State UP, 1976.

Wharton, Edith. *A Backward Glance.* New York: Appleton-Century, 1934.

Williams, Raymond. *Marxism and Literature.* Oxford: Oxford UP, 1977.

Winther, Per. "Minnetale over professor dr. philos. Per Eynert Seyersted." *Det Norske Videnskaps-Akademi.* Norwegian Academy of Science and Letters, 8 Sept. 2005. Web. 2 Jan. 2009.

Wood, Ann Douglas. "The Literature of Impoverishment: The Women Local Colorists in America, 1865–1914." *Women's Studies* 1 (1972): 3–46.

———. "The 'Scribbling Women' and Fanny Fern: Why Women Wrote." *American Quarterly* 23 (1971): 3–24.

CONTRIBUTORS

ROBERT D. ARNER is a professor of English at University of Cincinnati. He is the author of the first modern dissertation on Kate Chopin—published in a revised form as a special issue of *Louisiana Studies*—as well as other articles about Chopin. He is also the author of "Dobson's Encyclopaedia": The Publisher, Text, and Publication of America's First "Britannica," 1789–1803, and he has published articles on Ernest Hemingway, Nathaniel Hawthorne, Edward Taylor, Benjamin Franklin, Anne Bradstreet, Mark Twain, Ebenezer Cooke, and others.

THOMAS BONNER JR. is professor emeritus at Xavier University of Louisiana, where until recently he was W. K. Kellogg Professor and Chair of English. He has twice served as Distinguished Visiting Professor at the United States Air Force Academy. In addition to *The Kate Chopin Companion: With Chopin's Translations from French Fiction*, he has published books and monographs on William Faulkner, Edgar Allan Poe, southern fiction, and southern poetry. He has published and spoken on Kate Chopin and her writing since 1969.

LYNDA S. BOREN currently resides in Louisiana, where she teaches in the Louisiana gifted program. She is an independent scholar whose publications include *Eurydice Reclaimed: Language, Gender, and Voice in Henry James* and *Kate Chopin Reconsidered: Beyond the Bayou*, coedited with Sara deSaussure Davis. During her tenure at Northwestern State University in Natchitoches, Louisiana, she helped to organize the Kate Chopin International Conference and also chaired a special session on Chopin at the MLA convention in New Orleans.

ANNA SHANNON ELFENBEIN is an associate professor of English at West Virginia University, where she also serves as the resident faculty leader of a university residence hall. She is the author of *Women on the Color Line: Evolving Stereotypes and the Writings of George Washington Cable, Grace King, Kate Chopin* and a coeditor of *Engendering the Word: Feminist Essays in Psychosexual Poetics.* Inspired by the Chopin recovery movement, Elfenbein has also contributed to the recovery of Olive Tilford Dargan, another neglected woman author.

BARBARA C. EWELL is the Dorothy Harrell Brown Distinguished Professor of English at Loyola University New Orleans, where she has taught since 1984. In addition to her 1986 monograph on Kate Chopin, she has written articles on Renaissance poetry, various North American writers, and feminist pedagogy. Her coedited volumes include *Louisiana Women Writers: New Critical Essays and a Comprehensive Bibliography* and *Southern Local Color: Stories of Region, Race and Gender* (with Pamela Glenn Menke).

BERNARD KOLOSKI is emeritus professor of English at Mansfield University and has taught on the Fulbright program in Poland. He is the author of *Kate Chopin: A Study of the Short Fiction* and editor of *Approaches to Teaching Chopin's "The Awakening"* and of the Penguin Classics editions of Chopin's *At Fault* and *Bayou Folk and A Night in Acadie.* He is site editor of KateChopin.org, the Web site of the Kate Chopin International Society.

SUSAN LOHAFER teaches at the University of Iowa. She has published short stories but identifies herself mainly as a narrative theorist interested in cognitive poetics, empirical approaches to genre, and relations between narrative nonfiction and the short story. Her books include *Coming to Terms with the Short Story* and *Reading for Storyness: Preclosure Theory, Empirical Poetics, and Culture in the Short Story.* She is the coeditor of *Short Story Theory at a Crossroads* and one of the editors of *The Tales We Tell: Perspectives on the Short Story.*

MARY E. PAPKE is a professor of English and associate provost at the University of Tennessee. She is the author of *Verging on the Abyss: The Social Fiction of Kate Chopin and Edith Wharton* and *Susan Glaspell: A Research and Production Sourcebook* and the editor of *Twisted from the Ordinary: Essays on American Literary Naturalism.* She has published essays on feminist theory, postmodern women writers, Evelyn Scott, Sean O'Casey, and Marxist literary criticism in early twentieth-century America, among other topics.

BARBARA H. SOLOMON is a professor of English and women's studies at Iona College in New Rochelle, New York. In addition to editing the Signet edition of "The Awakening" and Selected Stories of Kate Chopin, she has edited or coedited sixteen other anthologies, including Other Voices, Other Vistas: Twenty-Five Non-Western Stories; Herland and Selected Stories of Charlotte Perkins Gilman; Critical Essays on Toni Morrison's Beloved; Once upon A Childhood: Stories and Memoirs of American Youth; and Zona Gale's Miss Lulu Bett and Selected Stories.

MARLENE SPRINGER is a University Professor for the City University of New York. She retired as president of the College of Staten Island, CUNY, after serving for thirteen years. She is the author of numerous articles and the following books: Ethan Frome: A Nightmare of Need; Thomas Hardy's Use of Allusion; Edith Wharton and Kate Chopin: A Reference Guide. She is co-editor with Haskell Springer of Plains Woman: The Diary of Martha Farnsworth and editor of What Manner of Woman: Essays on English and American Literature.

HELEN TAYLOR is a professor of English at the University of Exeter, United Kingdom. She is the author of Gender, Race, and Region in the Writings of Grace King, Ruth McEnery Stuart, and Kate Chopin, along with Scarlett's Women: Gone with the Wind and Its Female Fans and Circling Dixie: Contemporary Southern Culture through a Transatlantic Lens. She has also coedited Dixie Debates: Perspectives on Southern Cultures and published articles on American and British women's writing. Her most recent work is an edited Daphne Du Maurier Companion.

EMILY TOTH is a professor of English and women's studies at Louisiana State University–Baton Rouge. She is the author or editor of two Kate Chopin biographies, two collections of Chopin's unpublished writings, and the first edition of Chopin's last story collection. She is also the author of Ms. Mentor's Impeccable Advice for Women in Academia, Ms. Mentor's New and Ever More Impeccable Advice for Women and Men in Academia, and Inside Peyton Place: The Life of Grace Metalious. Her "Ms. Mentor" advice column appears on the Chronicle of Higher Education's Career Network site.